Thank You!

In appreciation for purchasing Jimmelynn's book, she would like to *gift* you the first chapter of her audiobook *free*. Scan the QR code and receive the first chapter. Narrated by Jimme herself, it will be like having a heart-to-heart conversation with her in person!

Do you have a friend you think could use some Jimme wisdom? Have that friend scan the QR code to also receive the first chapter of the audiobook.

Changing lives together . . . Thank you!

You can also visit JimmelynnGarlandRice.com/audio for this download.

Write a Review on Amazon

Thank you for investing in the global effort to change the lives of women and men of all ages. The message of *Letters from Jimme* is truly revolutionary.

You can be a part of sharing this powerful message and increasing its visibility worldwide by writing an Amazon review.

Thank you for helping us reach *as many people as possible* with this message of hope and encouragement.

"When I think of Jimmelynn, I think of how *selfless* a person she is. She is always thinking of others and how she can help them. Her strength knows no bounds and *her ability to relate to your challenges, struggles, or difficulties* makes her the *best friend you didn't know you needed.* I know that *firsthand.* Because of her loyalty and deep love, she is also the first to celebrate your successes and victories! Her teaching and this book should be in *every* library! *The power of her words will impact generations!*"

—**Charlotte and Forrest Lucas**, Executive Vice President, owners of Lucas Oil Products

"Sometimes, it's not just teen girls who need a Jimme in their life. It could be an NHRA Top Fuel Championship drag racer who had lost her way, was broken, confused, suddenly homeless, shattered, and one hot mess. I know. I was *that girl.* Even though I was a thirty-one-year-old adult woman with a spectacular career, Jimmelynn knew I needed a home, love, privacy, tender care, and a safe place to heal. She wrote personal letters to me leaving them in my bedroom encouraging, mentoring, and coaching me back to health and faith. This book, full of her wisdom and life-changing guidance, will do the same for you! *Letters from Jimme* is a MUST. Her words are life-giving, full of hope and joy!"

—**Leah Pruett Stewart**, 2x NHRA World Champion, NHRA Top Fuel drag racer, Tony Stewart Racing

"This book is a love letter to YOU! This is your guide and road map for life. Jimme will walk you through critical challenges of life we all face. Her honesty, realness, and love poured out on these pages will help you become the young lady God has designed you to be. Jimmelynn's capacity to connect with everyone she meets and share truth with such compassion and honesty is a very rare gift. She has also been a blessing to me personally during difficult times and professionally in my long career as a TV anchor. It has been an honor to walk alongside her in this mission and ministry, and I will continue to do so reaching as many young lives as we can. I've seen and experienced the power with which God is using her! This book is her heart's mission and God's handiwork. Countless lives will be transformed."

—**Fanchon Stinger**, 15-time Emmy Award–winning broadcast journalist, cofounder and CEO of Grit and Grace Nation

"As a dedicated physician and retired 2-star general, I have seen many young women dealing with the crippling effects of the mental, emotional, spiritual, and physical health crises that are so prevalent in our current culture. It has been powerful to see how God has progressively worked through Jimmelynn to pour into the lives of young women. Her passion and dedication, even in the face of personal adversity, have been an inspiration to countless girls in helping them identify, communicate, and work to resolve real-life issues. Do yourself and everyone you know a favor—BUY THIS LIFE-CHANGING BOOK!"

—**David E. Wilmot**, MD, FAAFP; chief medical officer Longview International Technology Solutions, major general, US Army (retired)

"As a superintendent of schools, I am constantly working with staff to address the academic, social, and emotional needs of our students. As you well know, the areas that are most challenging include the social, behavioral, and emotional areas. Assisting students with the issues that trouble them is critical to preventing and dealing with bullying in our schools.

"The compelling charisma, wisdom, and teaching of Jimmelynn Rice captivates everyone who hears her speak. This book, *Letters from Jimme: Life Lessons I Wish I Could Tell My Younger Self*, needs to be given to every student to provide them a road map of positive coping skills and life guidance, placing them on the pathway to success and enabling them to become the amazing leaders they were created to be!"

—**Jeffrey K. Butts**, PhD, superintendent of the Metropolitan District of Wayne Township, Indianapolis (largest school district in Indiana)

"As a primary care physician, I've watched patients struggle with debilitating chronic diseases for more than 20 years. The way that Jimmelynn has battled her advanced Lyme disease is the way she lives each day. She uses her God-given gifts of compassion and strength to tackle adversity head on with a clear mind, bravery, and perseverance. She is an inspiration to not only those struggling with serious illness but anyone looking for answers to the tough questions in life."

—**Angela Debord-Henriksen**, MD, board certified internal medicine physician, Indiana University Health

"Jimme is like a 'hug whisperer'—offering loving, passionate, healing hugs to those around her in EVERY. SINGLE. HUG! It's as if she touches your soul. Each hug is therapeutic—like physical and mental therapy. She not only writes these letters from deep within her soul but is also an on-the-spot wordsmith, always knowing just what to say and *how* to say it. She is a devoted and compassionate community leader and an inspiration to all, especially young women who are our leaders of tomorrow. For anyone who has or knows a teenage girl, BUY THIS BOOK! Share Jimme's words of wisdom."

—**Heather Davis**, attorney, vice president and senior trust advisor of Regions Private Wealth Management, TEAM GNI leader and advisor

"I was a young girl abandoned by my mother and left in a gas station restroom along with my little brother. Although I am now a successful businesswoman, I immediately resonated deeply with Jimmelynn when I first met her and heard her story of birthing Girls Nite In in a public high school girls' restroom. Just like someone rescued me, Jimme compassionately and decisively stepped up with a strategy to rescue teen girls from self-destructive choices. By creating a Safe Refuge offering hope, healing, and life-guidance, she has already impacted and changed thousands of lives all over the globe. Jimmelynn is so passionate and charismatic about changing the next generation of women, you can feel it on every page!"

—**Jessica Abeln**, philanthropist, founder and former co-owner of DEFENDERS; board of directors for Girls Nite In International

"I have journeyed with Jimmelynn for close to 30 years as my pastoral leader, greatest mentor, and heart-to-heart friend. I have also been beside her in the throes of her horrific, life-threatening health crisis when she was diagnosed with chronic neurological Lyme disease. As a nurse for over 45 years, I have *never seen anyone fight so hard for her life when it would have been easy to just give up!*

"This fierce fight to live has only made her resolve to share truth and hope ever so much stronger. This book is life-giving guidance for us girls of ALL AGES now and into the future!"

—**Cindy Modafferi**, RN, Indiana University Health Hospital, TEAM GNI leader and mentor

"Jimme is truly a dynamic mentor and leader to girls of this generation! *Letters from Jimme* will resonate with women of ALL AGES for generations to come! The rare, compelling, and loving voice of hope will impact your heart long after the words in this book are consumed."

—**Cindy Barnard**, oncology nurse, RN, BSN, OCN, CBCN, TEAM GNI leader and mentor

"Jimmelynn writes from the heart. More than that, she lives from the heart—a heart for God and a heart for young ladies. This book will be a great help for every young woman who reads it!"

—**Bruce W. Martin**, author, *Desperate for Hope*

"Undeniably the strongest and most compassionate person I have ever met! A fierce warrior who has persevered and fought weary through many personal and health challenges. This incredibly insightful book, *Letters from Jimme*, was written by an extremely courageous, brave, and obedient woman who followed God's calling to passionately mentor and empower teen girls to navigate the constant challenges they are facing.

"This must-read book will positively change your life as these heartfelt words of truth have already inspired and saved so many girls and women alike!"

—**Sharon Hammer**, Brownsburg Relay for Life Youth Engagement Coordinator and Silent Auction Chair, GNI International Fundraising Coordinator

"I'll never forget the first time I ran into Jimmelynn after I'd grown from the innocent little girl she had known to the woman I'd become. A woman with scars, with a past, with a story. As soon as I saw her, I wanted to hide. I was ready for the disapproving look of shame I'd received from so many from my past. But that is not Jimme. Jimme looked into my eyes, saw my shame, my hurt, my past, but she also looked deep into my soul and saw my future. She saw who I was meant to be, who I was slowly allowing God to make me. All I needed was that tear-rimmed smile, full Jimme hug, and message that I was loved to know that I could find my way back to wholeness and I could find a group of women to love me for who I was and who I would be. Fourteen years later, I now have the absolute JOY and pleasure of working side by side with Jimmelynn and Kristi for the mission of Girls Nite In International. A mission so close to my heart because I've experienced the healing that comes through it. The healing you're about to experience by reading the love-filled words in this book."

—**Valeri Abbott**, former GNI girl, GNI International community engagement coordinator, TEAM GNI leader and mentor

Letters From Jimme

Life Lessons I Wish I Could Tell My Younger Self

Jimmelynn Garland Rice

BROOKSTONE
PUBLISHING GROUP
Birmingham, Alabama

Letters from Jimme

Brookstone Publishing Group, An imprint of Iron Stream Media, 100 Missionary Ridge, Birmingham, AL 35242, IronStreamMedia.com

Copyright © 2023 by Jimmelynn Garland Rice

DISCLAIMER: *Letters from Jimme* is the sole undertaking of the author, Jimmelynn Garland Rice. No funds from Girls Nite In International were used for the production of this book.

Library of Congress Control Number: 2022918130

Cover design by Ashley Day

ISBN: 978-1-949856-87-3 (paperback)
ISBN: 978-1-949856-91-0 (hardback)
ISBN: 978-1-949856-88-0 (eBook)

1 2 3 4 5—26 25 24 23 22

Contents

Contents

Dedication

To you, my friend, the reader:

> A book is a long letter to just one person.[1]

Welcome! I'm excited that you're here. Thank you for joining me because I view this as a conversation between two close friends. *No matter our age, we all still carry that vulnerable little girl or boy inside. No matter our age, we all tend to revert to unhealthy ways of coping when life hurts. So, my friend, this book is for you. All of us.* I have written every word painstakingly with you in my mind's eye and carried you close in my heart with every single word written. Thank you for trusting me. *My letters are the most personal, vulnerable, loving gift I could give you.* I trust you find the hope, inspiration, and courage to embrace change and live the life you were created to live. We need each other. So, let's do this together, you and me.

To my adored and loved Girls Nite In International girls, past, present, and future: You are my reason for writing these *Letters from Jimme* the past fifteen years. You are my *why*. My *calling*. My *passion*.

To my Rodney, my hubby, life mate, and life partner: *We said, "I do" and we choose to say "I do" every day.* We just recently celebrated forty years of marriage and ministry. *That's who we are. A team.* We made a promise to each other, and we have kept it. When you marry, troubles will come. You don't look for a way *out*; you look for a way *through*. We did. We have cared for each other through sickness and health, in want or plenty, in laughter and tears, in joy and sorrow. Marriage reveals the *best* and *worst* in you and *challenges you to grow up*. Marriage is not so much about *finding* the right person as it is about *becoming* the right person. The good news is we *really* like each other now too. ☺ *I love you with all my heart.*

To my adored and adoring, loved and loving three children: Kristi, Jason, and Blake: You are my *life's work* and *greatest joy.* I have loved and cherish every moment being your mama. I am so proud of you and who you have chosen to become. *You stole my heart and own it. xoxo*

To my son-in-love and daughters-in-love: Tim, whom I affectionately nicknamed Dub, Staci, and Kayleigh whom we lovingly welcomed into *our family* and shared our greatest gifts, our children. You have made our family complete and are *deeply loved.*

To my adorable, deeply loved granddarlins! *You stole JiJi's heart the moment I laid eyes on you,* and you continually bring me the most joy, fun, laughter, and love. If you ever wanna run away from home, you know where to come! ☺ I ran away once. Packed my suitcase and everything. Made it to the end of our long driveway then realized I forgot two major necessities: money and food! Didn't take me long to realize that wasn't the smartest idea, and *I probably oughta do a 180 real quick and book it back home!* This book is for you with all my love. My lasting legacy to you. Always remember JiJi loves you! "From my heart to your heart." ♥

To my Mama, Ann Garland Munn: Thank you *for giving me life* as a young, beautiful sixteen-year-old girl. As Daddy always said, *"We grew up together."* Thank you for believing in me, being supportive of me through all the years, watching out for me, and loving me. Thank you for *helping to bring me back to life again* when I was so deathly sick fighting late-stage Lyme disease. You and Rodney literally took care of me when I had lost all neurological and physical functions and could not care for myself. *I am the most grateful girl ever to be alive. I love you "a bushel and a peck and a hug around the neck" and will always be your little girl.*

To my God: You are the *Giver of life and breath and restored my soul.* How could I not give you my all? You have my full attention and my full affection. *I love you, my Abba Father. I am Yours.*

Foreword 1

Kristi Hardin

"You are so lucky to have Jimme as *your* mama!"

As the saying goes, if I had a nickel for every time I've heard this throughout my life, I'd be rich. But it's true. I *am* the luckiest girl on the planet—and deeply grateful. I've had a front-row seat to observe one of the most brilliant, wise, discerning, motivated, hard-working, compassionate, strategic, and loving leaders and teachers. What a gift that I do not take for granted!

Mama leads by example in everything she does. As a young girl, I had the privilege of watching her serve behind the scenes, quietly and faithfully, making others look good and never wanting the spotlight. She balanced being a worship leader and pastor's wife, full-time musician and piano teacher, unpaid and sought-after counselor, and mama to three babies while my daddy worked sixty to eighty hours a week. And she still somehow managed to make sure we knew that we were her greatest joy and top priority.

Once grown, I watched her reluctantly and courageously step into her calling as a gifted public speaker and compassionate leader of a global nonprofit, impacting thousands of teens and women across the world.

Mama is the same person behind closed doors as she is on stage and in her socials. Her heart is as big as the globe and she feels emotion deeper than anyone I've ever known. A true *empath* before Gen Z made the term popular, she has the unique ability to feel others' emotions and uses strategic discernment and wisdom to compassionately guide them through life's messiness.

Now that I'm a mama, I find her words and actions shaping my thoughts as I parent my own kids. I'm so grateful for the lessons she has taught me:

- The most important lesson to learn is Gratitude.
- Forgive yourself. The goal for your life is progress, not perfection.
- Don't compare. Don't compete. Run your own race.
- Expect nothing. Appreciate everything. Nobody owes you anything. Be grateful!

My mama leads from a place of deep wrestling, deep heartache, and deep communion with God. Emotional and physical pain in her life has led her to truly seek God's face and heart. Her courage, hard work, and sacrifice is a tremendous inspiration and motivates me to live my life fully surrendered to His plan and purpose.

I'm so proud of Mama for the hard work and late nights she has put into these Letters. Her powerful words of hope will live on as her legacy, impacting generations, including my own kids and grandkids.

With deepest admiration and love,
Kristi Hardin

Foreword 2
Rodney Rice

I consider it one of my highest honors to introduce this book to you. I've seen this book fleshed out in real life before there were ever words on a page. I've witnessed this incredible lady with tears rolling down her cheeks, because of girls who were destroying their lives by one or more of these powerful topics. As Jimme still does to this day, she meets girls at all hours of the day or night because they're terrified, confused, empty, and begging for answers for which way to turn. The cries echo over and over, "If I could just talk to Jimme, I know she'll listen and be able to help." Or, "I just need a Jimme hug." I've seen Jimme up at night until two or three in the morning writing and pouring over many of these letters because she wanted every word to communicate raw *truth* to the thousands of girls whose faces and situations she couldn't erase from her mind.

God called Jimmelynn Garland Rice in 2008 to a task that she never would have chosen for herself. God placed His hand on Jimme for a job that forced her out of her comfort zone. Jimme has spent over thirty years as a professional musician, worship leader, music educator, recording artist, and ministry partner. God shook her world when He asked her to give direction, love, and guidance to girls in our culture who were making horrible choices and destroying their lives. This book is born out of a heart that God broke, redirected, and mightily empowered for a job that was far bigger than she ever anticipated.

So, what do you say when God rocks your world with a job that scares you to death? There's only one thing she could say. And that's *yes!* But then her questions began flooding in. "What am I going to teach? There's no curriculum out there for what these girls are dealing with."

Then God said, "You'll write it yourself, and I'll guide you! Don't sugarcoat my message. Speak Truth. Speak Love. Be real, honest, raw, and transparent. The girls will not listen to a phony. Get into their messes. Love them unconditionally. And most of all, make sure they know that **I love them**!"

That's how this book was born. Are you willing to take the challenge and allow your Creator to lovingly speak to you through the words of a woman who loves you more than you could ever imagine? Are you willing to take these words to heart? Because if you are, I can guarantee you, my friend, these words are packed with so much love, wisdom, compassion, and power that they will most definitely—as they have mine—*Change Your Life*!

Lovingly,
Rodney Rice
aka "Mr. Jimme"
Pastor, voice artist, musician, chef, and best of all, husband to this incredible lady, my college sweetheart and love of my life, Jimmelynn Garland Rice

Introduction
Life Redirected

Ms. Jimme, I was six years old. I knew my mama's boyfriend was in her bed. . . . I just didn't know he was comin' to mine.

Those chilling words forever changed the trajectory of my life.

Her trembling lips revealed a tightly held secret that pierced an arrow through my heart and riveted my attention like a thunderbolt, causing me to instinctively pull Sheronda close to my heart and wrap her in a warm hug of protection, compassion, and deep love. NO girl should ever have to experience this no matter what her age. This gut-wrenching abuse and betrayal of trust completely wrecked and broke my heart.

I was a public high school teacher and saw so many of my students making self-destructive choices either because of their own decisions or because someone was doing something *to* them that was destroying their lives. My students gravitated toward me because they knew I loved them and could be trusted as they poured out their hearts and deepest, darkest secrets while desperately confiding in me for guidance and counsel. They longed to be heard, seen, loved, and accepted.

I felt compelled to make a choice to begin intentionally taking my breaks in the girls' restroom rather than in the faculty lounge with my colleagues, knowing that the restroom is often a girl's safe place when she is vulnerable and hurting. That decision forever changed not only the trajectory of my life but that of thousands upon thousands of teen girls.

Every girl has a story if you care enough to listen. After lunch you'll hear girls purging, terrified they're pregnant, running into the restroom stall sobbing to escape a bully in the hallway. Girls paralyzed by crippling anxiety or panic attacks. Feeling trapped and alone, depressed with no hope. Toasting each other with water bottles laced with vodka because of what they have to deal with when they get home, girls covering up their arms while washing their hands so no one would see the self-cut marks ripped into their skin, or the worst, girls terrified to go home after school because the wrong kind of stepdad was waiting on them and mama wouldn't be off work for two or three more hours. Some of my girls were living in a home where they had a *different "uncle" every night* taking advantage of them.

I knew what that meant, and I could not get their stories out of my head—or my heart. I felt compelled to take action to make a difference, to throw a life rope of hope and start something that did not exist. I knew I needed to create this group, a gathering, a Safe Refuge providing help, hope, and healing. A warm, inviting place of trust, love, truth, and life guidance. A *family* where they knew they belonged, were loved, and were fully accepted. A *family* where they would know they were not alone no matter what they were facing, and they would not be judged because of their past or the shame they were wearing.

I already knew the name I would call this Safe Refuge: ***GIRLS NITE IN***—instead of Girls Night Out—partying. My intent was to design a tee shirt with our branding logo on the front to give to each girl as a *thank-you gift* for coming, and on the back of the tee, I would create a design similar to a rock band tour tee shirt listing the *date and topic for each event*. My goal was for these shirts to be a *walking billboard*, arresting the attention of teens and drawing girls in because of a particular topic they saw that "called their name"—a certain issue they  were deeply struggling with and needed someone who cared enough to help. My vision when starting Girls Nite In was to create a Safe Refuge of HOPE for teen girls and young women who desperately needed help, healing, healthy coping skills, an intentional strategy, life guidance, and most importantly, love.

I frequently share that I wish there had been a Girls Nite In when I was a teen growing up. I wouldn't have made some of the choices I made or allowed some people to do some of the things they did to me. But I wasn't fortunate enough to have something like Girls Nite In. So, I want to give others what I didn't have.

"*Our teens do not live in a PG-13 world but are trapped in R-rated and XXX-rated constantly!*"—a harsh truth I heartbreakingly see and share every chance I get when speaking.

It is so hard, as a teen, to keep your head on straight in this culture! Dang. It's hard for adults too. I don't care if you have a good support system, even one parent who actually cares about you and is involved in your life. The negative forces of darkness and the pull of this culture and friends, coupled with strangling anxiety and fear of uncontrollable events, has our teens opting to end their lives at an alarming, unprecedented rate. I see good kids fighting suicidal thoughts and turning to unhealthy ways to cope.

I couldn't escape the unrelenting, persistent fire and passion that God was burning within me to create this Safe Refuge for teen girls where we would talk raw, candid, and honest about real-life struggles they were facing and offer guidance that would enable them to make wise choices and be empowered with life-changing truth at a critical, pivotal time in their lives and decision-making process.

Our teens are bleeding internally. They may look great and well-adjusted on the outside, but the very real pain and brokenness they feel on the inside is ripping them apart. Many are raising themselves with little or no guidance. Often, they are modeling the behavior they see at home—which is not healthy—or sometimes, even legal. Because of their crippling anxiety, fear of the future, complexities, and difficulties of their everyday lives, they are turning to unhealthy coping behaviors to survive.

God kept wrecking and ransacking my heart. The burden became so strong and continued to build in my heart until I felt that I would be flat-out stiffing and dishonoring God if I didn't say YES and do what He was calling me to do.

My kitchen window faced the high school. Every morning, when I was unloading the dishwasher looking out the window, it seemed as though there were neon lights on the high school building flashing at me: *"the girls, the GIRLS, THE GIRLS!"* I would force the dishes a little harder into the cabinet with each thought as I told God *every* reason why He was talking to the wrong girl! I told Him every reason why I *wasn't* the one who should be doing this! There was nothing like this out there for teen girls in this culture! I knew. I had already looked! Besides, I already had a full, overflowing life as a high school teacher and a piano and vocal coach with more than fifty students, whom I loved. I was a professional musician and worship leader and served our community, as a pastoral team with my husband, of a growing, thriving megachurch. *And* I was mama to three, busy, involved-in-everything kids whom I loved and adored.

Besides, I reasoned, there were already plenty of resources for teens: coaches, camps, YMCAs, youth programs, counselors, therapists. Surely, that was enough. Why did God possibly need me?

I was having an all-out wrestling match with God.

The truth is, I wrestled with God . . . until He won! ☺

I remember well that summer day I walked out to check the mail in between teaching piano students. As I walked back up the driveway sorting through the mail, I came across a simple white envelope with the return address of a couple we had enjoyed dinner with weekly during that summer. As they got ready to leave that night, I asked if they would mind sitting back down around our table on the deck so I could share something with them that was burning inside me. I told them what I just shared with you and asked if they would pray for me as I felt that God was asking me to do this and that I was going to explode if I didn't! They assured me they would, as they saw the enormous need for this.

Their daughter was my piano student, so I opened that envelope that afternoon walking up my driveway thinking it was the tuition check for that month. However, much to my shock, inside was a check with a Post-it note attached. The note said, *"Jimme, go do what you have a passion to do! Use this check to help you buy the tee shirts for those girls."* The check was written for $100. I stood there with tears streaming down my face, held my hands, along with that check, up toward the sky, and said, *"Okay, God! I hear You! I give! I surrender! I will do this! But I'm telling you, You're gonna have to lead me every step of the way! 'Cause there's nothing like this out there! As soon as I teach my last lesson today, I'll head to Team Sports—the only custom tee shirt store I am aware of in town."*

I walked into that store, check tucked into my purse, and a voice greeted me. *"Can I help you?"*

"Sure," I kinda stammered. *"This is sort of an unusual, random request. I don't really need to purchase any sports team shirts, but I want to create a custom tee shirt. Do you do that?"* I started to explain the program and group I was about to start when Tim interrupted me, saying, *"I know who you are. You're Jimmelynn Rice, and you teach at the high school. I've heard about you, and you're getting ready to start a group called Girls Nite In, right?"* Well, I was completely stunned speechless! You could have blown me over with a feather. I had *never* met Tim, had *no* idea how he knew me, had *no* idea how he could possibly know what I was about to do.

I could hardly breathe except to ask him while shaking my head in total bewilderment, *"How on earth do you possibly know that!?"* Tim went on to explain that he had a high school girl who worked for him at the store, and she had come into work *so* excited because she had run into one of her favorite high school teachers at the ballfield. This teacher told her what she was thinking about doing: starting a group for teen girls to discuss the *real* struggles and issues they were facing in a real, raw, honest way—and asked if she would be interested in coming. Ashley (name changed to protect privacy) was so excited and said, *"YES! I definitely wanna come!"* and started naming a list of girlfriends asking if they could come too!

Tim said, *"I think you're gonna have more girls than you think and know what to do with when word gets out! So, what is your plan? Are you designing the shirt and then having the girls come in to purchase it?"* I explained, *"No. Actually, I don't want the girls to pay for it. I want to give the tee to them as a thank-you gift and encourage them to wear it to represent GNI and invite other girls to join us."* Tim asked how I was going to pay for them. So, I told him the story and said, *"I have a check here for $100 from this friend, and I'm planning to pay the difference."*

Tim replied, *"Jimme, I don't think you understand how many girls need this! I'm telling you; you are going to have more girls than you know what to do with because they NEED THIS DESPERATELY! I'll tell you this:*

Ashley has a difficult home life, and she needs this badly. If you can help girls like Ashley, I'll do everything I can to help you. How many tee shirts do you think you'll need?"

"*Oh, probably twenty,*" I replied.

Tim said, "*Well, actually we purchase tees in groups of dozens, so how about twenty-four?*"

I instantly replied, "*Duh! I should know that! My mama owns a men's clothing store in South Carolina, and I should know you always purchase by dozens. So, yeah, oh my! Twenty-four will be plenty!*"

Tim went into the back room, came out, and said, "*No, twenty-four is not gonna be enough. I think you need to order thirty-six!*"

I incredulously shook my head and said, "*Okay, if you think so, I'll go with thirty-six, but that will be* more *than plenty to last us through this school year!*"

Once again, Tim walked into the back room, came out and said, "*Nope, you need to go with forty-eight!*"

I shook my head in disbelief, but replied, "*Okay, if you really think so, I'll trust your judgment. But I'm tellin' ya, forty-eight will be* more *than plenty shirts to get us through this school year!*"

Then Tim said, "*Tell ya what! You give me the $100 check, you write me a $100 check, and I'll cover the rest.*"

I shook my head no. "*Oh, Tim! No, no, no! I'm not expecting a handout. My mother owns a small business, and I know how everyone comes in thinking and expecting she should give them a discount! I'm* not *that type of girl, and I don't expect that!*"

To which Tim replied, "*Oh, I know you're not. I can tell. That's why I want to help you. Besides, I believe in what you're doing!*"

I left there raising my hands up to the sky saying, "*WOW! Okay, God! If You'll lead me every step of the way, I promise You I'll do this!*" I shared my passion with ten of my girlfriends and asked them to join me on my team with specific roles for each. We were stoked and excited!

The Saturday before our very first GNI event on Sunday, I got a phone call from Tami, one of my close friends, whose daughter was a piano student of mine. Tami said, "*Jimme, Renee has told me about this group for teen girls you're getting ready to start. I just don't think you know how many girls need this! You know me. I don't normally do this kind of thing. But I feel like the Spirit of God is telling me I need to call you and open up our home to you to use for your Girls Nite In events. I just think you're gonna outgrow your basement and God will not leave me alone or let me get this off my mind until I do what He's asking me to do and call you to offer our home."*

Tami's husband was a respected physician and they had been blessed with a gorgeous, spacious, warm, and inviting home. She continued, *"Jimme, there are plenty of snacks and drinks anytime you want to use it! I'll give you my garage door code because we're not home on Sunday nights."* I thanked her profusely and told her I would definitely take her up on her offer *if we ever outgrew our space that year.*

I never dreamed that I would be calling her *the next day* to say, *"Tami! God must've told you a secret He hadn't let me in on yet! ☺ Haha! It's 3 p.m., and I've already gotten so many texts from girls who are coming and wanting to bring friends. I don't think we're all gonna fit in my basement! Did you really mean that? 'Cause if you did, I think I need to take you up on your offer TONIGHT!"*

So, I quickly put a major plan in motion! I called friends and asked them to come over to my house one hour before GNI was to start to give the girls that drove up in our cul-de-sac the directions I had printed off to Tami's house and a cell phone for them to call their parents or guardians to tell them the plans had to be changed and the new address where they were going to be. I instructed my husband and sons to run and buy flashlights to direct traffic and pink helium balloons to hang on the mailbox at Tami's house. When they spotted a car beginning to slow down driving on the country road toward her house, they would direct them up the long, hilly, gravel driveway where another son would help them find a place to park.

I will never forget standing at the front door of her house peeking out the side windows that November Sunday evening when it was getting dark by six o'clock and watching the headlights of car after car driving up the hill . . . choked up and fighting back tears of joy and disbelief that *so* many girls were coming!

I had goosebumps watching God orchestrating His plan and taking me *way* out of my comfort zone, because He was driving this movement and we'd never be able to keep up! My job had been to say YES.

Imagine my shock that first night when I expected ten to fifteen girls to meet in my basement, and instead, fifty-five teen girls showed up! Fifty-five! We didn't even have enough tee shirts for the *first* event, much less the rest of the school year! ☺

Throughout that first year, teen girls from seventeen different high schools across Indianapolis began to come, having heard about GNI purely through word of mouth or seeing our tee shirt with some topic arresting their attention and calling out their name!

I began to receive phone calls and emails from mothers, grandmothers, parents, and guardians begging for their middle school girl to be allowed to come. *"Jimme, if my daughter waits until she's in high school, it's going to be too late. She needs help now!"*

Former high school students, who were now in college, began texting, *"Jimme, is it too late for me to come to Girls Nite In? I used to see all those GNI flyers hung all over the walls when I was in high school, but I had too much anxiety to come alone or thought I didn't need it! Ugh, how wrong I was! Can I still come?"*

"Absolutely! It's never too late!" I enthusiastically replied. So, our doors began to swing wide open to include middle school, high school, college-aged young women, and young teen moms!

And, yes, we quickly outgrew that space, and another and another!

National Growth

A year later, a national radio network, K-Love, picked up my story and aired it across the country—unbeknownst to me! A sixty-second spot right before the news—every hour on the hour—for that entire day! They highlighted an inspiring leader across the nation who was making a difference in their community! I had never interviewed with them.

But, as a result, I began receiving emails and phone calls from other cities and communities begging for help as they had no proven strategy to rescue teens who were spi-  raling out of control making self-destructive choices. They pleaded with me to consider expanding the scope of GNI and make it possible to launch a Girls Nite In affiliate chapter in their city or community. It was apparent that we needed to become a registered 501(c)3 nonprofit organization immediately.

That summer, I began the arduous process of writing The Girls Nite In Affiliate Leadership Training Manual, Policy Manual, all the curriculum on each of our topics and creating all the GNI brand templates for advertising, database resources, hosting and everything needed to make Girls Nite In a complete turn-key program to multiply our reach and broaden the scope of this Mission and Message of HOPE to this generation! This exhaustive labor of love, blood, sweat, and tears provided the tools to help us train, mentor, and empower other incredible women across the country to launch a GNI in their own community!

At that time, we began training and launching GNI affiliates in multiple locations in seven other states.

Another exciting development is that we have launched GNI in public high schools, community and pregnancy centers, college cam-  puses, churches, homes, section 8 housing complexes, and at Indiana Women's Prison— where the inmates begged me to start a GNI in cities where their kids were living with relatives or in the foster system because they didn't want their kids to make the same choices they did.

International Growth

A year later, I received an out-of-the-blue completely unexpected email from Argentina.

> My name is Alice Peacock. I teach English as a second language and do mission work in Argentina. I've heard about your program—Girls Nite In—and the girls in Argentina desperately need this! Could you help us?

My reply: *"The answer is YES! The 'how-to' we'll figure out together!"*
And so it began . . . the spread of this movement across the globe.

This required me to do intense research and interviews with global organizations to create and lay a thorough foundation and structure to ensure our GNI International Mission Organization could remain repeatable, scalable, and sustainable. I also wrote and created The Girls Nite In International Affiliate Association so that we would not have "mission drift" as we began to expand.

Alice flew to the States that summer, and we spent a full day together discussing the details of what expanding into Argentina would look like. I shared with her the strategic method in which I approached each topic to make sure it would work and resonate in the Argentine culture. I mentioned that we didn't have the funds, as a young nonprofit, to hire a Spanish translator.

Alice leaned back in her chair, thought for a minute, then leaned forward and said, *"I'll do it!"*

Thus began the lengthy process of translating all the curriculum into Spanish until, one day, Alice reached out asking if she could engage the help of two of her colleagues, Gabriella from Uruguay, and Adrianna from Chile, to help as this was quite a lot of material. I replied, "I totally understand! I labored quite exhaustingly myself writing it all! ☺ Absolutely yes! Engage these two amazing women to help!"

Once we had Spanish translations completed of eight topics, and I was able to raise the funds needed, we launched *Noche de Chicas*

Internacional in Argentina in three large cities and three schools! When I was contacted by friends from Nicaragua and Panama, we were able to launch in those countries as well. Currently, we are working to launch in India, Germany, Dominican Republic, Mali, South Africa, and other countries as translation and funds allow.

Even just translating the name of our organization into Spanish, *Girls Nite In International*, became quite interesting! ☺

You must remember when I founded GNI, I was only planning for this nonprofit to be for ten to fifteen local girls meeting in my basement. *Never* in a million years did I expect it to become a global nonprofit and movement!

I had initially named my creation, mission, and movement *Girls Nite In*, a hip, catchy name just to attract girls in the Indianapolis area. However, it was becoming clear that we needed to add another word to our legal name: **Girls Nite In *International*.**

Imagine the horror of trying to translate our name into Spanish only to have it translate literally as "Nite Inside the Girls" or "Girls In the Night"—the *exact opposite* of what we stood for and our mission! So, we landed on Noche De Chicas Internacional and just dropped the word *in*. We had to laugh along the way, as this became problematic in more ways than one! Imagine the shock I felt listening to a voice mail from an irate wife who found our phone number in her unsuspecting husband's cell phone calls. Needless to say, she thought we were an escort service providing needs for men! NOT! But we could not convince her otherwise and she threatened us, calling us every vulgar name ever invented! So, we tried to imagine what it must have been like for her husband to come home that night to an irate wife who thought her husband was hiring an escort service called Girls Nite In International!

Thankfully, those incidents are rare.

But, what is not rare are the miracles and stories that happen. I have only told you two. But, I could write a spellbinding book just sharing all the unbelievable stories that have transpired in these fifteen years of continuing to say yes.

Messy. All-consuming. 24/7. Working into the wee hours of the morning. Exhausting. Fulfilling. Poured out. Filled up. Those are just a few words that describe my life living out this calling. What it is like to deeply love, offer long-term help and guidance not just to teen girls but to entire families, affecting generations.

In my *Letters from Jimme*, I address the heart. Because whatever is in your heart is going to come out in your behavior. You can pass all kinds of laws to legislate behavior, but you can't legislate the heart! If there is rage in your heart, it will come out in your behavior. If there is anger in your heart, it's gonna come out in your behavior. On the other hand, if there is love, compassion, and gratitude in your heart, that is also going to come out in your behavior. So, I address the heart. The root of every single issue.

I continue to be humbled that teens love me, trust me, feel safe with me, and allow me to speak truth into their lives at such a critical, pivotal point of life choices and decision-making that will affect the rest of their lives. There is such a limited window of time when our most important life decisions are made: Who do I want to become? Who do I allow to influence my life and future? How do I learn to think for myself? Who will I marry? What goals and outcomes do I want for my future—and how do I get there?

I believe that I have been given A VOICE! Words to articulate the pain and conflict churning inside this generation! Words they themselves can't articulate and needs they can't yet express! Whether internal conflict or external struggle! I feel a passion and strong call on my life to mentor this generation! A deep, compelling desire to point them to True Help and True Hope! I have grown weary watching too many self-destruct and spiral into the clutches of darkness. I believe that I have been given discernment and

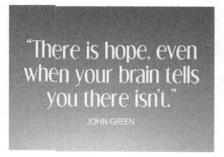

"There is hope, even when your brain tells you there isn't."

JOHN GREEN

insight to compassionately express the truth behind the struggle and pain that is causing them to derail into self-sabotaging behavior. An ability to define and articulate the compelling force of the negative cultural influence surrounding them and luring them down a dark path.

There is a way out! There is HOPE! There are answers—and I am called to share them!

What I have learned: Whether in my backyard, across the nation, or around the globe, I have learned that I am still a teacher. Only my classroom is now the globe.

What I want you to know: *The enormous impact and influence God has allowed me as I lead this global movement, my amazing TEAM GNI who volunteer and work alongside me as we mentor and pour our lives into these young women, and the Girls Nite In International Mission and Movement I founded that has had a life-transforming effect on the lives of thousands upon thousands of teen girls, young women, and adult women is truly humbling!* Their stories are gut-wrenching, truly remarkable, and I could write a book just sharing how their lives have been rescued and transformed through the nonjudgmental, unconditional love they receive, as well as learning positive coping skills, character-driven values, life guidance, and strategy through the *Letters from Jimme* that you now hold in your hands.

I first began writing *Letters from Jimme* as a personal message of love, practical tips, and life guidance starting at that very first GNI event in November 2008. A letter from my heart to theirs; important life lessons I wish someone had told me. After sharing the message of my letter at every GNI event, I give my GNI girls and GNI team a personal copy to take home with them to keep and have available when they need it most.

So many of my girls have shared with me that they took their notebook of *Letters from Jimme* with them to college, and those words of wisdom or life guidance helped them when they were really struggling. If a friend was struggling, they invited that friend to their dorm room, pulled their "Jimme" notebook off their shelf, and read the letter out loud to their friends, having their own little GNI in their dorm room. That made my heart melt and leap for joy!

I never intended or expected this to be a book. But throughout these fifteen years, men and women alike continue to ask for copies. Parents come to me with tears in their eyes saying how much they wish they'd known some of these life lessons when they were growing up. They wouldn't have made the wrong choices and mistakes they did. I have been inundated with requests for copies of these Letters from Jimme.

My goal is that my words will give *life* when you feel *worthless*, infuse *hope* when you feel *hopeless*, bring *clarity* when you feel *confused*, fuel *joy* when you feel *despair*, give *guidance* when you've *lost your way*.

In closing, I want you to know what God has burned into my heart as my personal life mission, the purpose for which I was placed on planet earth. Allow me to share with you these important life-changing words *I eventually trademarked as my personal life mission*. As you read them, please know I am looking deeply into the *eyes of your soul, my friend, and want you to know:*

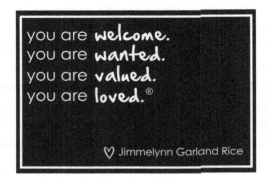

With more love than you can imagine,

Prologue

Life Interrupted

In 2015, my life came to a screeching halt and my former life stopped dead in its tracks. Life as I knew it was over. My life became a *living nightmare from hell.*

While following my calling and mission from God to lead Girls Nite In International, my own life took a drastic, devastating turn for the worse. After returning from a mission trip to Argentina to launch Noche de Chicas Internacional, my health began to rapidly and severely decline. I went from being a healthy, high-functioning, high-energy leader to feeling physically depleted and totally, utterly exhausted at the core level. Every cell in my body was not just tired but I had zero stamina or energy to do even a simple, basic task like taking a shower or writing a simple email that should have taken three minutes. I would find myself three hours later still staring at the computer screen in utter frustration because I could not put together one single sentence.

I woke up every single morning hoping to have strength to start the day but devastated to feel my tank completely empty. It was like plugging my cell phone in to recharge during the night, only to find it at 1 percent power the next morning—depleted of any energy whatsoever.

I began experiencing daily, excruciating, completely debilitating headaches. It felt like someone was taking a drill and boring into the temples on the sides of my head. Like a vise was attached to the top of my head squeezing my brain tighter and tighter. I kept saying, *"My brain feels swollen, like my head is going to explode."* The piercing pain was unrelenting 24/7, every day with no relief, turning into months and months. Dizziness and nausea made it difficult to do anything. I could only hold my head completely still to keep from feeling that the room was spinning.

When I tried to move, it felt as though my arms and legs weighed fifty tons and an elephant was sitting on my chest. The slightest movement to try to lift my arm or my body required such enormous energy and strength that it became impossible.

My adrenal system was crashing, but my central nervous system was on fire. Pain was piercing every raw nerve ending, every joint and muscle in my body. I felt excruciating pain all over—my mind screaming out with pain.

I began having extreme difficulty processing thoughts and trying to communicate. I would fight to find words and struggle to put sentences together or to answer simple questions. I eventually completely lost the ability to communicate, to speak, to read, or to write.

I could feel my body shutting down. I was terrified. I felt *scared and trapped,* unable to communicate to anyone what was happening and no longer able to make my body or brain function. It was sheer terror! *I knew my body. And I knew something was desperately wrong.*

Within a matter of months, I went from having it all to losing it all. Physically, cognitively, and neurologically. I became trapped in a body and brain that could no longer work or function.

I became a shell of the outgoing, energetic, full-of-life woman I used to be and could no longer participate in my own life. Completely sidelined.

My body felt like it was plugged into an electrical outlet, frying, burning and on fire. I began to experience body tremors and painful, electrical jolts. The overwhelming fatigue and weakness were so severe that I eventually became totally bedridden. I needed help to get from my bed to the bathroom and back to bed. I remember so many days when it was impossible to walk, and I would try to crawl to my recliner but couldn't, so my husband would have to pick me up and carry me.

I felt scared, angry, confused, and frightened because I could no longer communicate or work, and my brain couldn't retrieve or process words to enter conversation or engage in life on any level with my family or friends. I was absolutely terrified knowing something was terribly, horribly wrong with me.

My family took me from specialist to specialist desperate to find answers, only to have our hopes dashed again and again, as no doctor was able to diagnose or give us answers. *The utter frustration of seeking help and building up hope that THIS specialist was going to have the answer only to have them hang their head and say they didn't know how to help me was the most frightening thing.* Friends gathered to passionately pray for me and to pray over me.

Living in a nightmare, I desperately clung to the promise: Trust in the LORD with ALL your heart. Lean not on your own understanding. In all your ways, acknowledge him, and He WILL direct your path. I had faith that God would direct my path and asked everyone who loved me to pray for ONE. CLEAR. PATH.

That delivery came from Dr. Crozier, a physician, Lyme disease specialist and geneticist from Florida, who battles Lyme disease himself.

I remember the day of the phone call from Dr. Crozier in 2016 that gave me the diagnosis. Those words from my doctor paralyzed and gripped my heart with uncontrollable fear.

"Your tests have come back, and they confirm the diagnosis: You have three separate processes destroying your body and your brain. You have:

- *Advanced, late-stage Lyme disease*
- *An aggressive, invasive parasite infection [that invaded my body while doing mission work in Argentina launching the new Hispanic chapter of Girls Nite In International—Noche de Chicas Internacional]*
- *Heavy metal arsenic poisoning and mold because your body can no longer get rid of toxins on its own."*

Tests showed an *active, deadly bacterial infection* eating away the cells in my brain, invading my entire body. This tick-borne illness had been in my body, destroying it, for years without me even knowing I had been infected! Lyme disease, much like cancer, is diagnosed in stages. Caught early, it is much easier to treat. However, I was diagnosed with late-stage Lyme disease, and this active, vicious, deadly infection that had been destroying my body on the inside for years meant that treatment was not going to be easy.

"If you have any hope for survival or stand any chance of recovery, you need to start treatment immediately. I can help you, but you'll need to come to my medical clinic in Florida for seven months and begin aggressive, painful IV-infusion treatments that will feel like 'chemo on steroids.' These treatments are brutal, and you'll get much worse before you ever start getting better. These treatments are so severe they make grown men, who have been fierce military soldiers, cry."

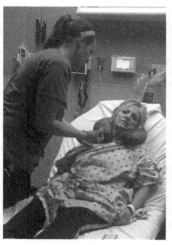

Dr. Crozier is a world-renowned Lyme disease specialist and geneticist, so I heart-breakingly made the decision to leave my kids and go to his functional medicine clinic to begin the painful treatments. My husband went to Florida to take care of me as the treatments made me violently sick, all while having to fly back and forth to Indy to pastor our church. My mama drove from South Carolina, alternating with Rodney to care for me as this was a day clinic, not a hospital, and we had to rent a hotel room to stay in throughout the lengthy months of treatments.

Since 2015, I have been in an ongoing battle, fighting for my life against this deadly disease and overcoming the damage done to my brain and body. I have worked hard in rehab privately to recover and to heal areas of my brain that were injured and to relearn skills I had forgotten.

Even though I had made progress, in 2019, I began to severely regress and was desperately fighting to hang on to life. It was sheer terror. The darkest, most difficult days of my life. There were many long months I didn't know if I would survive, and I had to push so hard to keep fighting and struggle for every single breath. My husband and family were scared that I was not going to make it and that they were going to lose me. But nobody was as scared as I was. I felt terrifying fear gripping every inch of my body. I was desperate for God and for His presence to hold me, sustain me, and carry me, to keep my hope and faith in Him alive and to trust Him with my life and my future. No matter what that might look like.

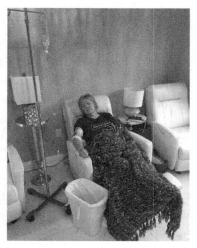

God has graciously answered the battle-cry prayers of an army of prayer warriors from across the globe calling out to God passionately on my behalf to bring healing to me. *I know I am a walking miracle, and I am the most grateful girl on the planet. God has literally spared my life and brought me from the jaws of death back to life.* He has provided measures of healing in my body and brain. It is a true miracle that I am alive and here with you today. I have made a lot of progress, but I am still fighting.

"God's Not Done" is a phrase of encouragement I have shared countless times throughout my life to encourage friends not to give up, to bring hope, counsel, healing, and fresh trust to many who were struggling, whether physically, emotionally, mentally, or spiritually. I have spoken that phrase to affirm God's plan and purpose for their lives and to inspire them to have the fortitude and courage to keep fighting,

to never give up and not to lose HOPE. As Kristi, my daughter, shares, "We had tee shirts made saying **#GODSNOTDONE— Team Jimme** and people literally all over the world proudly wore the shirt and posted on social media, offering prayers for Mama and thanking her for the impact she had made in their lives."

That very phrase I had used to encourage others became enormously life-giving—inspiring HOPE inside me as I clung to that truth when I was at my lowest point of fighting for my life in my battle against Lyme disease. I decided to have that phrase *trademarked*. It is the message of my life and the battle cry for a new movement I have begun to inspire hope and faith and share my story, as well as the story of others.

#GODSNOTDONE®
Team Jimme ♥

I have regained quite a bit of what was lost in the many years I was so deathly ill, but I still struggle to operate at the "old Jimme" level. What you see on the outside is not a true reflection of what is happening inside my body. On the inside, I am battling a very complex, different life. Sadly, there is no cure for Lyme disease in its advanced stage. Treatment simply works to fight the active, deadly bacterial infection to get to a place of remission. Some days are a real challenge physically as I have little strength or stamina. Other days are a struggle cognitively, as areas of my brain that have been deeply damaged are still healing. Often, preparing to speak and write this message and *Letters from Jimme* to you takes many months of long hours struggling for my brain to process the words I want to say.

In battling this disease, I have endured and fought a living nightmare from hell! God has literally brought me from death back to life . . . and spared my life. After many years of battling Lyme disease, I am the most grateful girl on the planet. Grateful just to be alive!

One of the debilitating effects of this disease and the active deadly infection in my brain was losing the ability to communicate, to read and to write. I used to love words. They are my life and one of the ways I love, minister to, and care for people. Now, I find myself hating words. When I have to write them, it becomes total frustration and endless exhaustion because they are trapped, and I can't retrieve them without agonizing hours, days, and weeks of trying. I can't find my voice anymore. For a writer, that is death. I almost would rather give up trying than face the torture of fighting to find the words and how hard it hurts and exhausts my brain. Which causes more pressure, anxiety, and stress.

I still deal with pain from the disease and intense IV treatments. But I am so grateful to God for the progress I have made!

> I choose to be grateful for what I can do instead of dwelling on what I can't do.

I am a fighter. I am not a quitter, and I will NOT give up! It really is quite remarkable how far I have come in the healing process. But I ask for your prayers as I am still in the heat of the battle fighting this disease. Healing one cell at a time.

My cognitive and neurological function has been operating off the charts. I have had great brain healing and recovery. Stamina is better. Although with pushing myself, I do hit a wall—and the stress takes a huge toll on my body requiring total rest for a day or two to recover.

The reality of living with this disease means an intense daily regimen, more IV infusion treatments for the rest of my life, and a complex protocol of about fifty pills and customized supplements every day to keep my body working. I have a new normal.

When speaking or sharing my story, I don't shy away from telling the truth of the devastation, despair, and hopelessness I felt, but I also share how my walk with God and deep communion with Him has deepened my faith, trust, devotion, and passion even stronger than ever. I continue to pray for healing every day. The Calling, Passion, and Purpose over my life only burns stronger—and one of those passions is you.

I want to ask you: what is the purpose and passion for which you were created? My hope is that this book creates a hunger inside you and helps guide you on the path to figure that out. Go *be* you. Go *do* you. Our world *needs* you! I'm in your corner *cheering you on!*

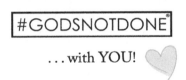

#GODSNOTDONE®

...with YOU!

> **"** If you have a talent, use it in every which
> way possible. Don't hoard it. Don't dole it
> out like a miser. Spend it lavishly, like a
> millionaire intent on going broke.
> —Brendan Francis Behan **"**

For more information about me and my battle against Lyme disease,
view these gripping, heartrending interviews.

FOX59 Interview   *Towne Post* Interview

1

Anxiety | Fear

Do one thing every day that scares you.

My Dear Fear-Filled Conqueror,

I placed this challenging quote on the desk in my office intentionally to stare me in the face every single morning when I walk in—daring me to face my fears head-on and do what I fear most.

Of all the topics I tackle, I am *highly qualified* to speak to you on this topic of ANXIETY and FEAR! You're lookin' at One.Hot.Mess.

Just sayin' . . . I could've earned a doctorate degree in Anxiety! The struggle is real! ☺

You have to know that it seemed like a *"you talkin' to me?"* moment—pretty much *Mission Impossible*—when God tapped me on the shoulder and placed this massive calling and vision on my life to start and lead this movement and mission called Girls Nite In International. I had spent my life and career as a teacher, a music educator, a counselor, a worship leader, a pastoral leader, and a professional musician and performer. I was very comfortable behind a mic, as long as it involved singing, performing, directing music, or playing piano—the instrument I passionately love!

However, the one thing that brought me terrible anxiety, to the point of making me physically sick, was *public speaking*!

I had always had a paralyzing, horrible, debilitating fear of speaking in public in front of a crowd of people. Talking one-on-one? No problem. Love that! But, put a mic in my hand and stick me in front of a crowd and I want to throw up. Or run!

Know what I'm talking about?

Even a simple thing like making a phone call can bring me terrible anxiety. In fact, my family laughs at me. It's a running joke around our house. If you see a lot of little three-by-five index cards spread out all over the kitchen counter, Mama must be gettin' up the courage to make a phone call. It is pathetic! I get so nervous about what to say, I literally have to script out my conversation. You think I'm kiddin'? I've probably had to do that before calling some of you. ☺

All this to be totally vulnerable with you and share the humbling fact that I did not arrive on the scene fully formed! It's been a journey that I am still on! I have worked with fierce intentionality and strong determination to change my "self-talk." I purposefully challenged myself through leadership development and personal growth to rise to the challenge, call, and purpose on my life to become all that God has created me to be. That has required fierce determination, deep resilience, and grit to grow and push through my fear. I set strategic goals to grow as a leader and a speaker as well as develop the business skills to lead and run a global nonprofit. All this required doing the hard work in my personal life to get a grip on my fears and crippling anxiety. So, when I speak on this topic, I am right there with you in the struggle.

Which brings me to a question: What are you afraid of? What do you fear? What gives you tight knots in your stomach? What stresses you out? What made you lose sleep and kept you awake last night?

We all fear something.

- Maybe you worry if you're going to have a prom date. Or you worry that "*she's gonna steal yo' man!*"
- If you're shy, you might be terrified of the teacher calling on you in class.
- Maybe your fear is college or having a career. Everybody's asking

what you're gonna do or what you're gonna be "when you grow up." And you don't have a clue!

- Maybe your fear is a result of your own stupidity and poor decision. You live in constant anxiety and dread over the consequences of a not-so-smart, not-so-wise choice you've made.
- Perhaps, you have very real fears about whether your family is going to stay together. The fights you overhear and the cruel words that are said play in your mind over and over.
- Or sheer terror may not be strong enough to describe the emotions surging through you every night because you don't know what your future looks like. Perhaps your mama—the only parent you have in your life—has been diagnosed with cancer or another life-threatening disease. And you really, really don't know what that means for her . . . or for you.

What I do know for sure: we all fear something. Some of our fears are real, and some are downright stupid crazy. But one thing is for sure. *Fear can absolutely paralyze us.*

What were your fears while growing up? The dark? Thunderstorms? Spiders? The monster under your bed or in your closet? Shower curtains . . . or what's hiding behind them? Yep. Ever seen the movie *Psycho*? Research shows that 90 percent of the things we worry about never happen.[1]

Anxiety does not have to define you.

So, how do we deal with our anxiety? Let's talk STRATEGY! I want to share with you six practical, action steps that will help you cope with stress, face your fear, and get a grip on your anxiety. If you can grab hold of even just one of these helpful steps and start to practice it, your life will begin to change. Game on!

Action 1: Name Your Fear

Well, duh! That might sound simple or even stupid, but you can't deal with something you're pretending doesn't even exist. Let's talk real.

What's stressin' you out? What are you afraid of? What are you scared to talk about? Say it out loud. Admit your struggle is real.

Action 2: Stop Catastrophizing!

What the whaaaaaat??? *Catastrophizing* is just a big word that simply means "to expect the worst." You know, when you're thinking about a situation and immediately your mind begins imagining and expecting the worst. You start thinking of

> **People hear what they fear. Logic tends to whisper, whereas fear tends to scream.**
> —Mike Berry

all the what-ifs. All the horrible things that *might* happen. Obsessing about all the terrible things that *could* happen. Like playing softball and striking out in your mind before you even get to the plate.

Or psyching yourself out of auditioning for the school play because you're afraid you'll forget your lines and make a complete idiot of yourself.

Determine right now to break your old habit of always thinking and expecting the worst.

Stop making yourself the victim of catastrophic thinking: allowing your mind to obsess and imagine the absolute worst. "OMGOSH! But what if . . . ?"

What do you spend your time and energy thinking about? You ARE spending it somewhere. In either a negative or positive way. Thinking requires energy. Obsessing requires energy. You must make a choice and say, "I refuse to park and stay stuck in this negative headspace! Negative thinking does me no good! It serves no purpose whatsoever!"

Negative thinking steals time. Moments I will never get back.

> Fear does not have to control your life or ruin your life.

Make a deliberate choice. Choose to retrain your brain—one thought at a time—to focus on healthy, positive thoughts, not trapped in all the negative self-chatter and drama that will destroy you. "God has not given us a spirit of fear, but of power and of love and of a sound mind" (2 Timothy 1:7 NKJV).

When an unreasonable fear starts stressing and freaking you out, call yourself out: "Nope. Not today. What in the heck am I doin'! Stop! Seriously!" You gotta call yourself out and be tough on yourself.

No buts. If you're not willing to do this, you're essentially willing to put up with your life just like it is.

> Self-talk matters. What you tell yourself
> day-to-day plays a major role in your anxiety level.

I remember when I was in high school and completely stressing out over something trivial and insignificant, one of the best things my mama taught me was to ask myself this question: *Five years from now what will this matter?* That one question will put a lot of your short-term stress in perspective.

> You can't change the stress,
> but you can change the way you respond to it.

For example, petty drama on social media is an absolute waste of your time and will destroy you. Don't get sucked into it.

What you feed your mind determines who you will become.

What music is your jam? Which artists are on your playlist? What type of shows and movies do you binge-watch? What you feed your mind *is* who you will become.

Feeding your mind truth is so important! Otherwise, you will stay trapped and stuck in the same emotions, the same toxic thoughts and beliefs that have kept you from growing into who you want to become.

I work intentionally to strengthen and focus my mind by writing positive affirmations and placing inspiring quotes all over my house, by reading biographies of strong leaders I admire, and selectively choosing what music, news, and information I let permeate my world.

We've got to infuse our minds with truth because, honestly, we *don't* think right.

> You *become* what you *believe.*

God will bring healing to our deepest fears and anxiety when we ask for His help and trust Him. Over and over, God's Book of Truth shows that God is sensitive to our fears and wants to give us courage and strength to rise above them.

Don't be ashamed to admit you're broken. Can I tell you the truth? We're all broken. God specializes in "broken."

> God accepts you just as you are,
> but He has very real plans to change you.

The LORD is my light and my salvation;
Whom shall I fear?
The LORD is the strength of my life;
Of whom shall I be afraid?
—Psalm 27:1 NKJV

I find that comforting. God knows we will experience fear, but He doesn't beat us up and condemn us for that. I don't know about you, but that brings me great peace and comfort. Instead, God gives us a *strategy*. A *plan* to overcome our fear and anxiety!

We have two choices when we are scared and afraid: fear *or* trust.

"When I am afraid, I will put my trust and faith in You."

Clearly, God is acknowledging that we *will* be afraid and *feel* legit fear. But He doesn't abandon us and leave us alone panicking in that fear that is strangling us. Read the phrase one more time.

"When I am *afraid*, I will put my *trust* and faith in You."

There are two strong emotions described:

1. Afraid [which feels like fear]
2. Trust [which feels like safety]

But then, we have two action choices. The choice is *yours* to make. When I *am* afraid, I *will* trust in You.

MY CHOICES	
FEAR	TRUST
When I am afraid [Fear]	I will put my trust and faith in You [Trust]

Trust is an active choice of your will. I must *choose* to stop obsessing about my fear and actively *choose* to trust God. Maybe you're thinking, *Jimme, I'm just not feelin' it.* Same. I don't *feel it* many times either. That's when it becomes an active choice of your will. Act anyway! Choose to allow your faith to be bigger than your fear.

Action 3: Stop Panicking!

Fear always produces a physical reaction. It might be fear of bridges, elevators, clowns, heights, or being in a crowd when you have social anxiety. The fact is, we *feel* our fear.

Ever had a panic attack? What happens physically when you have an anxiety attack? Let's name some of the physical symptoms or reactions we experience:

- stomach knots up
- sweating like crazy
- knees weaken
- heart beats faster
- body trembles
- breathing accelerates
- muscles tense up and tighten

Did you know there are specific things you can do—*on purpose*—to alter the physical reaction of your body when you feel fear? Because I have spent my career as a professional musician, teaching and performing, I have learned some practical tips to reduce the physical reaction of my body when I feel fear or stressed out with anxiety.

Allow me to share these practical coping strategies with you:

- *Monitor your breathing.* What happens when you panic? You begin shallow chest breathing. Then, you feel the need to breathe more quickly, which causes you to hyperventilate. So, how do you counter that? Practice deep abdominal breathing. Let your stomach relax, and then inhale slowly and deeply for ten seconds. Hold your breath for several seconds, then slowly blow it out through your lips—like letting air out of a balloon. This one technique, alone, helps you gain control of your body.

- *Relax muscles that you tend to tighten.* The next time you feel panic coming on, make a point to notice how your muscles respond. Do you clench your hands? Cross your legs tightly? Squeeze your butt cheeks? ☺ Fold your arms? Tighten your stomach muscles? Clench your teeth? All these reactions just *increase* your stress level. Make a conscious decision to do exactly the opposite. Intentionally relax your muscles when you are tense. Move your head around to loosen your tight neck muscles. Open your mouth and let your jaw hang limp. Relax your butt cheeks. Open your clenched hands and let them hang loosely. Then, shake your whole body. "Shake it out, shake it out!" ♪ ♪ ♩ ♪

- *Do something physical.* Physical activity helps reduce stress when you're filled with anxiety. For example, walk, run, skip, shoot hoops, play sports, dance, or play with your dog! Anything that will bring you joy and make you LAUGH! Laughter truly is the best medicine!

When we panic, we only make the situation worse.

Action 4: Confront Your Fear

Stare the lion in the face. At some point, it is necessary to do the very thing that frightens you, the thing you fear most. We have to face our fear head-on. Conquering any fear begins with facing the fact that fear itself cannot be fully avoided. Take small, baby steps forward.

> If you think you need to wait until you're no longer afraid, you will never conquer your fear.

You don't cure a fear by analyzing it to death but through experiencing it . . . in baby steps. For example, maybe you have a fear of heights or elevators or bridges. You might need to ask for the help of someone you trust such as a friend or mentor to help you gain courage to step into the situation that causes you fear. Their assistance and encouraging words can give you courage. Sometimes, we need someone to come alongside us to encourage us to move forward and do the very thing we fear!

I have always been terrified of dogs. I was bitten by one when I was little, and that made me scared to be around dogs or to trust them. Well, one day a few years ago, I was teaching piano lessons in my studio and in the door walked my handsome twenty-something-year-old son, Jason. I ran over to greet him with a great, big hug! Jason had his coat pulled suspiciously tightly around him, and he slyly grinned at me while proudly announcing, "G-ma, meet Tyson. Tyson, meet G-ma!" as he slowly opened his coat to reveal an adorable little black ball of fur—an abandoned puppy named Tyson. Needless to say, as he placed Tyson in my arms, it was love at first sight!

He had me at hello, or rather *woof*. ☺

That was step one. Jason also has another rescue dog named Champ. Well, I was absolutely terrified of Champ and certainly would not dare think of reaching my hand down in front of his slobbery, growling, menacing teeth to feed him! ☹ But, Jason was determined to help me get over my fear of feeding the dogs. So, what did he do? Jason took my hand in his. He put a dog treat in it. As he calmly talked to me, he gently encouraged and instructed me that *together* we were going to feed Champ that treat. I'm not gonna lie, it took several attempts (well, maybe a lotta!) before Champ got that treat! But Jason came alongside me, eased my fear by taking my hand in his, and helped coach me to be less afraid to put my hand close to that dog's mouth.

So, just maybe someone coming alongside you is exactly what you need. Don't be afraid to ask for help. WARNING: That help might just come in the name of Champ or Tyson. ☺

Action 5: Find a Safe Person You Trust and Talk Through Your Fears

Confide in and talk with someone you trust. If you are struggling with fear or anxiety, the presence of someone you trust—with whom you feel safe—is huge. A quote I share so often:

> **"The best present you can give someone is your presence."**

Don't ever underestimate the power of presence. The presence of someone you trust. Or *your* presence when someone needs *you!*

Ultimately, the safest refuge is God's presence. I have learned that personally, deeply, in a profound way. "God is my refuge and strength, an ever-present help in trouble" (Psalm 46:1 NIV).

After my Lyme disease diagnosis, God's Spirit and His presence are so alive in me and are the only hope I have to face the unknown of my future. He will be your hope too.

> In God alone my *soul finds rest*,
>   my salvation comes from Him.
> He alone is my rock and my salvation.
>   He is my fortress;
>   I will never be shaken.
> > —Psalm 62:1-2 BSB, emphasis added

> Have mercy on me, O God, have mercy,
>   for *in You* my *soul* takes *refuge*.
> > —Psalm 57:1 BSB, emphasis added

GOD'S PRESENCE really is the only true security we have to help calm our deepest, darkest fears and to face the future.

Action 6: Control Your Fear by Reshaping Your Thoughts and Identifying Your Triggers

We control our fear by learning to reshape our thoughts. You are what you think! If you constantly dwell on your anxiety, it will overtake you. If you allow yourself to obsess because you have anxiety, you will stay just that: anxious. FEAR will paralyze you.

Identifying My Triggers

I realized I have carried a high level of internal anxiety since I was a little girl. No one talked openly about emotions and feelings in my family, and I certainly didn't have a name to put to what I felt. I had a lot of stomach issues, kept all of my emotions tightly locked up inside my little head, and lived with a constant sense of dread and fear. I now realize a lot of my anxiety and fear was rooted in expectation. Daddy's expectations.

My daddy was very difficult to live with, a rigid perfectionist who was incapable of expressing affection and was verbally abusive and impossible to please.

Daddy's impossible expectations of me created an inner turmoil of never measuring up, always longing to be accepted and loved, and never feeling safe because I didn't know when the next verbal explosion of insults was coming. All the demons from his past that he was personally fighting made our family life *hell*. Rigid rules and impossible standards about *everything*! There was *one right way* to do everything—his way. Daddy was OCD to the extreme. And he expected us to read his mind, automatically know *his right way*, with no explanation. The scalding, demeaning, heart-piercing, soul-shattering words he said when I didn't do something right, by his unreasonable standards, even though I was constantly trying my hardest to please him—trying not to upset him or set him off—still ring in my head and affect how I think about myself: *"What are you? STUPID? Hot Almighty! You 'bout a dumb one! You stupid! Get out of my way!"*

Those cutting, insulting words deeply shaped me and defined who I thought I was. *Stupid* and *incapable*. That has carried over into the thoughts that immediately flood my mind as an adult and how I view myself when I don't live up to the expectations I have set for myself.

Growing up in fear and a lack of security deeply affected my lack of confidence and belief in myself.

Internal Expectations I Have of Myself

I have also come to realize I transferred that wrong view onto myself and a lot of my anxiety comes from putting unrealistic expectations and high demands on myself. Impossible expectations that are unattainable and impossible to reach cause me to beat myself up and hate myself.

- I never feel good enough.
- I give others grace, but not myself.
- I feel I have to do things perfectly.

I have realized a lot of that wrong perspective is rooted in trying to meet Daddy's impossible, unattainable expectations. So, reversing my mindset and perspective has been a conscious goal. Sometimes I succeed. Other days, I fail. But, I keep trying.

I have worked extremely hard all my life because of the high standards I have set for myself. God has gifted me to be an extremely high-capacity person with a high capacity for leadership and life. God also gifted me with a high capacity for relationships and loving others deeply because He apparently created me with a heart the size of the globe.

Because of this, dealing with the "new normal" and limitations of my life while fighting and living with chronic, advanced Lyme disease has been devastating and creates a tremendous amount of extra stress. Sometimes, I set impossibly high expectations on myself and have trouble forgiving myself if I cannot meet them. Or if people get upset because I don't meet their expectations and unrealistic demands! So, I meet with God every morning and give my body, my brain, my life, my hopes, my plans, my day to Him. To do with me as He pleases. All that really matters is the Approval of One. The Voice of One. His Favor over my life.

> I choose every day to be grateful for what I *can* do,
> and not dwell on what I *can't* do.

I have had to realize my life now is no longer about *time management*, but about *energy management*. I love so deeply and so fiercely that it grieves me profoundly not to be able to care for and spend time with people loving on them, mentoring, counseling, and ministering one-on-one as much as I used to . . . and still long to do.

Although the scope and influence God has given over my life has become far-reaching, the most important thing that matters to me is the approval and smile of God's pleasure over my life.

As I have worked painfully hard to rehab my body and my brain and to reenter life and leadership on the days that my body has stamina and my brain has healed enough to regain some capacity, I am facing a "new normal." I *miss* the old me. Many days, to be perfectly honest, I *hate* the new me. The struggle is still very real and the wrestling match that goes on in my mind is fierce. I start beating myself up when I can't do what I used to do and the lies start bombarding my mind:

- You're worthless.
- You suck.
- You're useless.
- You don't have what it takes anymore.
- You're not worth loving.
- Maybe you should just go away, throw in the towel, and give up.
- It's over, girl. God's done with you.

God has to remind me every single day that those are lies meant to destroy me. He has to gently remind me of the very same words I trade-marked and lovingly say to you:

> *You are* welcome.
> *You are* wanted.
> *You are* valued.
> *You are* loved.®

You are loved . . . just as you are. In all your brokenness. In all your weakness. In all your struggles.

If you came over to my house, you would see Post-it notes placed strategically all around my house: in my kitchen, on my bathroom mirror, and in my treatment room where I get medical IV infusions to keep fighting this disease. Affirmations from God's Book of Truth and inspiring, positive, motivating quotes to intentionally focus my mind and thoughts! To stop the negative, self-defeating thoughts that bombard my mind as my body and brain continue to heal. Truths that remind me I don't need to be fearful, scared, or afraid because God loves me, cares for me, will protect me, and will never leave me, abandon me, or forsake me.

I share all of this to be honest, raw, and real with you so that you know you are not alone. You are loved. Just like you are. You are loved, wanted, valued, and accepted. The struggles may be very real, but God does have a plan and purpose for your life.

What Really Causes Our Anxiety?

If you really get to the root of anxiety, it is fear of the unknown. Not being able to control your situation. The major reason we panic is fear we are losing control.

Let me share with you what God has to say about anxiety and worry. God told us exactly what we need to do when anxiety and panic set in. Because they will! But the good news is that God does not leave us alone to deal with our fears. He teaches us how to work through our anxiety. When we are gripped with fear or worry, He tells us exactly what to do to be flooded with peace and less afraid of the future.

God shares this amazingly tender and simple truth about anxiety.

> This is why I tell you not to worry about everyday life—whether you have enough food and drink, or enough clothes to wear. Isn't life more than food, and your body more than clothing? Look at the birds. They don't plant or harvest or store food in barns, for your heavenly Father feeds them. And aren't you far more valuable to him than they are? Can all your worries add a single moment to your life?
>
> And why worry about your clothing? Look at the lilies of the field and how they grow. They don't work or make their clothing, yet Solomon in all his glory was not dressed as beautifully as they are. And if God cares so wonderfully for wildflowers that

are here today and thrown into the fire tomorrow, he will certainly care for you. . . .

So don't worry about these things. . . . Your heavenly Father already knows all your needs. Seek the Kingdom of God above all else . . . and he will give you everything you need.
So don't worry about tomorrow. (Matthew 6:25–34, emphasis added)

> Worry and fear paralyze us! When you worry, you freeze!
> You are no longer living in the present.
> You are either regretting what happened in the past
> —*which you can't change*—
> or dreading what might happen in the future
> —*which you can't control.*

God gives us very specific help, a very specific plan when fear, anxiety, or panic threatens to overtake us:

Don't worry about anything; instead, pray about everything. Tell God what you need, and thank him for all he has done. Then you will experience God's peace, which exceeds anything we can understand. His peace will guard your hearts and minds as you live in Christ Jesus. (Philippians 4:6–7)

The Old English word from which we get our word *worry* literally means "to strangle or choke." That is exactly what worry does. It is a kind of mental and emotional strangulation. Have you ever been so consumed with worry and severe anxiety over a situation that it feels as though you are choking, you are strangling, and you, quite literally, feel as if you can't breathe? A true panic attack!

Worry is the greatest thief of a peaceful mind. Even God recognizes and knows that it is not enough just to tell us to "quit worrying," because that will never get to the root of our problem.

Don't worry. Instead pray! Pray your worries to God. Leave the rest to Him. Trust God to be faithful, just like He promised.

Just like the theme song from the Disney movie *Frozen* says: "Let it go. Let it go." Or as my little granddarlin', Trey, belts out from his car seat, "Let it go. Let it go . . . *me don't care.*" Actually, pretty wise advice from a three-year-old! "Me don't care" meaning "I'm no longer worrying or trying to control the outcome of the situation."

> [God,] You will keep in perfect peace
>> all who trust in you,
>> all whose thoughts are fixed on you!
>>> —Isaiah 26:3

Dealing with fear and anxiety is an ongoing process. New circumstances or challenges will come into your life that will unexpectedly and legitimately accelerate your struggle with *fear* versus *trust*.

Whenever you start to worry, ask yourself this question: ***Am I dwelling on the problem or working on a solution?***

When we're consumed with worry and anxiety, it really is a slap in God's face.

What you fear *most* reveals where you trust God the *least*.

- Worry says I don't think God can provide.
- Worry says He is not powerful enough to handle my problems.
- Worry says I can solve my problems by stressing constantly. (Really?)
- Worry says: "God, You are not capable of trust!"

So, the real question is: *Do I trust God?*

Listen to these words from Jesus Himself: "Not a single sparrow can fall to the ground without your Father knowing it. And the very hairs on your head are all numbered. So don't be afraid; you are more valuable to God than a whole flock of sparrows" (Matthew 10:29–31).

If you came over to my house and joined me for a cup of coffee at my kitchen table, you would see a framed quote hanging on my wall in very prominent view with these words:

> Fear not tomorrow;
> God is *already* there.

You know why? *Because my heart needs to see that truth every single morning.* I am so prone to fear. How about you? Next time you're feeling helpless, hopeless, or scared, remember:

God has shouted His love to you from the cross.

Do you need Him to remind you that He cares? That He knows your name? All you gotta do is look out your window and watch a little bird. Does that little sparrow worry about her next meal? No, God provides. Not a sparrow falls from the sky without Him knowing.

> 66 Worry does not empty tomorrow of its sorrow. It empties today of its strength.
> —Corrie ten Boom 99

Or take a look at those gorgeous wildflowers. They're not fretting and filled with anxiety about whether they're gonna have clothes. *"Will I have one petal today or five?"* God dresses them in radiant splendor and breathtaking colors. And they're here today but gone tomorrow. Pouffff!

Do you not think He cares for you?

God's got you.
With more love than you can imagine,

 Jimme

2

Toxic Relationships | Drama

My Dear Conflicted Friend,

> Not every person who wants to be in your life should be.
>
> Not every person who wants to be in your life should have permission to be in your life.

I realize that sounds really harsh and cold, but the truth is, I sure wish someone had told me that when I was fifteen.

It was the beginning of my sophomore year in high school. My family had just packed up all our belongings into a crammed U-Haul and moved from South Carolina to Chattanooga, Tennessee. I was fifteen. Not an easy age to move, and for sure, not an easy age to start a brand-new high school.

The high school I was getting ready to attend was four times bigger than the one I left! Talk about anxiety! I had this terrible crazy mix of fear combined with humongous excitement and anticipation! I mean, four times the size of your old high school also means four times the possibilities of new guys to meet, right? I'm not stupid! I didn't know anyone at this new school. No one knew me. I was excited about this new adventure but completely terrified at the same time.

How many of you have ever moved? Or changed schools? Ever watched the movie *Mean Girls*?

That's what I'm talking 'bout!

I was that new girl. Didn't know exactly where or if I was gonna fit in. I mean, I knew who I was at my old school and people knew me.

I knew where I belonged. I was a basketball player and a cheerleader. I loved playing piano and singing in choir, musicals, and other productions. Sports and music were my world. But no one knew me at this new school, and it's scary being the new kid.

You're dying for somebody to notice you and invite you in. I mean, there's nothing worse than sitting by yourself—ALONE—at the lunch table! Just somebody—ANYBODY—please talk to me! You feel the stares. The other girls checkin' you out, looking you over, sizing you up, deciding if they're gonna talk to you or not, determining if you are a threat to their territory!

High school can be the most terrifying, lonely place. All because of the absolutely exhausting *drama*. The lies. The rumors. Incriminating photos. Bullies in the hallway. Bullies in the lunchroom. The nasty, cruel texts and posts.

Haters. Girls can be straight up cruel, mean, and vicious! The confusing thing is that sometimes it's not overt; the fighting is sneaky! Girls out to completely sabotage and destroy another girl, whether out of jealousy, hate, or their own insecurity.

Our goal is to take a deep dive and an honest, raw, hard look at toxic relationships.

Unhealthy relationships. A relationship with a girlfriend, perhaps. Or it could be a family member who is incredibly difficult and hard to live with. Or possibly, a boyfriend who is controlling and abusive. Or a creeper!

There are basically three types of toxic relationships:

- A toxic friendship
- A toxic dating relationship
- A toxic family relationship

Maybe you have questions and are wondering if you are in a toxic relationship. You see red flags and warning signs, but you're really confused. Or perhaps your heart is heavy because every single day you deal with a difficult, cruel family member. You live with a parent who is very damaged and in need of deep healing herself/himself. Or just maybe, for the very first time, you might realize that YOU are that toxic person!

Maybe you're the bully!

So, warning! Straight up. I am going to say some very difficult things.

How do you know if you are in a toxic relationship? What are the warning signs?

A toxic person is jealous, overly possessive, domineering, tries to control you. They constantly belittle you, criticize you, put you down. They demand all your time and energy. They might have violent mood swings and a really short temper, blaming you for everything they do wrong. "It's your fault. If you hadn't done that, I wouldn't have to act this way!"

Very angry with you one minute, but sweet and apologetic the next so you won't leave them.

They isolate you from anyone who cares about you. They get jealous and make you feel guilty for hanging with your friends. They spy on you, stalk you, and take advantage of you big-time. They make you feel ugly, stupid, and incapable of making any decisions apart from them.

They demand to know your passwords and check your phone and social media and are jealous of any other relationship. They may physically hurt you. If you are feeling used or controlled by a toxic person, we are going to get real about some decisions you may need to make. Steps you need to take to get your life back to a healthy place again.

It may be time to cut ties with that toxic person.

I love you and don't want you to destroy yourself or allow someone to destroy you. If you'll accept my help, I want to share some Life Lessons: Things I Wish I Could Tell My Younger Self.

Truth 1: Not every person who wants to be in your life *should* **be.**

Not every person who wants to be your friend *should* be your friend.

The people you choose to allow in your life will either build you up and encourage you to grow into a better person, or they will pull you down to their level of immaturity and drama.

Don't feed the drama. Don't get sucked in.

I have done some really stupid things in my life looking for acceptance from friends and guys who didn't really value me.

When you start seeing value in yourself,
you won't tolerate toxic people in your life who do not value you.

No person is worth sacrificing your dignity and values. Ever.

Truth 2: You cannot change other people. You can only change yourself.

I often see girls tolerate certain behaviors within dating relationships or friendships and I wish that I could pull each of them aside and say, *"You are worth so much more than you are getting right now. If you could see the value I see in you, you would realize that you don't need to settle. You can set the bar so much higher with the people you let into your life."*

Sometimes, the most toxic person in your life is YOU!

You are your own worst enemy. Don't believe the lie that you're worthless.

No person can give you worth. No person can make you happy. It is not their job. Nor is it your job to make someone else happy and validate their worth. Only God can give you the security you crave and show you how much you are loved and valued.

You're losing relationships that REALLY matter, and the people who really *do* love and care for you. Don't hate yourself. Just decide right now that some things need to change.

So, what does that mean in real life? On a practical level? Once you recognize you are in a toxic relationship that is destroying you, it's time to be proactive.

The choice of friends in your life is yours. Choose carefully.

We literally become like the people we hang out with. Friends influence our thinking and choices.

God's Book of Truth points out how important our friends are:

> Walk with the wise and become wise;
> associate with fools and get in trouble.
> —Proverbs 13:20

It's incredibly important to choose your friends wisely. Let's look at some traits of a healthy friendship versus the traits of an unhealthy friendship.

Healthy Friendship	vs.	Unhealthy Friendship
Care		Disrespect
Trust		Lies
Love		Control
Honesty		Jealousy

Truth 3: Neediness is not friendship.

Your attitude should be: *"I'm okay with you; I'm okay without you. But I want you in my life and I choose to be a part of yours. Both of us are better people as a result of our friendship."*

Some really simple but good advice: *"If you want a friend, you must show yourself friendly."* In other words, if you want a friend, *be* a friend.

There are two types of people in the world: givers and takers. Which one are you? *If you are a taker—a bully:*

You are selfish. You are demanding. You are not grateful. You expect, expect, expect! You demand, demand, demand! It is your way or no way.

If you recognize you are a taker, *you are* that toxic person we are talking about! Determine, with God's help, you are going to become aware of your actions—aware of your behavior—and begin the hard work to change. And I'm not gonna lie to you. It will be some of the hardest work you have ever done in your life!

Quit making excuses for your anger! Healthy people learn how to manage their emotions. They might feel angry, but they learn effective ways to express their feelings without blowing up and attacking someone else.

> If you don't get a grip on your anger now, I can guarantee that you are going to have deep trouble with every intimate relationship in your life!

Every single one of us has legitimate reasons to get angry about something or at certain situations. But it's how you handle your anger that matters.

> A toxic, angry person will leave a trail of broken relationships their whole life.

Dealing with your emotions is a daily battle. You can't stop the emotions from coming, but you *can* control your response. In fact, your success in life depends on it.

> If you discipline yourself, no one else will have to.

Truth 4: Place healthy boundaries around yourself.

- 💜 Healthy boundaries will protect your mind, your body, and your heart.
- 💜 Healthy boundaries will keep you from being manipulated.

> People treat you the way you allow them to treat you.

Boundaries

Let's talk specifically about boundaries you may need to place in two distinct relationships in your life. The first is with a *toxic family member*. The second is with a *toxic friend or relationship*.

Toxic Family Member

Maybe you live with a parent who is an alcoholic, an addict, or mentally ill. Some days are okay. But when your mom or dad is drinking heavily, you have to basically *be the parent*. You're put into the position of covering and lying for him or her to keep them from losing their job, or worse yet, the house. You have to make excuses for him or her because their behavior is so unpredictable, freakin' erratic. They explode over the least little thing. You don't feel safe having friends over because you never know what your parent might say or do. You're humiliated because you don't know what your friend might see or hear.

It's exhausting to basically function as the grown-up and be the parent of the family. With a toxic family member, you will have to learn how to establish boundaries that will protect your heart from more hurt and disappointment. It will be important to think, plan ahead, and rehearse how you will deal with "hot button" issues. How you will react when you are in the heat of the moment. You cannot change the other person, but you can change the way you handle and deal with the situation.

> If you cannot honor the person, honor the position.

If you cannot respect the person, respect the position. Start with respecting the principle: honor your father and mother.

That does *not* mean you agree with or condone their behavior. It is not okay! But the posture of your heart is important.

You may have legitimate reasons to disagree, but you can show honor through the way you talk by not sassing or being disrespectful, hot-headed, and angry. At times, when the situation is becoming heated and volatile, you may need to walk away to keep the situation from escalating into violence.

However, let me be very clear. I am not condoning abuse! That is something entirely different.

No one deserves to be abused. Please find the courage to speak privately to someone you trust if you are being abused verbally, physically, emotionally, or sexually. You do not have to take that. It is NOT your fault . . . and that is not okay!

If you do need to confront or challenge your parent about a situation, make sure you are clearheaded and in control of your emotions. An angry person is looking for a fight. Keep a cool head. *Do not get pulled into their drama.* Then, when you do have that tough, difficult conversation, you will not have regrets about YOU.

It does not necessarily always mean there will be resolution. But you will not have regrets about *yourself.* About how *you* behaved. About how *you* handled the situation.

> Toxic family relationships may take a lifetime to resolve.
> Or, they may never resolve, especially if there is no desire to be mature on their end!

But, remember this: the *only* person you are responsible for is *you.*

> You cannot fix someone who doesn't want to be fixed, but **you can ruin your life trying**.

You do not want to repeat some of the behavior you have seen modeled in your family. Begin *now* to choose a much different life for yourself.

Let me assure you that however bad your circumstances are right now, your life doesn't always have to be this way. The life you choose for yourself as an adult can look very different if you choose to be intentional now about the kind of life and future you want to create.

> Sometimes the best education you can get is what you *don't* want to become!

Toxic Friendships

> Not everyone DESERVES a front row seat in the theatre of your life!
> Some should be placed in the back row or not even allowed in!

Accept people as they are, but place them where they belong.

Friends are the family we choose. You don't get to choose your family, but *you do choose your friends.* Maybe you have a toxic friend who only wants you when she needs something from you. She doesn't ask. She demands. She texts you over and over 'til you finally answer. She has no consideration for your time or your schedule. If she needs a ride, she expects you to drop whatever you're doing and drive across town to get her, and she never offers to help with the gas and never bothers to say "thanks."

I had a "best friend" in high school who stole from me, faked my identity, and created all kinds of lies and false rumors about me trying to turn my close friends, trusted youth leaders, and teachers against me. She even faked a whole series of disturbing letters mailed in my name and sent to this boy who liked me and was interested in dating me—because she didn't want him to like me and she wanted to date him. All this happened behind my back . . . while I totally trusted her, had her back, loved her like a sister, and confided in her when my parents went through a very difficult marriage and public scandal. I felt totally betrayed and humiliated and had difficulty knowing who and how to ever trust again.

It may take a while to recognize that not everyone has your best interest at heart. You may need to distance yourself from "friends" who manipulate, lie, and try to control or destroy you.

As hard as it is, you DO have to start putting some boundaries of protection around yourself.

> Not everyone deserves unedited access into your life.

And that's okay! Can I give you a little *Jimme* advice?

Truth 5: "When someone shows you who they are, believe them the first time."

Those words from Maya Angelou are so true! Quit lying to yourself. If your best friend or your boyfriend is jealous, critical, possessive, controlling, and manipulative, admit it to yourself. You do not have to put up with being abused, controlled, threatened, told you are worthless and useless, and treated like crap.

You are not worthless. Do not let someone stop you from seeing or talking with your friends or family. Do not let someone control where you go, what you wear, what you do. Do not let someone force you to have sex, blame you for hurtful things they do, threaten to kill you, or hurt you if you leave them.

That is not love. That is control.

You are not worthless. You do not deserve that. Do not be held hostage to that person. Tell someone. Ask for help. Get out! Don't be embarrassed.

Short-term shame is better than a lifetime of pain!

When someone shows you who they are the first time, believe them! Let me share some practical ways to put boundaries around yourself:

1. Learn to say no.
2. Develop a "code word" when you need help getting out of a situation.
3. Have an escape plan so you don't get stuck in dangerous situations.
4. Don't be alone with a guy or a girl if you notice "red flags."
5. Decide before you get pressured *how far* you will go; what you *will* or *won't* do.

Truth 6: Choose your team carefully!

The people closest to you help determine your future. It's a fact—so choose your team carefully!

Truth 7: Show me your friends and I will show you your future.

For example, the head coach of the Indianapolis Colts, or any NFL team, has one goal. WIN!

If the coach wants to have a winning team, with the ultimate goal of winning the Super Bowl, he can't choose just any old football players. He must choose elite athletes who are competitors at the top of their game.

In the same way, YOU are the COACH of your own team. Mine is TEAM JIMME. You choose your team. Your closest friends become your team. You are responsible for choosing the best! GO "TEAM [insert your name]!"

Who you spend your time with *is* your team.

If you surround yourself with people who are positive, hard-working, generous, kind, and have intentional goals for their life, you will start to pick up those qualities in your own life. We affect each other. Maybe I should say . . . we "infect" each other! ☺ Who are you allowing to affect and infect you? Surround yourself with people who have what you want to "catch." ☺

Find some good role models and mentors. Ask them to be part of your life, to mentor and walk alongside you.

Stay away from toxic people. "Friends" who are worthless pieces of #@%! Those who use you, exploit you, and live reckless lives, destroying people, property, and your possessions with no remorse. They will drag you down. Every time. You won't pull them up. I promise. No matter how good your intentions are. I have watched too many girls go back to these same "friends" only to get used, beaten up, lied to, stolen from, and their lives ruined.

If those "friends" have issues with anger, you'll start having issues with anger. If they're negative, you'll be negative. If they're moody, you'll be moody.

If they use and deal drugs, you're more likely to start using and dealing. If they party every weekend and get wasted, you'll start partying every weekend and get wasted. Simply because you wanna hang with them and you desperately want them to like you and accept you.

> Being in a relationship with the wrong people
> can literally ruin your life.

If that means you need to cut some people and activities out of your life, do it. Walk away from toxic people, or you will "catch" what they have.

> Cutting unhealthy people out of my life doesn't mean I hate them. It means I respect me.

- You don't have to be rude or mean. Just begin to spend less and less time with people who are always negative or critical. People who love and thrive on drama. *"Ain't nobody got time fo' dat!"*
- If you are in a toxic dating relationship and you have legit fears for your safety because of the manipulation and control this person has over you, talk to someone you trust. *You deserve help. You are not worthless and useless. You are not damaged goods.*
- For others of you, perhaps for the first time, you have come face-to-face with the horrible realization that *you are that bully. You are that toxic person.* And you hate yourself for it. Can I tell you there is HOPE. You CAN CHANGE! You are not hopeless!

There is nothing you have done that cannot be forgiven. There is no shame in admitting that you are broken.

We are all broken. We all need help, hope, and forgiveness. You might say, "Jimme, I just can't do this freakin' life anymore." You are exactly right; you can't!

You were made to need Jesus.

True Love comes not in the shape of a diamond but of a cross.

> Jesus *gave* His life to *save* yours.

His arms are stretched wide open in the shape of a cross, welcoming you into a relationship with Him! God does have a plan and purpose for your life! You were made *on purpose . . . for a purpose. Remember:*

- You're not a mistake.
- You're not worthless. God says you're worthy.
- You're not useless. God says you're useful.

Run to the cross. This is your moment of decision. The most important decision you will ever make.

Trust Jesus. Invite Him into your life to become your personal Savior and Life-Guide. You weren't created to do this life alone. You were made to need Jesus, Your Maker and Creator. Place your life in His hands.

He has the power to change you from the inside out.

God is the God of second chances . . . and third and fourth! ☺

It's *never* too late to start over.

> God accepts you just as you are;
> But He has very real plans to change you.

With more love than you can imagine,

 **Jimme**

3

Body Image | Acceptance

My Dear Self-Critical Darlin',

Our topic, body image / body shame, hits home with every single one of us. An area we ALL struggle with—guaranteed!

Most guys think every girl's dream is to find the perfect guy. Pshhh! NOT! Every girl's dream is to eat without getting fat! ☺

> You are your own worst critic!

I love the quote hanging in my kitchen: *Life is short. Eat cookies!*

What I've learned is sometimes, we just gotta laugh and remind ourselves that life is way too short to spend it worrying and obsessing over things that don't matter to the point we stop enjoying and living life! Refuse to give it any more headspace!

> **"**
> Life is too short
> for self-hatred and
> celery sticks.
> —Marilyn Wann
> **"**

In all my years, I have yet to meet one woman or girl who completely loves her body. I have yet to hear one girl say: "Mmmm! Lookin' good! You go girl! You are slayin' it! LOVIN' this body! These thighs, these abs! Girl, what you talkin' 'bout?!"

Instead, we have this little voice, our own inner critic, whispering inside our head:

- You're too fat.
- Your thighs are disgusting. They *so* rub together when you walk.
- You're not good at anything.
- If you were skinnier, maybe people would like you.

Have you ever been bullied? Bullied for the way you look, the way you walk, the way you talk?

You know who the WORST bully in the room is?

The worst bully you will ever deal with is that face staring you right back in the mirror—you!

I call it your "body bully." The voice in your head that beats you up every single day, reminding you why you're not good enough. That you suck. Why you don't measure up or fit in.

Truth is:

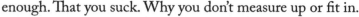
You are your own worst enemy!

My goal is that you will learn to see yourself through kind eyes, not eyes of criticism and self-hatred, but eyes of compassion, even eyes of love.

I remember growing up I never felt like I fit in or belonged. I had so many insecurities. I wanted to be everybody else but me.

When I was a little girl, my daddy always made a big deal about how much he loved and was attracted to small, petite, dark-haired, brunette, brown-eyed girls. My inner little girl interpreted that as: *Something's awfully wrong with me. I guess my daddy doesn't love me. I don't have dark hair. I don't have brown eyes. And I'm definitely* not *small.*

The only thing "little" about me is my "bird legs." I used to get teased and bullied about them all the time. In fact, I passed that family trait and those same legs on to my good-lookin' sons. Sorry, boys!

But I can laugh about my bird legs now and even had my hubby take a photo of me at the beach one summer when a huge flock of seagulls swooped in, surrounded me, and landed beside me in my beach chair. So, I just stood up with the seagulls and posed. It looked like the *Bird Leg*

Convention had convened on Myrtle Beach! And their keynote speaker had just arrived! ☺

I remember one particular vacation when I was little. My parents had saved and saved to be able to take my little sister and me to Walt Disney World. It was a big deal because our family didn't have much money. We stayed at a gorgeous, tropical hotel called the Polynesian Resort, which was the closest our family would ever get to pretending like we were going to Hawaii!

One evening for dinner, we went to a Hawaiian luau. OMGOSH! I was totally mesmerized and smitten with those gorgeous hula dancers! I loved watching their beautiful bodies dance and sway so gracefully and gently to the lush island music. I was totally smitten! 100 percent. I knew *exactly* what I wanted to be when I grew up. Only problem—of course, once again—they were dark-haired, brown-eyed girls!

I begged God—why couldn't I have been born in Hawaii and be one of those gorgeous, dark-skinned, dark-eyed, perfectly tanned hula dancers? One year for Christmas, I even asked for the video "Do the Hula with Tula!" Never have watched it one time, but one of these days my dream *will* come true and I am gonna do the hula. (But, probably not with Tula!)

I bet just like me you've struggled and wished *you could be anybody but you.* It takes a lifetime to understand and accept: nobody can beat you at being you.

So maybe, like me, you need a little body image adjustment—a fresh new set of eyes to really see the truth about yourself.

Whose eyes are you looking into to find your worth, your value, or if you even matter? Maybe you're trusting the wrong set of eyes. The wrong mirror to determine how you feel about your body. Whether you feel worthy . . . or worthless. Valued . . . or useless.

There are three different mirrors—eyes—you may be using to judge yourself:

- the mirror of your own eyes
- the mirror of everyone else's eyes
- the mirror of God's eyes

The greatest gift I wish I could give you is to see yourself the way I see you. The way God sees you.

Through eyes of love.

God outdid Himself when He made you! I don't want you to spend your life hating and despising yourself.

Body shaming is such a trap for girls. Whether you are feeling that shame yourself because you hate your body or you are experiencing it from others who are rippin' into you, bullying you to make themselves look better, we're gonna tackle this body-shaming struggle and help each other!

So, let me ask: Where do *you* look to find your value? Which mirror? Which set of eyes are you trusting to define you?

The problem isn't with your body, the problem is what you think of it... And what you think of yourself.

1. The Mirror of Your Own Eyes

Maybe the mirror you believe about yourself is kind of like one of those snapchat filters!

I'm afraid some of us have that crazy snapchat filter inside our own heads. When you look into the mirror every day, what you see in your mind is not reality.

- You hate yourself so badly, you don't want to go to school.
- You hate the color of your skin.
- You cut yourself because you don't think you fit in or belong.
- You believe the lie that skinnier people are happier or better. So, you're starving yourself to find out.
- You look with disgust at your body at what you perceive as flaws.

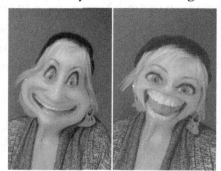

- You begin to compete with other girls and never feel like you measure up.
- You avoid participating in certain activities because you're afraid of how you look.

Or, maybe the mirror that you struggle with is not so much the *mirror of your own eyes*, but rather . . .

2. The Mirror of Everyone Else's Eyes

You constantly scan and read the mirror of other people's eyes to see what they think of you. You look into their eyes to see if you're accepted or rejected. Their eyes tell you if you're beautiful or less than, if you're popular or a loser, if you're smart or just plain stupid.

Please hear me, my beautiful girls!

If you only listen to the voice of the culture around you, you will waste your whole life feeling like you never measure up!

You will believe the lie that you've gotta be perfect and look perfect to be accepted.

You will believe the lie that your worth and value come from your appearance. The problem with all of us is: it's all about the "-er":

- I don't just want to be thin. I want to be thin*er*.
- Not just smart, but smart*er*.
- Not just hot, but hot*er*.

It's all about the "-er." And that's a miserable way to live. Don't let the "-er" destroy you.

When your looks and outward appearance are all that matters to you, your self-worth and self-confidence will be reduced to two things:

1. comparing yourself to others
2. competing with others

If you spend the rest of your life obsessed with those two things, you're in for a miserable life. You'll end up screwing up every valuable relationship in your life if you believe *everyone is a threat to you*, because you will live constantly competing and comparing.

The truth is we all long for approval and to know that we matter. And that's okay. That's normal. But where we look to find that approval really matters.

You will have to fight the message that says *your value = your appearance*. You'll have to reject the lie social media, Insta, and those magazine covers tell you. The lie that says the only way you can be accepted is when you are as perfect and beautiful as the model on that cover.

> Want to know the real truth about the model you envy on the cover of that magazine?
> Her body has been airbrushed to look perfect and starved to be accepted.

You will never look like the girl in the magazine. The girl in the magazine doesn't even look like the girl in the magazine.

You will never look like that filtered girl on Insta. The girl on Insta doesn't even look like that filtered girl on Insta.

The TRUTH is there is Only One Set of Eyes that really matters. Only one place where you will find the real love and acceptance you crave.

3. The Mirror of God's Eyes

God says, *"You are not a mistake. You are not worthless. You matter because I love you and carefully made you, inch by inch."* In fact, He knows the very number of hairs on your head, He sees your tears, He knows your fears, He hears your cries, and He knows your name.

Here are His words of 🖤 to you from His Book of Truth:

> I have cared for you since you were born.
>   Yes, I carried you before you were born.
> I will be your God throughout your lifetime—
>   until your hair is white with age.
> I made you, and I will carry you.
>
> —Isaiah 46:3–4

You are an original. Never has been, never will be, another just like you. My favorite quote says it best:

> Be yourself. Everyone else is already taken!
> —Oscar Wilde

You are ENOUGH. You don't have to compete. Just. Be. You.

> I'm not beautiful like you.
> I'm beautiful like me.

A smile is the most beautiful curve on a woman's body.

Every day you choose to compare yourself to someone else, it stops you from being you. Stop being afraid to be the person God has designed you to be.

Accepting your body begins with valuing it, not for its appearance, but for the amazing, incredible feats it performs for you every single day.

Don't take your body or your health for granted. I know, firsthand, things can change overnight. You can go from being perfectly healthy, to having everything stripped and it all taken away. If you have a body that works, be grateful.

You better believe my thinking about my own body has radically changed. I no longer view my body just for how it looks. I value it for what it does for me every single day—day in and day out.

I have learned to really appreciate and admire my body for how it takes care of me!

God first brought this fact home to me when my daddy suffered a severe, life-altering stroke.

Daddy had just retired and went to the hospital to have a long-overdue knee replacement surgery. After surgery, he came home and then woke up the next morning to go to rehab. While he was getting ready, brushing his teeth, he felt the whole side of his face go numb. He tried to take a few steps to call for my mama, but then he just fell over and collapsed against the wall. Over the next couple of days, Daddy had two strokes. His life, as well as the life of our family, was immediately altered—forever.

My once very strong, able-bodied, independent daddy was now paralyzed, confined to a wheelchair, dependent on Mama for the very life skills he used to take for granted! Watching him work—everyday—so long and hard at rehab, trying to gain back some of the body movements that he had lost due to his stroke, I became deeply aware of what my body does for me. Stuff my body does for me every day without me so much as being aware, much less grateful! Movements I took for granted, commands my body obeyed when I asked it to do something—these were all things my daddy's body could no longer do.

Things we expect our bodies to automatically do, my daddy's body no longer did. Simple tasks like lifting a fork to his mouth to eat or raising his arms to pull on a tee shirt over his head were commands his body no longer responded to. Daddy couldn't even get up from a chair by himself to walk from one room to the next. He had to call for help, wait for Mama to move him from a chair into his wheelchair, then roll him into the next room.

He could not simply wake up in the morning, get dressed, and head to the kitchen for a cup of coffee. He had to be dressed by someone else.

To spend time with him and help take care of him was the single most riveting experience of my life. I've always considered myself an extremely grateful person, but after watching him, my gratefulness skyrocketed through the roof! It was, for me, an eye-opener and a life-changer!

You better believe my perspective about my own body radically changed. I no longer view my body just for how it looks. I value it for what it does for me every single day—day in and day out!

I am pretty much in awe of it. When I wake up in the morning, I always now think:

- *WOW! I can roll my own body over and sit up on the side of the bed without waiting for someone to come help me.*
- *I can stand without help and walk to the kitchen to get a cup of coffee.*
- *When I am hungry, I can feed myself.*
- *I can walk to my Jeep, climb in, and drive myself to my office, the store, or a rehearsal.*
- *I am not dependent on someone else. My body has not failed me.*

I have learned to really appreciate and admire my body for how it takes care of me!

- It digests my food.
- It moves my arms, legs, and feet when I ask it to.
- It breathes without me reminding it to.
- I can see.
- I can taste, I can chew, I can swallow.
- I can run, I can skip, I can throw, I can dance!
- *Well, sort of!* ☺

All the impressive, incredible feats my body performs daily and has performed for many years, I never really stopped in amazement to say, "Thank you!"

However, with Lyme disease, my gratitude has skyrocketed as the reality of these gifts have hit home to me in a deeply personal, deeply painful way.

On the other hand, I have spent wayyy too much time being concerned about what everyone else sees when they look at my body. A lot of time concerned what they think. Concerned that someone else has a much flatter tummy, not-so-wide hips, and a curvier booty.

Embarrassed that other girls look so much better in their swimsuits than I do!

I'm not gonna lie! There are some girlfriends I wouldn't dare go on vacay with because they *actually do* look good in a bikini! I'm not *that* secure yet! ☺

But I have made progress. My new goal is to be uber grateful I have a body that works!

Maybe the thing you fear most—the thought that grips your heart with fear—is the negative opinion of other people. It keeps you awake at night, racked with anxiety and worried sick because you can't stand to feel rejected, not to be accepted, or not to have the approval of the people who matter the most to you.

Well, I will be the first to tell you that having faith in God won't totally silence that fear. But, what will happen as you gradually let go of all those fears and place your trust in Christ is that God will gradually make what He thinks about you much more important than what others think about you.

- You will no longer have to look into the mirror of everyone else's eyes to see if you matter or you belong.
- You will begin to look into the eyes of your Creator and find the approval, the love, and the acceptance you crave. The only opinion that will begin to matter to you is that of your Savior. The deeper you know Him, the more secure you'll be.
- When you finally understand that your worth and value is found in Him, you no longer need the approval of others. You will begin to live for the approval of One: your Maker.

My intention is to help you set these new goals for *your* life.

GOAL 1: Find a reason *every* day to be grateful for your body.
GOAL 2: Focus on who you *are* rather than on who you're *not*.
GOAL 3: Instead of finding everything *wrong* with your body, how about finding something *right* with it.
GOAL 4: Be grateful you have a body that *works*.

Maybe you find yourself identifying deeply with these words: "For a long time, I prayed that God would change the way I looked so I could learn to love myself. I asked God to help me diet, to find the right clothes, to make me anyone *but me*. I had it all wrong. It was my heart, not my body, that needed to change."

Let's choose to embrace that last sentence. Instead of focusing on being pretty, we should do as Rob Dial suggested: "Be bold. Silly. Strong. Confident. Independent. Intelligent. Brave. Fierce." Become a beautiful person, not simply a pretty girl.

> She was beautiful for the way she thought. She was beautiful for the sparkle in her eyes when she talked about something she loved. She was beautiful for her ability to make others smile, even when she was so sad. No, she wasn't beautiful for something as temporary as her looks. She was beautiful deep down in her soul.
>
> —Natalie Newman

How's your heart?

It's okay to not be okay. But I encourage you to . . .

Run to God in your pain, not away from Him.

At the end of your life, the approval of One is really all that matters.

With more love than you can imagine,

4

Sex | Self-Respect

My Dear Vulnerable Girl,

Our topic is Sex | Self-Respect. We're gonna keep it real and you're gonna help me. As I realize and share so often:

> Our teen girls do not live in a PG-13 world but are trapped in R-rated and XXX-rated constantly.

It's so hard as a girl to keep your head on straight in this culture! That's why this topic is so important. I care about you and don't want you to destroy yourself or allow someone else to destroy you.

Maybe you've gotten yourself into one hot mess. One quick sext or DM and you can get yourself trapped in a dark hole that seems impossible to climb out of. It can all start so young and so innocently. One of my little fourth-grade friends got an iPhone for Christmas this year. It was her first phone, so of course she was totally stoked and glued to her phone, adding friends and apps.

Not yet aware of the dangers, she innocently posted a pic of herself on TikTok and added this message with her cell number, "Text me if you wanna be my boyfriend," not realizing she had just made herself an easy target for an online predator. Thankfully, someone in her family saw it, reported it, and had it immediately removed to keep her from danger. To her, it was just an innocent, honest fourth-grade post.

There is so much pressure to fit in, to belong, to not feel left out. We all long to stand out and be noticed, to find approval, to be accepted and loved. That's normal.

Movies, Netflix, advertisements, and social media reinforce the belief that girls are nothing more than sex objects. Our bodies are judged constantly and used to sell everything from cars to fast-food burgers.

You know how much I love you, care about you, and want the very best for you. My goal is to help you learn how to think for yourself. To take care of yourself. Because maybe no one else will. Like the Under Armour slogan says: "Protect this house."

You gotta protect *your* house. No one else will.

> Your body.
> Your rules.
> Protect your house.

You matter. Your life matters. You're worth it. It is not too late to change your direction. You are not damaged goods.

> Your past does not define your future.

If your first experience was being molested or raped, that does not define you. Your past history does not define you. Your future direction does.

I can guarantee you that at some point, you are going to be placed in some sort of compromising situation. If it hasn't happened to you yet, it will. Whether it's oral sex, hookups, experimenting with a same-sex relationship, porn—whatever. The truth is you can quickly find yourself caught in one hot mess.

Maybe it's that text you got that said, "Come on over . . . this party's gonna be lit. It's gonna be a banger!" Or maybe your guy is asking you for nudes.

Problem is: Once you send him that pic, you just got set up. What you thought you did in private just got shared with all the guys in the locker room. Now it's the property of the whole world. You sent it 'cause you think the jerk actually cares about you. But with one password, the whole world of creepers, pervs, pedophiles, jerks, thousands of guys now have access to basically a photo gallery with you in it.

You think you're sending it to one guy—in private. Well, once you hit send, IT AIN'T PRIVATE! Anybody and everybody has access to you.

Girls, what I'm trying to say is that you have to think for yourself and keep your eyes wide open. Several years ago, I heard about a group called the Freshmen 500. Apparently, some of the upperclassmen guys—some of the jocks—had a competition! Their game was to see how many of the incoming freshman girls they could sleep with, "get with," hook up with. Don't be stupid, my girls! Don't be naive! Don't get used!

- All you are to him is a conquest, a challenge to be conquered!
- Then, he's movin' on to the next girl.
- You have just become nothing more than a body count.

I'm not dumb. I get how common it is now to "hook up," to be a side ho.

But, here's the reality. Let one girl share with you what it's like to live with that shame:

> Since I was fifteen, I've had a few relationships here and there, but for the most part I've had "friends with benefits." I liked kissing guys and making out with them, but of course they'd want to have sex, too, so I'd usually go along. I figured I had to give these guys what they wanted if I was going to get what I wanted. After a while I became addicted to hooking up with guys. You know, "Come over. It's gonna be lit." Every weekend I would go to a football game or a party and see someone that was hot and go mess around with him, often giving out oral sex like it was candy or something. I didn't care if I knew him. In fact, it was better if I didn't because then I wouldn't have to worry about awkwardness or "strings attached" later on. The problem that came from all of this lack of good judgment is that I've struggled with depression,

anger, jealousy, lack of self-confidence, and feeling worthless. I began to hate myself and seriously considered suicide.

Reality is you start hating yourself because you believed the lie: you think you gotta give a guy what he wants so you can keep him.

'Cause if you don't, there's another girl waitin' in line who will.

Well, let me tell you, that's a bunch of BS. You don't need him. That's not love. Protect your house! Tell him where to go and how fast! Get rid of him. He doesn't deserve you. The wrong guy will use you and move on, leaving you behind wearing nothing but shame and regret and beating yourself up for being so naive and so easy.

Let me tell you about a situation that happened right here. Some of my middle-school girls came over to my house to hang and spend an evening with me because they were scared for themselves and their friends.

Apparently, there was a birthday party for a guy in middle school. The party took place at his house and was attended by both girls and guys. While the mom left to go get pizza, one of the girls was called back to her boyfriend's bedroom. A group of his guy friends was there, laughing and telling her they were going to blindfold her so she could give her boyfriend his birthday present. She agreed to be blindfolded, and then the boyfriend unzipped his pants and the girl was forced by the other boys to give him oral sex.

This makes me furious for you girls because what girl wants to look like a fool in front of the guys?! So, she went along, not knowing what was gonna happen, but then, left feeling humiliated, dirty, and full of shame because of what she was forced to do.

So, let's talk *raw* and *real* about how you can protect yourself physically, mentally, and emotionally. My goal is to guide you as you develop an intentional strategy for *your* life. I want to suggest a few practical ideas to help you think for yourself and put some healthy boundaries in place to protect your house.

TRUTH 1: I know of too many girls who had sex when all they really wanted was someone to hold them.

It is not wrong for you to crave love and to want to be noticed and to be wanted. We all do. God placed that desire in you. It is perfectly normal.

But some guys will say or do whatever a girl wants so that she will be willing to give him her body, even if it means saying, "Mmmm, baby, I love you. You my boo. I want you so bad! You're hot as *@&!" He'll take you out, buy you things, tell you all kinds of BS if he thinks that'll help him get some! He'll tell you how much he loves and cares for you, tell you that if you *really* love him, you'll give him some. A guy with no values will take advantage of you and have sex with you without one thought whatsoever of committing his heart to you.

What these types of guys take, they never give back. Each time they have sex with a girl, they take a piece of her heart and soul. My darlin' girls, don't be stupid and naive! You've only got one you to give. Don't let him have you!

Better yet, give me his name. I will be all over him in a heartbeat. *"You leave my girl alone! If you think you're too sexy for your shirt, I can put you down in a nanosecond! Yeah, I might be all nice, kind, and loving, but you mess with one of my girls and I'll flat take you out in one hot Google minute! Don't be messin' with my girls! NOPE."*

> When you really get how much God loves you and values you, you'll be more able to recognize a cheap substitute.

Please don't give yourself away to just anybody.

I want to offer five more practical ideas to help you think for yourself, put some healthy boundaries in place, and protect your house.

TRUTH 2: Set boundaries now—it's preparation for the future.

Just because you get married and get that ring on your finger, it doesn't mean your days of being *hit on* and *seduced* are over. Hardly! Ask any married woman or man. Boundaries are never over! You never get to a place where you don't have to put boundaries of protection around yourself.

You have to be the one to protect your house because no one else will.

If you don't decide beforehand how far you want to go physically, chances are that the guy you're with is going to decide for you, and it will probably be much further than you wanted to go.

Perhaps you are headed to college. I want you to begin thinking now about the kind of boundaries you are going to place around yourself. You are going to face situations you haven't had to deal with before. If you don't have a plan, you are going to find yourself in the trap several of my college-age friends have found themselves. A guy who rocks your world can also leave it in shambles if you don't have some firm physical boundaries in place.

Allow me to share Makayla's story:

> He was everything I had dreamed of: handsome, six-pack abs, you name it. I ended up riding home with him that night, and when he invited me in, I accepted his invitation. We talked for a couple of minutes and then began kissing. Then we started rubbing against one another, grinding our bodies together as if we were having sex with our clothes on. Within minutes, the clothes came off, and I was giving my virginity to a guy that I had just met a few hours before. I'm not sure why I didn't stop him. It all happened so fast that I really didn't have time to think about it.

That's why I want you to think about your personal boundaries now. Sex is as common on college campuses as iPhones. Somebody described college dorm–living like this: *"College is screwed up. It's not real life. They take six thousand of us who are in our sexual prime and cram us into dorm rooms where there's nowhere to sit except on the bed. Guys and girls in co-ed dorms right next door to each other. . . ."*

I want you to know that many young women and young men are choosing to live with integrity—setting boundaries for their own protection. So, don't think it can't be done. But, it will take strong intentionality and a bold decision to think for yourself! To protect your house, guard your heart, guard your mind, guard your body.

You can either resent boundaries, or you can view them as protection.

Got a question for you. Why does our highway transportation department build guardrails along the side of the road?

Shortly before our young little family moved to Indianapolis, we were making a trip from Cincinnati to Indy to visit some friends. Rodney and I had both worked a long day and couldn't leave until late in the evening. Jason and Kristi were toddlers and were sound asleep in the backseat of the car. Rodney and I were both extremely tired. Every few miles, I kept asking Rodney, *"Are you okay? Gettin' sleepy? Want me to drive?"* Rodney said, *"No! No! I'm fine."* Another twenty miles, same question. Same answer. *"No! No! I'm fine! I got another hundred miles in me!"* So, I finally allowed myself to relax and barely dozed off in the front seat.

It wasn't five minutes later we were jolted awake by the crash and the horrible sound of steel scraping steel at seventy miles an hour! Rodney had fallen asleep behind the wheel and we had drifted off the road and crashed into the guardrail. As horrible as that experience was, the guardrail kept us from driving off into a one-hundred-foot ravine below.

Thank God for that guardrail. It scared us to death, but that guardrail saved our lives! Needless to say, I didn't sleep a wink after that!

In the same way, boundaries are a guardrail to keep you from getting hurt. Getting used. Embrace those guardrails. Don't resent them!

Set your boundaries *now*—your non-negotiables—before you get caught in the heat of the moment when your guard is down.

TRUTH 3: Don't advertise what you don't want to give away.

We wanna be careful. Don't advertise what you don't want to give away.

> If it ain't for sale, quit puttin' it on display.

We all get to choose how we present ourselves. If you're a foodie, you might have heard on the Food Network: Presentation is everything! To that statement I would add—not just with *food*, but with your *body*.

Hey, we all know guys are visually stimulated by what they see. When a guy sees something visually stimulating, the visual center in his brain lights up. But that does not give him a license to exploit you! He is responsible for his own actions.

Equally, girls, you are responsible for your own actions. We get to choose how we present ourselves every single day. What a girl wears can reflect how she feels about herself and how she projects her personality to the world around her. You choose the vibe you wanna give off by your attitude, your body language, your clothes, the way you respect or disrespect yourself.

Take ownership and responsibility for how you present yourself. I'm not talking about dressing like a prude, but with all due respect, don't dress like a ho.

Like the quote I saw on Insta:

> Dear girls: Dressing inappropriately is like rolling around in manure.
> Yep, you'll get attention, but mostly from pigs.
> Sincerely,
> Real Men

Please let me be clear, I am *not* talking about being *molested* or *raped* or any kind of *abuse*. That is *not* your fault. That is entirely different from what we are talking about here. You did not bring that on yourself. You *never* deserve that! Unfortunately, I understand all too well. #metoo

It was the summer I turned sixteen. I was groomed, coerced, and sexually molested by a sleaze-ball youth pastor whom I should have been able to trust. He knew *exactly* what he was doing to innocent young teen girls. It all started with little "fun" truth-or-dare games to break down my guard. Then he called and invited me over to his house because he saw "leadership potential" in me and had decided to hold a casual, spontaneous "Bible study"—only there was *no one else* invited, and it *wasn't* a Bible study he had in mind. I was too scared to tell anybody . . . and scared of him.

That summer, I worked as a counselor at our church camp. It was in the thick, sweltering hot, humid, southern, one-hundred-degree heat—and our cabin in the woods had no air-conditioning, just screened-in windows. Of course, after sweating profusely during the day, at bedtime we wore the thinnest pajamas so we weren't drenched in sweat and could breathe through the thick air. I was awakened that night, startled and scared by a pillow smothering my mouth and the filthy hands of my youth pastor roaming all over my body. He had the gall to break into my cabin while all my girls and I were asleep. He told me he had been watching me every night through our cabin windows and he couldn't get enough of looking at me in my spaghetti-strap nightgown, how beautiful I looked, how much he just had to have me—and how much he loved me. I was totally disgusted and terrified and kept telling him no. I didn't want anything to do with him and wanted him *out*! But, I was too scared and terrified to tell anyone and scared his wife would find out and blame me. Plus, I knew there were four more nights left before camp would be over.

I was terrified to go back to that dark cabin out in the woods with my little girls not knowing if he would come back. He was also the "head security," making rounds of all the cabins each night to make sure we were *safe*. Oh, how I wish I had known it was *okay to tell someone*, but who? I mean, he was my youth pastor, for crying out loud! Oh, how I wish I had *screamed*. Even if it scared my little girls! But I didn't want them to be afraid. And oh yeah! This man would be speaking to them the next morning, and I shouldn't ruin their trust in what he had to teach them. Right? Oh, how I wish I had someone I could *trust* who would *talk real* to me like I'm talking to you! Oh, how I wish I had something like Girls Nite In when I was growing up! That's why I feel so *passionate* and *determined* to *give you what I did not have!*

I am so grateful sexual abuse is talked about much more openly now. However, it still comes down to the fact that our culture is flooded with porn, guys and girls, men and women who are obsessed with the wrong expression of sex and have no problem exploiting you to meet their selfish needs! I will keep telling you and myself not to be afraid to tell, to own your voice, grow the courage to speak up and speak out, don't let someone else silence, hurt, and destroy you!

I am talking about the only thing you have control over: you.

Your body.
Your rules.
Protect your house.

I love you fiercely and I want to help you take care of you and to learn how to navigate this insane, sex-crazed world!

TRUTH 4: Teach people how to treat you.

You either teach them to treat you with respect, or you allow them to treat you with disrespect.

Remember, that Under Armour logo—protect this house? Ask God for wisdom to protect your house. He will guide you.

I gotta say, some of the posts I see girls post on social make me sick to my stomach and terrify me for you. Explicitly putting yourself out there, in vulgar detail, saying how you will use your body sexually to get a guy off. . . *Is that really the standard you want to set for yourself?* The type of relationship you want to attract? You *deserve more.* You are *worth so much more.* Don't settle!

> There will be times in your life when you have to choose between being loved and being respected.
>
> Always pick being respected.

Perhaps the thoughts or even anger raging through your mind right now is: *I don't want anybody telling me what to do! I wanna be free to sleep with whomever I want, whenever I want, however I want, and nobody's gonna tell me what to do! It's my body and I'll sleep with whomever I want, thank you very much. It's my choice and I'm free!*

Well, let me tell you something, darlin'! That love and freedom you think you're wrapping yourself in actually has another name. Know what it is? It's called Shame. Mental bondage. What you thought you had control of is actually controlling *you.*

The best way I know how to illustrate this truth is with these real-life examples. If we were all together, I would invite three girls to join me on stage to assist me. One girl would stand in the middle while her two friends "wrap" her up tight like a mummy—one sheet at a time—while I read these true-life stories one at a time. Each different colored sheet represents and symbolizes sleeping with five different crushes. The more "sheets of love" she is wrapped in, the more physically her body experiences being bound tightly like a hostage, unable to move or live freely because of being "in bondage" emotionally and mentally to these lovers. Representing the mental and psychological damage and anguish that builds up when giving your body over and over again sexually to someone without any commitment involved.[1]

Allow me to share with you these five sheets-of-love stories:

1. THIS IS JOSH.

We met during college on Spring Break at Daytona Beach.
You know the saying, "What happens in Vegas, stays in Vegas"?
Well, *it* happened.
I gave myself to some guy who doesn't even remember my name!
This is Josh.

2. THIS IS ADAM.

Adam and I have been childhood friends since first grade.
We were both going through really tough family situations.
Kinda found refuge and comfort in each other's arms.
Didn't really mean to go *there*, but we did.
This is Adam.

3. THIS IS TYRONE.

We were with a bunch of friends.
Shootin' heroin.
I passed out.
When I woke up, my friends said we had sex.
This is Tyrone.

4. THIS IS LA'TAISHA.

La'Taisha and I met at the alternative high school. We both had been expelled for destructive, rebellious behavior. Both our dads are serving time for murder. Actually, we just call them our "sperm donors" because they were never involved in our lives like a real dad should be. We have pretty much couch-hopped from place to place because our mamas are working two jobs and out all night at the bars looking for love themselves. La'Taisha and I felt an immediate connection, like we "got" each other because our lives are so much alike. Both trying to raise our younger siblings because our mama isn't around.

La'Taisha and I started messin' around with each other and experimenting in sex acts, frankly because we don't trust "no man." To be honest, I've always felt more attracted and comfortable with girls. I dunno . . . I'm kinda confused about a lotta stuff.
This is La'Taisha.

5. THIS IS JUAN.

Juan is uhhhhh-mazing! He has these incredible, mesmerizing dark eyes that just draw you in and a way of looking at you and making you feel like the most gorgeous girl on the planet!
Like you're his . . . one and only!
Only later, you find out you're one of his *many*.
He's moved on. And you're left wrapped in shame and disgust at yourself. . . for being so easy and such a fool.
This is Juan.

Truth is, that "freedom" to do whatever you want, whenever you want, with whomever you want is actually not so freeing after all. It has wrapped you in layer after layer of mental bondage.

- Thoughts of jealousy
- Feelings of disgust at yourself and shame for being so stupid and so easy
- The reality of having to deal with an STD or fear of an HIV infection
- The bitter sting of rejection and rage at the "other girl" who is now in his arms

Can I be honest with you? Can I tell you the truth? Something maybe nobody else will? The truth about that fairy-tale married life you dream about? Here's the real truth. One of these days when you finally marry "Mr. Right":

> Every time you make love to your man, you will be taking Josh, Adam, Tyrone, La'Taisha, Juan, and everybody else you've slept with to bed with you.

You're thinking: *When I was with Josh, he did this. Or Juan held me like this.* You can't enjoy the beauty of how you're being loved because you're having flashbacks of Josh and all those other lovers.

I have seen too many young girls sink into deep depression and even try to kill themselves because of the shame and humiliation of these destructive relationships. My gorgeous girls, please, don't give yourself away to just anybody.

Don't forget this truth:

> ### The wrong kind of guys give love to get sex, and girls give sex to get love!

When all you *really* wanted was just to be held. Dangerous combination!

When you make a decision to have sex with a guy who is just exploiting you, who doesn't respect you, who doesn't have wholesome values, who is not willing to commit to God's protective boundaries, that's why you feel used . . . like a piece of you dies. When two people have sex, whether they're married or whether it's a hookup, God's Book of Truth says they not only merge body parts but also merge souls. That's how powerful and serious sex is. Sex is never just a physical thing. It's not just two people gettin' off! It's a connection that is binding.

Listen to these words from God Himself, the Lover of your soul:

> There's more to sex than mere skin on skin. . . . As written in Scripture, "The two become one." . . . We must not pursue the kind of sex that avoids commitment and intimacy, leaving us more lonely than ever—the kind of sex that can never "become one." (1 Corinthians 6:16-17 MSG)

If you've already crossed a line and gone farther than you wish you had—whether sleeping around or doing everything but—you know the truth of these words.

What you did may have felt good at the moment, but something changed afterwards. That's why what seemed like something that was no big deal before became such a big deal later. You didn't just walk away with memories; you walked away with a strong emotional attachment.

That's why our Maker, God, gives us this warning out of love and protection in His Book of Truth:

> Run from sexual sin! No other sin so clearly affects the body as this one does. For sexual immorality is a sin against your own body. Don't you realize that your body is the temple of the Holy Spirit, who lives in you and was given to you by God? You do not belong to yourself, for God bought you with a high price. So . . . honor God with your body. (1 Corinthians 6:18-20)

The guardrails and boundaries of protection are there to keep you from destroying yourself.

It's not about keeping something good from you. It's about giving you the absolute best. God is not trying to withhold pleasure. He *created* it. Every instruction He gives is His attempt to protect you.

"You have to trust Me. Trust My heart," He implores us. Otherwise, it becomes all about a set of rules. God's Book of Truth is in reality a life manual. Given to you, so you don't screw up and destroy yourself. When you realize that behind the "rules" is Someone who actually cares, Someone who *actually* gives a rip about you, then you will know:

God's asking you to wait until you're in a committed marriage relationship because He doesn't want you to have scars. Consequences.

He's not asking you to wait so you can become some statistic in some dumb abstinence poll. He's asking you to wait because when you don't, you get hurt. Just ask some of your friends. You have scars. You get used.

I want to go a step further. As good as a dating relationship might possibly be, there is *no* guy or girl—no other person—who can meet and satisfy your every need. No one. He's not supposed to. It's not his job. And you can never fully satisfy a guy.

A guy or a girl cannot make you happy. If you're not able to take care of yourself and be happy without one, you'll not be happy *with* one either.

Your value, your worth, your hunger to be loved, your desire to be respected are met in one place. Your security is found in Christ. No one can fill that God-shaped hole in your heart. No guy and no same-sex relationship.

Maybe it's time to hit pause. Invest in yourself. Take time to discover Y.O.U. Don't adjust yourself to whoever your crush wants you to be. List your strengths. List things you want to accomplish in your life. Discover your favorites. Date yourself for a while. Take yourself out to movies, dinner, or a concert. Try something new. Go rock climbing. Take a dance class. Spend an afternoon hiking. Keep trying new things to figure out what really brings you joy. What are you passionate about? What is important to you?

Get to know YOU. You are quite amazing! Aren't you exhausted from trying to twist yourself into the person someone else wants you to be instead of being the real, true you?

I see you.

> Hold out for someone who will respect you and not exploit you.

Someone who will value you and, most importantly, long to please God. Great dating philosophy:

Run as fast as you can toward God,
And if someone keeps up,
Introduce yourself. ☺

With more love than you can imagine,

Jimme

5

Addiction | Trapped

My Dear Enslaved Overcomer,

These words from a celebrity and well-known actress arrested my attention:

> The first time I tried heroin, I was instantly hooked. I FELL IN LOVE! Heroin is my lover. It tells me what I'm gonna do that day. It tells me how I'm gonna make it. I wake up each day wondering and plotting how I'm gonna get my next fix. How am I gonna get money to pay for that fix! It just feels good to be numb.

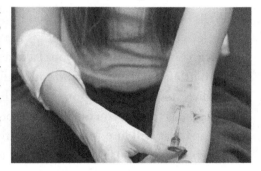

Truth is sometimes life sucks.

Maybe you're really on the struggle bus right now. How do you deal with the crap real life throws at you? Like this celebrity, all of us have ways of coping. Some healthy, some not so healthy. Truth is, we all have addictive personalities! A tendency to turn to some substance, some activity, some person, or some behavior to help us cope when life sucks!

Be real a moment. Let's say you found out your parents are getting a divorce or your best friend has stabbed you in the back and is spreading vicious rumors about you. Or your boyfriend is cheating . . . again!

Where do you go to find comfort, to get relief?

Do you cut? Injure yourself? Call a friend? Work out? Take some pills? Have sex? Smoke or vape? Grab a bag of chips or start stuffing your mouth with cookies?

Face it! No one likes dealing with rejection, pain, loneliness, or the emptiness you feel when you're alone, with no one else around, when it's just you and your thoughts. Perhaps if we knew the real truth about you right now, we would know that you hate yourself. You feel dirty. Worthless.

You feel trapped, embarrassed, and downright ashamed of some of the choices you have made or things that have happened to you.

> But what you're doing to self-medicate, numb your feelings, or escape your pain has got you in one hot mess!

Well, I care, and I don't want you to destroy yourself!

So, let's talk real about some traps that have been set to bait you, lure you, suck you in, and destroy you. Like a soldier fighting in a war zone on the battlefield, there are landmines all around you. One step in the wrong direction and you're gonna suffer lifelong consequences.

My goal is to help you make wise choices, avoid, and walk away from those traps that will lure you in and destroy you!

Maybe you're abusing Adderall or painkillers or "toasting" other girls with your water bottle filled with vodka between classes. Maybe your "fix" is the need to be in somebody's arms even if that means giving yourself away again and again to just anybody. You're jeopardizing your health and your future big-time with your risky behavior and putting yourself in reckless situations leading to STDs and other sexual diseases. But, you think, anything has got to be better than feeling this P-A-I-N.

The reasons you are doing so are straight-up real:

1. The pain you deal with at home daily is almost unbearable. Your parents fight nonstop or have made some screwed-up choices and now you have to live with the consequences of their mistakes.

2. Maybe you've had to bury your best friend 'cause she took her life. After a while, it becomes easier to try to forget the pain for a block of time and escape the reality of what you deal with. So, smoking weed, snorting coke, shooting heroin, poppin' painkillers you find in the medicine cabinet, or binge drinking is your way to drown out the pain when you're sick and tired of dealing with the junk sucking the life out of you.

3. Maybe you're just done with feeling like you don't belong. Anywhere. You so desperately want to fit in. Your heart hurts because you just want to be accepted. Your so-called friends constantly bully and harass you. You're craving love and think that maybe you might get some attention—people will notice you—if you just get sloshed and become the party girl. So, you decide—just this once—what the heck! I'm gonna go party like there's no tomorrow! I mean, really, you only live once, right? YOLO! Bring it on!

4. Maybe your closest friends don't get you anymore. They don't understand what you've been through. You've had to hold everything together at your house and take care of your little stepbrother and sister 'cause your mom just got her third divorce and now her new boyfriend has moved in and you're supposed to be happy and just love him too?

5. Perhaps your world has just been turned upside down because everything you innocently believed in when you were little has just come crashing down around you. You thought you were a family forever, but your dad just walked out on your mom and the rest of your family because he found somebody else he thinks will make him happy.

There are lots of real reasons girls begin using, vaping, drinking, or getting wasted. It's not because they made a decision to grow up and become an alcoholic or an addict. But, one bad choice leads to the next bad choice. One not-so-smart decision leads to the next not-so-smart decision. Then, habits are formed, addictions take hold, and a lifestyle is ignited from which it is hard to break free.

Perhaps some of you girls are feeling a little cocky right now—a little full of yourself—because you don't think you have any issues with dependency. You're not a user. You don't drink. Well, let me ask you some questions.

- How about your "addiction" to social media like Insta, Snapchat, or TikTok? What if you couldn't do socials for a week? A month? Would you go through withdrawal?
- How long can you turn off your phone and just exist without 24/7 contact with your friends?
- How long can you survive without being in touch with your friends or your boyfriend?

> "I never knew I was addicted . . . until I tried to stop."

We all have a "drug of choice" when life sucks: whether partying, cutting, drinking, rollin' a blunt, shopping, bingeing on Netflix, porn, stuffing doughnuts, or sleeping around.

> The point is, if you're using your addiction to *numb* your pain or *run* from your pain, you are just *prolonging* your pain.

It *will* catch up with you and you will have to face your pain head-on at some point.

> "No one chooses to be addicted . . .
> You're just trying to escape your pain."

A quick question. What is an addiction? An addiction is:

- A dependence on a substance [alcohol, weed, coke, heroin, inhalants, vaping]
- A dependence on a person [boyfriend, girlfriend, best friend]
- A dependence on an activity [cutting, shopping, gambling, social media, compulsive overeating, sex, hooking up]

Every addiction begins with a lie.
Just. This. Once.

You experimented with a behavior that you only meant to be a temporary fix, but now you realize that fix has become a necessity.

66

I couldn't seem to get enough drugs, alcohol, or sex to drown out the pain and anger.
—a GNI girl who is a recovering addict

99

When your addiction is the first craving you have when you wake up, when you plan your whole day around how you're gonna get your fix, when you have to lie and manipulate to cover up your addiction, when what you used a month ago is not enough today—you might have a problem.

Someone once wisely said:

A bad habit, if not resisted, soon becomes a necessity.

Let's take a quick look at the progression of an addiction.

1. Experimentation

Using the chemical or substance to take the edge off of your anxiety. Example: Vaping or smoking weed before a party.

2. Misuse

Chemical or substance begins to interfere with your life. Example: You're pretty much high or wasted every weekend.

3. Abuse

Reliance and dependence on the chemical controls your life and your thoughts. Example: You miss school or work because you can't function. All you can think about is getting your next fix.

4. Addiction

"I have to have more. What can I do to get more?"

Your body has now become dependent on your "fix" for survival. Your body craves it. Your body needs it. You don't just enjoy it; you *need* it.

Your mind is consumed with these thoughts:

- Where can I get some?
- How much should I get?
- Who can I trust to buy from?
- Who can I trust to use with?
- Where can I hide my supply?
- Where can I sneak away to do it?

That, my friend, is when you know you have a problem.

Maybe your struggle is not a substance but breaking free from a compulsion, a certain behavior that your mind obsesses about. That might be:

- sex
- porn
- compulsive overeating, bingeing, purging, or starving yourself with calorie counting and food restrictions (anorexia)
- social media (how many likes or how many followers you have)
- compulsive exercise to punish and beat yourself up when you screw up
- cutting, self-injury

You might ask: How do I know I have a problem?

You have a problem when your relationship with your obsession becomes more important than any relationship in your life!

Unhealthy addictions will not just destroy your relationships; they will destroy you.

However, I have good news! There is *hope*!

You *can* change. Your life can turn around. You don't have to be controlled by your addiction. You don't have to be held captive by those dark, obsessive thoughts that replay like a nightmare loop over and over in your mind. There's no fixin' at the bottom of that bottle or the end of that straw or that glass pipe.

Maybe you've relapsed—too many times to count—and think you're destined to be stuck in this addiction for the rest of your life. That there's no way you can get freedom from these chains.

That's a lie! Because of having to deal with all this crap going on in your life, maybe it's time to sit down and ask yourself, *Who am I? What kind of life do I really want?*

You have to want to change. No one can do the hard work for you. So, let's talk strategy—that is, the real steps necessary to change.

Step 1

Take ownership of your life. You alone are responsible for it. Own it.

Step 2

Admit you have a problem. Quit living in denial. Admit this truth: "I can't stop cutting. I can't stop using. I can't stop sleeping around."

Step 3

Admit you need help. You cannot do it on your own. Changing behavior and retraining your mind and body is hard work. If you have a chemical dependency, you may need professional help. Medical help might be necessary because your body is now dependent on this substance you have been feeding it. You gotta be weaned off of this substance.

So, admit you need help. There is *no shame in that*. In fact, that will be one of the smartest decisions you have ever made!

Step 4

Find a safe person to talk to about what is ripping you apart inside. Whether that person is your mentor, a counselor, a pastor, your trusted friend or adult, find that safe person.

I know many of you live extremely difficult lives in horrific, challenging situations. I have the utmost respect for you. Maybe your parent is incarcerated or the family member you live with is a user, abuser, or an alcoholic. The stress you face every single day is very painful and exhausting.

I would like to suggest that you find a safe place to talk and get that pain *out*. Otherwise, it will eat you alive.

Many of you are bleeding on the inside *from deep emotional wounds that no one can see.* Ask for help. Please. It is extremely important to get your heart cared for. Someone who cares who will wrap you up, help stop the bleeding, put dressing on your wounds, and help you start the road to healing.

We are not supposed to do life alone. Don't be afraid to reach out. Let someone in.

Step 5

Surround yourself with friends and family who want the best for you.

Surround yourself with people who *really* care about you. People who want you to be whole and healthy, such as a role model you look up to, your mentors, and healthy, positive friends.

Some of you are *very* fortunate to have family who actually care for you and want the best for you. You sure need to be grateful. Don't ever take that for granted.

But for others of you, your family is *not* a safe place. In fact, the behavior you see modeled at home is exactly what you *don't* want to become. You cannot control or choose family, but you do get to choose your friends. Who you hang out with really matters. Your friends have a major influence on you.

> Good friends bring out the best in you,
> not the worst in you.

Peer pressure is powerful. Negative peer pressure can drag you down and destroy you. Show me your friends and I'll show you your future.

But, you say, *"You don't understand! It's hard, Jimme!"*

Oh yeah?! Then quit hanging out at that place you know is gonna get you in trouble. Quit hanging with that same bunch of friends. Quit going to that same party where that same guy is after the same thing: a piece of you. *Run!*

God's Book of Truth says:

> The temptations in your life are no different from what others experience. And God is faithful. He will not allow the temptation to be more than you can stand. When you are tempted, he will show you a way out so that you can endure. (1 Corinthians 10:13)

I love what my good friend says: "The best equipment you have when battling temptation is your running shoes. *Run!*"

On the other hand, the *right* kind of peer pressure can be a positive influence.

Good friends can come alongside you when you're struggling, allow you to vent, encourage you, and help you to make wise decisions and to stay on track so you won't live with regrets.

I have finally learned the importance of having my tribe. My people. My best friends to do life with. We have each other's back and want the best for each other. We laugh together, cry together, play together, pray together, work together, and do life together.

The load you are carrying is *too heavy* for you to bear alone. It is too much.

> Trust people who are the right people to trust—to help you carry your load—to do life with.

I admit I have not always been the best at this. I have been betrayed badly and hurt deeply at a very vulnerable time in my life during which my family went through a very difficult, painful, public scandal. I trusted my "best friend" who betrayed my confidence and made light of me at a very vulnerable time. So, it became much easier for me to just stuff my feelings and keep my mouth shut. Then, nobody could judge me. Much safer. Much less vulnerable.

I have had to learn to trust and be okay with people knowing that

I hurt. That I'm not perfect. That I can't be everything to everybody. I have a breaking point too. If people get mad or upset because I can't be everything they need 24/7, then I have to be okay with them not understanding.

No one person can meet all your needs. No one person can meet all your expectations. They're not supposed to. It's not their job. Ultimately, we must all run to the same place.

God is our refuge and strength, an ever-present help in time of trouble.

Our only Safe Refuge. Our only Healer.

Only God can meet your deepest need, your deepest loneliness, your deepest insecurity, your deepest doubt, your deepest fear.

Step 6

Run to God with your pain, not away from Him. That one choice will save you from a lifetime of regret. *We have two choices:*

1. A lifetime of dependency *on painkillers*. These are counterfeit comforts along with the constant need of $$$ to support your habit and addiction so you can deal with life.

- Shootin' heroin
- Snortin' coke
- Cutting
- Poppin' painkillers
- Binge eating
- Binge drinking

These are all pain-dullers! Eventually you come back to the source of your pain and have to face it head-on again.

2. A lifetime of dependency *on God*. Dependency on God is a good dependency. Exactly where He wants us. "I can do everything through Christ, who gives me strength" (Philippians 4:13).

> Our goal is to trade self-dependency for God-dependency.

This inspiring quote, hanging purposefully on my kitchen wall, has helped me so many times when I find myself scared and full of fear.

Fear not tomorrow: God is *already* there.

I cannot promise you the pain will go away. In fact, a critical part of growing up is learning to live with pain.

Sometimes the circumstances do not change. But I can promise you something far better. Our God will walk through your circumstances with you. He will never leave you, abandon you, or forsake you.

Our culture wants you to believe that life is all about being happy. But God's goal for your life is *character development*—becoming who He wants you to be. God doesn't provide quick-fix solutions. He allows those dark, difficult times of testing and adversity to bring us to the point of recognizing that *we can't do life on our own.*

Who do *you* trust? Who is *your* God? *You?* Good ol', miraculous you? How's that workin' for you? Just maybe your Creator has a better plan for your life. Our entire life boils down to one word: TRUST.

> Trust in the LORD with all your heart, and lean not on your own understanding; in all your ways acknowledge Him, and He shall direct your paths. (Proverbs 3:5-6 NKJV)

So, don't take the easy way out and do everything you can do to avoid dealing with pain. God never wastes our pain.

Some of you are afraid to talk to God about your pain. You're afraid to say out loud what you're dealing with. Afraid God would be disgusted with you and want nothing to do with you.

Then, you obviously haven't done too much reading in God's Book of Truth.

Believe me, there is *nothing* you have done or have lived through that would surprise God. Nothing!

Quite the opposite.

Run to God with your pain, not away from Him.

The Lord promised to be near to those who have a broken heart and humble spirit. He hears your cry. He sees you. He knows your name.

So, how *do* you turn your life around?

1. *Admit you have a need.* Tell God the truth. He already knows anyway. Tell Him, "I have screwed up big-time. I am straight-up one hot mess. I admit it. I am a sinner."
2. *Admit you need a Savior.* Say to Him, "Oh God, I give up. I can't save myself. I've tried. Epic fail every time. I need you to help me—save me."
3. *Invite Christ into your life.* Admit to Him, "I'm tired of feeling empty and alone. I know I am lost and hopeless without You. I ask You to come into my life to save me. Thank You for dying on the cross to take away my sin. My shame. I need You in my life to be my Guide."

Jesus Christ stands with outstretched arms ready to welcome you, save you, and give you a new beginning—a fresh start.

Who controls your life?

That one choice will make all the difference . . . now and for eternity.

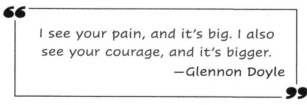

> I see your pain, and it's big. I also see your courage, and it's bigger.
> —Glennon Doyle

God doesn't just want your *attention*, He wants your full *affection*.

With more love than you can imagine,

Jimme

6

Depression | Suicide

My Dear Weary Fighter,

To anyone who has battled depression this year, I'm glad you're here.

To anyone who has had suicidal thoughts this year, I'm really glad you're still here. ♥

On particularly rough days, I like to remind myself that my track record for getting through bad days so far is 100 percent, and that's pretty good! ☺

We all know the alarming urgency of our topic: Depression | Suicide. I promise you, there is no need to hide what is tormenting you inside. In your thoughts. In the depth of your soul. I beg of you! Let's quit pretending so we can talk real. About massive bouts with depression, mental illness, and thoughts of suicide or suicide actually being carried out.

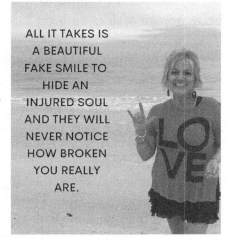

ALL IT TAKES IS A BEAUTIFUL FAKE SMILE TO HIDE AN INJURED SOUL AND THEY WILL NEVER NOTICE HOW BROKEN YOU REALLY ARE.

We're not gonna hide in the uncomfortable. We're gonna step out of isolation and into community where we can be honest about who we are and what we are struggling with.

> Silence is the most powerful scream.

- Choose HOPE.
- Choose LIFE.

Because hope is real. Help is real. You are important. Your life matters. I want you to know that you are wanted. You are seen. You are valued. You are loved.

I don't believe anybody takes their life because they want to die. You get desperate enough to end your life because you feel trapped, stuck, with no hope and no way out. The fear and darkness strangle you, and the voice of the enemy whispers, "There. Is. No. Hope."

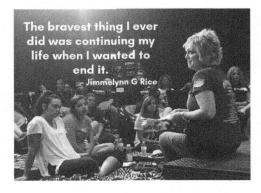

Your pain is real. God knows that.

Me too. I get it. It's okay not to be okay. The bravest thing I ever did was continuing my life when I wanted to end it. Is it possible to be a courageous, brave woman of deep faith yet battle depression at the same time? Yes, it is.

Ann Voskamp, a gifted, well-known writer, wrote these words about her own struggle:

> Depression is like a room engulfed in flames and you can't breathe for the sooty smoke smothering you limp—and suicide is deciding there is no way out but to jump straight out of the burning building....
>
> That's what you're thinking—that if you'd do yourself in, you'd be doing everyone a favor.
>
> I had planned mine for a Friday.
>
> ...You don't try to kill yourself because death's appealing but because life's agonizing. We don't want to die. But we can't stand to be devoured.[1]

The pain of depression is like a dark hole sucking you in and threatening to consume you. I'm asking your permission. May I please climb into that dark hole with you? You are not alone. We will dive into that darkness, and that darkness will not consume us. What I know is this: Light wins every time. Light invades the darkness. There is hope. There is life waiting on the other side. Jesus promised, "I have come to give you life." "Come unto me, all of you who are weary and carry heavy burdens, and I will give you rest" (Matthew 11:28).

Depression is a very lonely illness. But I want you to know that you are not alone. We are in this together. And your life has value, dignity, and worth, no matter how deep your struggle. We all need a Safe Refuge. A safe place to fall. A place to be real with our struggles, our hurts, our pain. Otherwise, the burden becomes too great, and the only option we see is a way out. Permanently.

Suicide is the second leading cause of death in teens.

The enemy of your soul has come to kill, steal, and destroy you. He will even try to convince you to believe the lie that everyone will be better off without you. Let me tell you, *no one will be better off without you*. You choosing to take your life will trap everyone around you, who loves you deeply, in an unending, horrific pain for the rest of their lives.

> Suicide is a terribly permanent solution
> to your pressing struggles.

There is no going back. Let me be very clear. *Every one* of us has the blues or feels sad or depressed occasionally. It is not wrong to feel depressed. The difficulty and danger come when we shut down emotionally and can't express or feel any emotion, or we feel only one emotion predominantly, such as deep, painful sadness.

I want to respect the power of the grip of darkness that you or someone you love may be struggling with. Depression does its best work in the dark. Scientists say that more suicides happen in the dark of night—that dark night of feeling hopeless. I know personally that depression tightens its grip in the night, in loneliness, and in isolation.

What have I learned from persevering and fighting deep struggles, excruciatingly painful disease, and adversity in my

own life? What hope, help, practical tools, and life-giving truths can I share with you to help you cope with depression in a healthy way? Allow me to share with you . . .

**Life Lessons with Jimme
Things I Wish I Could Tell My Younger Self**

Having a healthy mind is just as important as having a healthy body.

God created us—mind, body, and spirit. All three areas must be healthy to be whole.

A broken mind needs healing just like a broken body.

To be strong and healthy mentally, you must feel safe emotionally.

What do I mean by that? I have finally understood this truth myself after struggling through some very difficult teen years, analyzing my own life, making personal growth a priority, working extremely hard to master and discipline my approach to life, choosing daily to positively focus my energy and reframe thoughts in a healthy, life-giving way, and discerning who does not deserve unedited access into my life. The healthiest relationships are ones in which you feel safe. I'm not just talking physically. In fact, much deeper. I'm talking emotionally safe. Your heart.

If you do not feel safe, you cannot trust.
Relationships are built on trust.

When I sensed God's call and mission for my life to start Girls Nite In International, I longed to create a Safe Refuge where you would find love, be accepted, know "you are welcome, wanted, valued, and loved."® My goal was to create a safe family that had each others' backs; drop our masks so we could be real, raw, and candid; as well as provide practical teaching where you would find hope, healing, and life guidance.

If we lived in a perfect world, a family would be a safe place. Unfortunately, the reality is that many families thrive on drama and create the very stress, anxiety, and depression we are talking about. I know the difficult reality many of you live in and my heart breaks for you.

When a family feels safe, we are free to open our hearts to one another without fear of shame, guilt, control, manipulation, criticism, comparison, and judgment.

> Healthy families are able to talk about their feelings, whereas unhealthy families tend to act out their feelings.

There are no perfect families. We are *all* broken. Every family is dysfunctional. No doubt, some more than others. Just like other struggles, depression can run in families and, without you even being aware, become a learned pattern of coping with stress. However, my goal is to help you become better equipped to cope with real-life struggles in a healthier way. My heart aches because I know many of you do not have a safe family. Your parents are very broken and damaged themselves, emotionally, and do not yet have the capacity to love effectively. My prayer and goal is that they will find healing as well. Let me share with you one of the most important truths I have learned and teach:

> Sometimes, the best education you can get is what you *don't* want to become!

If the behavior you see modeled at home is not healthy and makes you bitter and angry, let me encourage you to redirect that anger in a positive direction by learning *what you don't want to become*. Discover what you can do differently so you don't grow up and become just like the very behavior you despise. Determine your life will be different and take steps now to make that your goal.

> Take your negative past and turn it into a positive future!

If you are suffering from dangerous depression and suicidal thoughts, I beg you to seek help. You might need to see a medical professional for help and even begin medication to help restore the depleted chemicals in your brain and body so you can begin the process of healing emotionally and physically.

You are not crazy. There is no shame in saying, "I need help."

I can relate. When I was in my early thirties, I went through a very dark period in my life. I won't go into all the details, but it was a deep, dark time when the circumstances around me seemed utterly hopeless. Adding to that, I was very much alone, in a big new city, with my three little kids—one of whom was a newborn. We had just moved to Indianapolis, and I was working feverishly to help my two older kids get adjusted to moving, leaving friends, and changing elementary schools in the middle of the school year.

My husband was gone all the time with his new ministry job, which left me physically and emotionally drained and feeling stuck and all alone, as our marriage was deeply struggling. I was working full-time—teaching forty students during the day—and getting no sleep day or night while caring for my three-month-old screaming, colicky baby who was constantly sick and in terrible pain, could not be comforted, and cried inconsolably for three years straight. Yes, *years*! No doctor could help with his colic and I thought I would lose my mind. Or that one of us wasn't gonna make it—either my baby Blake or me!

I felt myself sinking deeper and deeper in that dark hole of depression as I had no family around or new friends to help. I was emotionally and physically worn out and depleted, and I did not see any way out or hope for things to ever be different. I felt like I was drowning in the middle of the ocean, the waves crashing over my head, pushing me deeper and deeper, further and further into the black hole, until I could no longer come up for air. I was so deeply depressed, I really did just want to end my life . . . and tried to figure out a way I could. But the only thing that held me back was that I just couldn't bear the thoughts of leaving my babies behind without their mama.

One morning, my little girl, Kristi, and my husband found me curled up in a fetal position in the shower sobbing my eyes out, deep depression and utter exhaustion overwhelming me. Although I was embarrassed and mortified to ask for help, I did seek medical care from my doctor who treated me with medication for several months to help restore my body physically and heal from severe depression. No one had told me about postpartum depression—added to all the stress, lack of sleep, moving to a new city and trying to start all over building a new life and ministry.

I once heard a quote that greatly affected me and my outlook on life:

Never be afraid of a scar.
It simply means you were stronger than whatever tried to break you.

This quote has stuck with me through some of my darkest, most difficult times and still helps me to this day. You see, the deep depression I suffered in my early thirties was not the only dark period of my life. More recently, I suffered deep, dark depression and battled suicidal thoughts while desperately fighting for my life the past several years in an incredibly difficult battle against late-stage, advanced Lyme disease. This vicious disease and active deadly infection invaded my body and brain, causing excruciating pain and stripping me of the ability to even engage or function in life.

Even though I was determined to be a fighter and not give up, the darkest, deepest struggle was yet ahead. As the disease continued to take over my body and a new treatment regimen was begun, I began the most terrifying fight to survive. My body started to shut down because I had a severe allergic reaction to a stem cell transplant, causing me to desperately fight for every breath.

Those long months of sheer terror took me to the darkest, scariest place I have ever endured. My family didn't know if I was going to make it or not, and I didn't either. Not being able to breathe or make my body move or brain function—I was terrified and scared. THAT was when I felt completely helpless, hopeless, trapped, with no cure and no way out. I was so deeply scared, feeling sheer terror and desperation, that I began trying to think of a way to end my life.

I remember begging God to please just take me if this is how the rest of my life will be and I can't do anything to "will" myself out of this or help myself. I didn't want to leave my babies and everyone I loved, but I was terrified of dying this painful, torturous death and fighting so hard to breathe.

That is why I *know* that no one takes their life because they want to die. You get desperate enough to end your life because you feel trapped, stuck, with no hope, and no way out. The fear and darkness strangle you, and the voice of the enemy whispers, "There. Is. No. Hope."

Only through the passionate, fervent prayers of friends and family across the globe calling out to God on my behalf, pleading with God to spare my life, am I still alive today. I was taken back to the medical clinic in Florida for new treatment to save my life. I know I am a walking miracle, and I am the most grateful girl on the planet to be alive. I thank God every day for the gift of life. Although there is no cure yet, I will continue to fight and not give up because I know #GodsNotDone®!

That is why I plead with you, if you are struggling with depression or suicidal thoughts, there is no shame in asking for help. There is *help* and there is *hope*. If you broke your arm, you would go to the doctor to have it treated and reset so your body could properly heal. If you are diabetic, you go to the doctor and take insulin so you can live. Give yourself permission to get professional help through medical care or counseling if you are struggling with depression so deep you are seriously questioning if you want to live. You are worth it. Choose life.

I want to help you. So, let's talk strategy. What daily changes can we make—what steps can we take to tackle depression and get rid of destructive, negative thoughts?

Strategy 1: Discover the root of your depression; admit your feelings

Ask the hard question. Why do I feel down? Is there a particular event, strained relationship, loss, grief, physical condition, or circumstance that is causing me to feel depressed and lonely?

Maybe you have recently suffered a great loss or experienced gut-wrenching trauma in your life:

- Your parents are divorcing.
- You moved to a new city to live with your parent who has custody, changed to a new school, and left all your old friends behind.
- Your parent is an alcoholic, addict, or in jail; and you have to fend for yourself and take care of your younger siblings.

- Your parent has a severe mental illness, and the instability, uncertainty, unpredictability, and insecurity of your life means you never feel safe.
- You just found out your mother has cancer, and you are scared.

No matter what is happening, you need to be honest with yourself and admit what you are feeling and why.

Strategy 2: Don't isolate yourself

Depression is very lonely. When you are depressed, you will tend to avoid other people and isolate yourself; when in reality, that is the exact opposite of what you need to do.

Solitude—being alone—only feeds depression. Staying in confined spaces for long periods of time is not healthy. Locking yourself in your bedroom behind closed doors with the lights off and a playlist of depressing music is the worst thing to do. Or binge-watching endless depressing Netflix movies! Choose to be with people who will encourage you, build you up, rather than give in to those dark feelings when you know you are struggling. Create a playlist of positive, upbeat encouraging music to lift your spirits. Faith-filled worship music will feed truth into your mind.

Strategy 3: Talk with someone you trust

There are times when we should not fully trust our own thoughts. This is especially true during a deep, clinical depression when we tend to have a distorted view of reality. When you are vulnerable, whether in body or mind, you can be sucked into depression and lose perspective. Relying on someone you trust can help give you a reality check. Their words can pull you out of the pit of negative, destructive thoughts and help redirect your perspective to a healthier, realistic view.

Now more than ever, you need that true, trusted friend or caring mentor with whom you feel safe. No judgment. That person who loves you, will let you cry, will listen to you vent even when you are one hot mess and the emotions are all jumbled up inside—even while you struggle to explain the depth of darkness and despair in your spirit.

Strategy 4: One of the ways to get strong again is to set the words free

One of the main reasons I created and founded Girls Nite In International is because I wish there had been something like Girls Nite In when I was growing up. I wanted to give you what I did not have. Many of these topics I teach on just about destroyed my life. I had no one to talk to who cared enough to help me navigate through some very difficult things in my childhood and teen years. I desperately needed it and my life would have been so much easier if I'd had a leader, speaker, or trusted mentor who talked out loud about the real struggles I was dealing with, listened to me, and shared real tools and guidance to help me deal with the tough things I was facing and fighting.

This is the reason I agonize over every word and work so hard when writing *Letters from Jimme* to share with you. I am determined to give you practical coping tools, real-life advice, strategy, and life-direction that I wish someone had given me.

But another reason I labor so hard over the message I share with you is because I want God to do the deep healing in me too. So, I choose to bare my soul and be vulnerable, transparent, honest, and real even when it hurts and is humiliating, or I risk being judged, criticized, and misunderstood for being so real, all because I know the power of being transparent and setting the words free to help bring healing to others and to the broken, deep, hurting, painful areas of my own soul that need God's healing. I choose to take the risk to be vulnerable and honest—to help you be vulnerable and real—so you can start to heal.

Because the truth is . . . we are all broken. We all need healing.

There is power in journaling, writing out your story and setting the words free. Saying the truth out loud is one of the most powerful steps toward healing. Admitting the truth first to yourself, then with someone you trust. Keeping all the pain or anger inside is a poison that eats slowly and destroys you. If you, like me, tend to hold everything inside, this is one of the hardest things to do. Especially if you have taken the risk, only to be betrayed by the one person you thought you could trust. That is why it is important to be selective and be wise with whom you share your innermost self. Someone you trust who has your back and your best interest at heart.

I pray you find that safe person.

Strategy 5: Choose joy

Find the joy again. Learn to laugh. Joke. Don't take life so seriously. Do fun things that bring you joy. Play games. Watch a funny movie. Play with little kids and become a kid again. Run, skip, swim, kick, throw, paint, sing, laugh, create. Anything that brings you joy and helps you smile again. Your body needs to rebuild its supply of those endorphins that come from joy.

Strategy 6: Don't let feelings rule your life

Don't trust your feelings. Feelings lie. They can change by the minute and make you one hot mess. Ask any girl. The switch can flip instantly based on whatever drama is on social media, your friends, or how many likes or followers you have (or *she* has)!

It takes hard work to overcome a lifestyle and pattern of negative thinking. But you can do it.

Retrain your brain by reframing your thoughts in a healthy, positive direction, instead of dwelling and obsessing on negative emotions. Discipline and retrain your mind.

I refuse to live in negative energy, griping about things I cannot change or allowing people to suck the joy and life out of me. You need to do the same.

Let go of negative habits. Unfollow negative people.

We need to base our validation and worth on who God says we are. God loves you. Your worth is not based on how many friends you have or how many likes or followers you have. You are the object of His affection. He loves you. Period.

Strategy 7: Feed your mind healthy thoughts

When you see things as being much worse than they really are and stay trapped in that downward spiral, your thoughts become poison.

When your head starts going to the dark place, it is very important what you feed your mind.

What you think about . . . you will become.

You will not be able to fix everything in your life. Change what you can. Let go of the rest.

You cannot change your circumstance, but you can change your attitude toward it. You cannot change another person, but you can change you.

When you start worrying and obsessing, remember:

> You cannot change the past.
> You cannot control the future.

Live fully in this moment.
That's all you have.
Relax into God's strong arms. He's got you.

> Fear not tomorrow. God is *already* there.

Strategy 8: Run to God for help

He has promised to be there no matter what you're going through. He will never leave you or forsake you. He will never abandon you. Cry out to Jesus!

I cried out, "I am slipping!"
  but your unfailing love, O LORD, supported me.
When doubts filled my mind,
  your comfort gave me renewed hope and cheer.
—Psalm 94:18–19

Give all your worries and cares to God, for he cares
about you.
—1 Peter 5:7

Strategy 9: Memorize God's Book of Truth

God's Word is the only hope that will transform and change your thinking. We don't think clearly on our own.

> *Trust* in the LORD with *all* your *heart*,
>   *do not depend* on your *own understanding.*
> Seek *his will* in *all* you do,
>   and *he* will *show* you *which path* to take.
>   —Proverbs 3:5–6, emphasis added

If you feel lost, scared, and confused, God has promised to hear your cry, give you direction, and provide light for your path.

One idea I want to suggest is to write verses from God's Book of Truth on Post-it notes where you will see them and memorize them every day so you can focus your mind on truth when you are struggling and believing lies. Placing God's truth and positive affirmations and quotes all around you will provide focus and redirect your thoughts every single morning.

Just sayin'... my home looks like a boutique gift shop because I have so many inspiring quotes, signs, scriptures, and graphic artwork in every room to focus my mind and to motivate and inspire me each day. *Trust me. It is life-changing. It helps.*

Strategy 10: Bring healing to others

God can use you and your story to bring healing to someone else. Open your arms, reach out, and offer that same love, hope, and healing you have found to someone else as we continue to build a movement, a family, a community locking arms together all across this globe!

> God does not waste your pain.
> Run to God in your pain—not away from Him!

Need hope? God has plenty to go around. Wanna know how much He loves you? Just take one look at the cross.

> Do not fear, for I have redeemed you;
>   I have summoned you by name; you are mine.
> When you pass through the waters,
>   I will be with you;
> and when you pass through the rivers,
>   they will not sweep over you.

When you walk through the fire,
   you will not be burned;
     the flames will not set you ablaze.
For I am the Lord your God.

                          —Isaiah 43:1-3 NIV

There's a Doctor in the house. It's the wisest and the bravest who cry for help when lost. There's no stigma in saying you're sick because there's a wounded Healer who uses nails to buy freedom and crosses to resurrect hope and medicine to make miracles.[2]

                          —Ann Voskamp

Jesus has come to heal the brokenhearted and to set the captive free. Jesus has promised: "I am the WAY, the TRUTH, the LIFE." Do you feel lost? Jesus promises He is the **way**. Do you feel confused? Jesus promises He is the **truth**. Are you scared, desperate, and at the end of your rope? Jesus promises He is the **life**.

What I know is this: *light wins every time.* Light invades the darkness.

There is **hope**. There is **life**.

NO more shame.

NO more fear.

NO more hiding.

God offers **hope**.

God offers **life**.

The choice is yours.

Choose **hope**.

Choose **life**.

YOURS!

With more love than you can imagine,

 **Jimme**

7

Jealousy | Envy

My Dear Insecure, Like-the-Rest-of-Us Girl,

There's a saying that goes, "When guys get jealous, it can be kinda cute. When girls get jealous, World War III is about to begin!" Although that's kinda funny and there might be a little truth to that, fact is: jealousy doesn't look good on anybody. Girl or guy!

Jealousy is an ugly trait and haters will always be around. And as they say, hating me isn't gonna make you pretty. There are no pretty people in the eyes of jealousy.

If you have to make somebody else look bad to make yourself look good, then maybe you're the problem. Haters only hate the people they can't have or the people they can't be. Isn't it kind of crazy to think that tearing someone else down builds you up?

> Haters don't really hate you. They hate themselves because you're a reflection of what they wish to be.

When it comes to envy, a person hates you for one of three reasons:

1. They want to be you.
2. They hate themselves.
3. They see you as a threat.

If you have ever been around two little kids playing together, you know what I'm talking about. When you hear two little kids arguing and fighting, you know the real issue is not the toy, the ball, or who gets to sit in what seat. The real issue and problem is that two people want their own way, and one's not getting it!

105

Kid 1: Mine.
> I deserve this.
> I worked hard for it.

Kid 2: I want something.
> I didn't get it.
> I'm taking it.

Kid 1: Somebody stole it.
> No fair.
> I hate you.

We have cute little phrases that express this feeling now in a humorous way:

- Don't be a hater!
- I'm jelly.
- Can't touch this!
- It's okay, I'd be jealous too.
- You just hate me 'cause you ain't me!
- You dreamed it, I did it. You're jealous, admit it!

The truth is . . .

> Jealousy is real.
> I struggle with it.
> So do you.

Why is it so much easier to say you struggle with anger than to admit you struggle with jealousy? I guess 'cause it just sounds so petty, so junior high-ish or so middle school. *Have you ever jumped in on a little online hate?*

At one time or another, all of us have wanted what someone else had, that we didn't have. When we scrutinize and compare where we stand in the world—as compared to where others around us stand and measure up—that feeling can usually be boiled down to one word: *envy.*
Here's how it happens:

- We see what someone else has, and we want it for ourselves.
- If we think that we deserve the object of our desire more than the person who has it, our envy then blossoms into jealousy.

Put simply: envy is when you resent God's goodness in other people's lives and ignore God's goodness in your own life.

It's when you think: *They've got it and I want it. They don't even deserve it. They shouldn't have it in the first place.*

Our culture thrives on envy.

- "Seriously, I kid you not! If I had *those* jeans . . ."
- "What's up with that? When did she get *that new* iPhone?"
- "Just sayin'. If I had *that* hot guy with those abs?"

If we took every ad or commercial seriously, we'd never have one minute of satisfaction in our entire life. We'd never enjoy what we do have, because we'd always be wanting more and what someone else has.

Yep! That's the way the advertisement industry is designed to work. To ensure that we're never happy!

Wanna learn how to be content? Wanna learn how to quit being a hater? How do we achieve our goal of living a life of contentment? Here is how one writer described contentment: "I have learned to be content whatever the circumstances. I know what it is to be in need, and I know what it is to have plenty. I have learned the secret of being content in any and every situation, whether well fed or hungry, whether living in plenty or in want" (Philippians 3:11–12 NIV).

So, what robs us of peace and a life free from jealousy? Well, before we can talk about the solution, let's first look at our problem. Jealousy and envy are like cousins.

> Jealousy: I fear that someone will *take* what I have.
> Envy: I *want* what someone else has.

- Do you get upset when other people get an award, recognition, or scholarship?

- Do you find it difficult to celebrate the success of someone around you?
- Do you sometimes feel that God has disappointed you and let you down?
- Do you find yourself often thinking, *If only I could have had* _____ [fill in the blank with what you wish were different in your life], *my life would have been so much better!*
- Do you feel the competition to be the fashionista who always has the hottest clothes, shoes, hair, or looks?
- Do you find yourself being critical or judgmental of others?
- Do you find that you are not content unless you are "best" at something? Whether sports, music, talent, academics, achievements, or recognition?
- Do you worry that your best friend is going to take your boyfriend?
- Do you sometimes wish you could sabotage the good things happening to someone you know?

Envy and jealousy can cause some of the biggest wounds and are futile attempts to control and fill the ache in our hearts to be significant, to feel like we matter, or to feel secure by having what someone else has.

Like the famous movie line, "I'll have what she's having."

At the deepest core, jealousy is not the problem. Jealousy is actually the symptom of a broken heart. Your broken heart. A heart that shouts, "Hey, wait a minute! What about me? No fair. I did not get what I deserve!"

Here's what God says:

But if you harbor bitter envy and selfish ambition in your hearts, do not boast about it or deny the truth. Such "wisdom" does not come down from heaven but is earthly, unspiritual, demonic. For where you have envy and selfish ambition, there you find disorder and every evil practice. (James 3:14–16 NIV)

What causes fights and quarrels among you? Don't they come from your desires that battle within you? (James 4:1 NIV)

Whatever is in your heart will come out of your mouth eventually. Jealousy comes from a terrible battle inside our own mind. Within our own heart. The root of jealousy is motivated by one thing: We didn't get our way. We didn't get what we wanted.

You can overcome these dark feelings that plague your mind and eat at your heart. But before we examine the solution, let's identify our problem. Why do we struggle?

Jealousy displays its ugly head in one of these three powerful emotions:

- fear or insecurity
- comparison to others
- anger

1: Fear or insecurity can destroy you.

My fear is that there's not enough to go around. A scarcity mentality:

- If she gets this scholarship, there won't be anything for me.
- If she gets this guy, there won't be anyone for me.
- If she gets this recognition or promotion, there won't be any for me.

Your fear can be any number of things. Your fear may be that there won't be enough:

- love
- acceptance
- recognition
- praise
- accolades

- talent
- jobs
- careers
- room for you

The lie that we believe because of this fear—the faulty thinking that gets embedded in our mind—is this: *If there's room for you, then that means there's no room for me.*

Remember *Toy Story*? Woody and Buzz Lightyear?

Woody, a good-hearted cowboy who belongs to a young boy named

Andy, sees his position as Andy's favorite toy jeopardized when his parents buy him a Buzz Lightyear action figure.

The old-fashioned, adorable cowboy, Woody, who has always been this little boy's favorite toy, gets caught in the conflict with Buzz Lightyear, the new modern space ranger who may replace him. In the beginning, Woody feels like "this town ain't big enough for the two of us." Woody feels left out, hurt, and jealous when Andy chooses Buzz to play with instead of him. He later confesses his hurt feelings to Buzz: "Why would Andy ever want to play with me, when he's got you?"

If we're all honest, we have to admit that there's a little Woody mentality in all of us. Woody is saying, *I'm scared if there's room for you, then that means there's no room for me.*

Not true. A lie! Don't believe it. That lie of envy is a trap.

2: Comparison to others can destroy you.

Healthy competition is good. Competition can spur you on to become the best version of you. Whether in sports, talents, academics, goals, or achievements. However, very quickly good ambitions can turn a dark corner, and envy takes over and becomes a stronghold in your heart.

I'm sorry. I'm just the jealous type.
I'm just scared someone better is gonna take my place.

As long as you live, you will wrestle with the struggle to compare yourself to others. Whether at school, at work, at home, in college, or on the job. I just recently led a leadership conference with some powerful women who are strong leaders in their community and workplace. These women admitted and lamented the fact that the jealousy, hatred, and workplace war that takes place in their office between women who are always competing against each other is undermining and defeating. It can get downright ugly and can destroy and sabotage good people. The truth is Haters never go away and you will always have to choose the healthy way to deal with competition.

Just be you. There never will be another you ever created. Don't rob this world of you. Just be the best version of you God ever created.

3: Anger can destroy you.

When we have been wronged, anger rises up inside of us and begins to boil with these types of thoughts:

- I have been the good girl. The good daughter. You should see my brother.
- Because of his behavior and bad choices, now I can't
  _____.
- I have worked hard; worked my butt off. Now this? You've got to be kidding me!
- Can't he leave me alone? Isn't it enough that he already has his? Now he wants mine too! No fair! Keep your dang hands off!

Sometimes, the anger and jealousy that arise during a situation are real because we truly have been wronged.

I deserve this. I worked hard for it. She got it. Why can't I?

Jealousy says, *"God owes me. I deserve this."* Jealousy is really dissatisfaction with God. Dissatisfaction that He will meet your need. Or that He met your friend's need and not yours. When we think of jealousy, we think of all the things others have that we don't—looks, talent, health, height, money, awards, scholarships, recognition. So, we think we have a problem with the person who possesses what we don't. But, as we know, God could have fixed all that. Whatever He chose to give to your friend, He could have chosen to give you as well.

Bottom line: If God had taken care of you the way He took care of your friend, you would be in so much better shape—or that's how we think.

So, your real problem isn't with people whose stuff you envy; it's with your Creator. God owes you, and you're holding a grudge against Him. And until you face up to this simple but convicting truth, jealousy will continue to terrorize your life and wreak chaos in your relationships.

God says there is only one answer: "What causes fights and quarrels among you? Don't they come from your desires that battle within you?" (James 4:1 NIV).

So, apparently our external battles are the direct result of internal battles. Our external conflicts are the direct result of an inner conflict that has worked its way to the surface.

God's Book teaches that if you and I find ourselves in an argument, it will be because a battle inside of me has spilled on to you or—vice versa—a battle inside you has spilled on to me. According to God's Word, there is conflict within me, and if you bump me too hard, what's going on inside of me is going to come spilling out all over you.

How do you overcome these dark feelings that plague your mind and eat at your heart? How do we move beyond and get rid of the bitterness and rage eating at our insides? How do we move past the jealousy and envy that threaten to destroy us and distract us from the true purpose and goals for our life?

> A sound heart is life to the body,
> But envy is rottenness to the bones.
> > —Proverbs 14:30 NKJV

> Do not let your heart envy sinners,
> > but always be zealous for the fear of the LORD.
> > > —Proverbs 23:17 NIV

Read those words again. This time pay attention to the word *heart*.

God says the key to overcoming envy is a peace-filled heart. What is a peaceful and peace-filled heart? And how do I get one?

First, I must address and be truthful about the condition and posture of my heart. *Whatever is in my heart will come out in my behavior.* If I have rage and anger in my heart, it will spill out in my behavior.

The next key to overcome or stop envy is to be intentional to trust God all day long. I must be passionate and devoted to commit my heart to God all day long, every single day. There are no free passes. *None of that "well, I'm just not feelin' it" allowed.* It is not an emotional choice. It is a conscious decision. Our entire life revolves around the word *trust*. You *must make a choice to trust God with your life every single new morning*, over and again throughout the day as new situations and challenges happen. I'm not saying it's easy. It's not.

The real truth is that when we are full of envy, we are really angry at God. We don't trust Him.

Let me offer this suggestion if you are dealing with envy. Work with me for a moment.

Take the person—the face—completely out of the picture.

What emotion is fueling your envy? Is it:

- fear or insecurity
- comparing yourself to someone else
- anger

If you're like me, check, check, and check. I deal with all of those emotions! To have a peaceful heart, we must deal with the conflict within. How can we have peace and deal with the wrestling inside our hearts? How can we have victory and overcome this internal struggle?

Let me share with you a few things I have learned. The hard way. And the truth is, I am still learning them and asking God to help me.

Five Things I Wish I Could Tell My Younger Self

1. Be content with who God made you.

Comparison is the fuel of jealousy. It will eat you alive. Be content with the gifts and talents God has placed in you.

Say it with me and believe it: *Be yourself. Everyone else is already taken.*

2. Run your own race.

Instead of looking at everyone running around you, run your own race. Sheeesh . . . I will admit that is a tough one. But it is the only way to peace.

Run your own race.

It does not mean you stop striving to be the best you. Determine to work on your personal growth goals. Monitor yourself and listen to the words you say. Become more positive in your outlook on life, braver, and more courageous. Allow someone to mentor you in areas you need help, grow your leadership skills so you can become all God has created you to be. But always remember, God only made one you. So . . .

113

> Don't compare.
> Don't compete.
> Run your own race.

3. There is room for all of us.

You have a big God. Reject the lie that says there's no room for the both of us. Just because someone got a big piece of the pie doesn't mean there isn't a slice for you too. ☺ Who knows . . . maybe God's going to create a whole new pie just for you!

4. God will provide for you.

You serve a Big God who will provide your needs. Trust Him. Your whole life will revolve around the word *trust*. God will teach you over and over through big struggles and small ones that He can be trusted.

You won't learn it just one time and be done. Your heart will wander away and begin to doubt if He really cares and has your best interest at heart.

But I promise you. He does. There is not one thing that happens to you that escapes His notice or attention.

> God will always do a deep work in us
> before He does a deep work through us.

That will involve some pain, some struggle, some failure, some disappointment (in ourselves even), and always—always!—growth.

Just think of a caterpillar as it transforms into a butterfly. Breaking out of its cocoon is a difficult struggle. Growth always involves struggle.

So, don't be discouraged. Admit to God the truth in your heart. Own it. Name your struggle out loud. He's a big God. He already knows. He just wants you to admit it to yourself. In fact, that is the first step to victory.

> God will remind you that He's got you. He's got this situation.

All that you need to accomplish the purpose God has designed for your life, He will give you.

> God made me. There will never be another me.
> For as long as the world has existed, and as long as it spins,
> God made one me for one purpose.
> No one else will steal my purpose.

5. God has not forgotten me.

I need to continue to place my fears and restless heart in His very capable hands. Pray my fears out loud to Him. Name my deepest struggles. Own them.

GOD is the Source of everything He will ever ask me to do! Because someone else gets something, doesn't mean I have nothing. God will always provide all you need. *Always.*

I choose to trust God.

So, what are my action steps? How do you continue to get rid of a jealous heart? A goal that takes a lifetime? Realize that jealousy is a waste of emotions! "Jealousy is a terrible disease. Get well soon!"

How do you begin to get well?

1. Pray blessing over the person you have a struggle with.

This will be the hardest thing you have ever done. Trust me. Sometimes, it's all you can do just to say that person's name out loud. Much less pray blessing on them. But the beginning of the path to forgiveness and freedom is to take the sting out of your own heart.

2. Congratulate them on their success.

Jealousy happens when you count someone else's blessings instead of your own.

> **"**
> The worst part of success is trying to find
> someone who is happy for you.
> —Bette Midler
>
> People will wish you all the success
> in the world, and then they hate you
> when you get it.
> —Unknown
>
> It is in the character of very few men
> to honor without envy a friend who has
> prospered. Few men have the natural
> strength to honor a friend's success
> without envy.
> —Aeschylus
> **"**

3. Even harder than honoring the success of a friend is honoring an enemy.

Tough stuff. Tough to talk about. Even tougher to do.

Let me close with the most powerful true story of forgiveness from the life of an incredible woman of faith and courageous World War II hero named Corrie ten Boom.

Corrie ten Boom was a Holocaust survivor who, along with her family, helped many Jews escape the Nazi Holocaust by secretly hiding them in her home, affectionately known as The Hiding Place. After saving over eight hundred Jews from certain death in Nazi concentration camps, Corrie and her sister, Betsie, were themselves captured and imprisoned in a horrible camp and tortured by a Nazi guard who regularly stripped them naked, beat, and humiliated them.

Just two years after her release from this horrific torturous camp, in 1947, Corrie was speaking in a church basement in Munich to a group of solemn, defeated Germans who desperately needed to hear her message that God forgives. Corrie reminded them that when we confess our sins, God casts them into the deepest ocean, gone forever.

The solemn German faces stared back at her, not having the courage to believe. One by one they stood up in silence and left the room.

"That's when I saw him." Corrie described the moment she saw *him* working his way forward against the crowd. She saw the overcoat and the brown hat; but next, in her mind's eye, she saw that blue uniform and cap with its skull and crossbones. All the torture and memories came flooding back with a vengeance—she could feel the rush of emotions exploding inside her. Her mind flooded with the horrific memories of being stripped, naked, humiliated, shamed, and tortured.

Corrie now stood face-to-face with one of her prison guards and tormentors.

There he stood in front of her, his hand thrust out. He thanked her for her penetrating message and remarked how good it was to know, as Corrie had said, that all our sins are cast into the bottom of the sea! Never to be held against us!

Corrie vividly describes how she, who had spoken so easily of forgiveness, now fumbled in her pocketbook rather than take hold of his hand. He did not remember her, but oh how she remembered him. That face was indelibly filed in her memory.

He mentioned that Corrie spoke of being in Ravensbrück concentration camp in her talk and that he had been a guard there. However, since his time there, he had become a Christian and knew that God had forgiven him for the terrible, unspeakable torture he had put the women prisoners through. However, he was compelled to ask her forgiveness. Point blank, he asked Corrie, "Will you forgive me?"

Corrie vividly describes the deep wrestle going on inside her as she vacillated, mustering up the forgiveness, strength, and courage it would take to genuinely speak the words "I forgive you" to her former captor. Here are Corrie's own words about this defining moment.

> Those who were able to forgive their former enemies were able also to return to the outside world and rebuild their lives, no matter what the physical scars. Those who nursed their bitterness remained invalids. It was as simple and as horrible as that.
>
> And still I stood there with the coldness clutching my heart. But forgiveness is not an emotion—I knew that too. Forgiveness

is an act of the will, and the will can function regardless of the temperature of the heart.

"Jesus, help me!" I prayed silently. "I can lift my hand. I can do that much. You supply the feeling."

And so woodenly, mechanically, I thrust my hand into the one stretched out to me. And as I did, an incredible thing took place. The current started in my shoulder, raced down my arm, sprang into our joined hands. And then this healing warmth seemed to flood my whole being, bringing tears to my eyes.

"I forgive you, brother!" I cried. "With all my heart!"

For a long moment we grasped each other's hands, the former guard and the former prisoner. I had never known God's love so intensely as I did then.[1]

Not sure you have the power to do that? You don't.

The path to freedom and forgiveness always starts with admitting the truth to yourself, then to God. He alone will give you the strength and power to forgive others . . . and yourself.

Run to God—our Only Hope—for cleansing. Forgiveness! When we ask God for cleansing, He forgives us and never throws it in our face again.

Take yourself out of prison today. "Being resentful is like taking poison and waiting for the other person to die."[2] The only person you are destroying is you.

While you're sanitizing and wiping everything down, be sure to wipe hatred out of your heart. That's a virus too.

Free yourself by refusing to live in the chains of jealousy, envy, and hatred. Let God heal and restore you as you let go and choose to trust Him.

Forgive yourself.
The goal for your life is progress.
Not perfection!

With that in mind, every day:

- Ask God for forgiveness.
- Forgive yourself.
- Forgive others.

With more love than you can imagine,

 Jimme

8

Divorce | Blending Families

My Dear Aching Girl,

Let me encourage your broken heart with this truth:

> That which does not break me only makes me stronger.

This topic is a tough one that hits home for so many of you: divorce and blending families. I am not gonna lie or pretend. This is so difficult! There are no easy answers. It's heartbreaking and complicated.

The truth of the matter is this is not a situation you chose for yourself. You didn't ask for this.

Sometimes you find yourself angry, resentful, and asking the questions:

- How come I'm forced to deal with my parents' mistakes?
- This sucks! I didn't pick him. I didn't pick her. You both picked each other.
- So, why am I the one stuck in the middle of all this?

Truth is: this reality affects you and those closest to you pretty much every single day. I want to say straight-up! It is not my intention—in any way—to bash either one of

your parents: your mama or your daddy. It is not my intent to pass judgment at all.

What I do intend to talk about is the position you now find yourself in. I want to acknowledge the reality of your situation. But, most importantly, I want to help you answer the questions:

> How do I heal my heart?
> How do I find hope?
> How do I move forward from here?

We're going to talk honestly about the confusion, the mixed-up emotions, the thoughts you haven't said out loud to anybody.

There are no simple or easy answers for dealing with the fallout of your parents' failed marriage. But I do want to help you find courage and hope to face the future. Some practical answers to some not-so-easy situations.

Maybe a particular inner struggle you are facing. Perhaps an issue you need to discuss with one of your parents and don't know how to approach it without offending them. Maybe a question about how to work through your bitterness and move forward.

As I say to you often, this particular topic may not apply to your life at all right now. However, at some very unexpected point in the future, it may. Just ask some of your closest friends.

If you are fortunate enough to live with your original, bio family, go home and thank your mama and daddy! Whisper a prayer of gratitude and thank God right now.

But, whatever you do, listen and learn. Because I can guarantee you, if you are not dealing with this, one of your close friends is.

Be a friend who listens and cares. Choose to be a Safe Refuge for each other. We need each other!

At some point, many of you heard these life-changing words: *Sweetheart, there's something we need to tell you. We're getting a divorce. But you're going to be okay. I promise!*

You remember this moment always. I don't care if you were three years old or thirty. It doesn't matter if your parents have been divorced for two days or ten years. You never forget this moment. In this moment, life changed. Their life. Your life. Forever.

One writer used the word *split* to describe her life after she heard those words. *Split*: life became defined by one pivotal moment in time.

The moment my parents split, *a new me* was created. From that moment forward, all my identity was formed and fashioned by the fact that I came from a divided family.

There was life *before* the divorce and life *after* the divorce.

Tim Baker, the author of *Broken: Making Sense of Your Life After Your Parents' Divorce*, shares his experience of hearing those life-changing words:

> I remember a lot of laughing. Not the kind of laughing you hear after a good joke or when you nail someone with a water balloon. More like the nervous kind of laughing you might hear at a funeral or at the bedside of someone trying to be funny in the emergency room. . . .
>
> To be honest, I have no idea what the words were. Maybe this is one of those protecting things our minds do when we've experienced something too painful.
>
> The idea was pretty clear: Moving out. Taking stuff. Won't be back for a while. . . .
>
> "Okay," I say, feeling my face go blank. What kind of expression should I have? Should I make a speech? Maybe I should throw myself on the floor, and scream and cry! Really I don't know what to do.
>
> How are you supposed to respond to your world falling apart?!
>
> Maybe you've had the same thoughts as this sixteen-year-old me: I totally blamed myself when my parents separated. In my eyes, the only connection between my parents was me—so, the divorce must have had something to do with me. But, it doesn't. It doesn't. It doesn't. Does it???[1]

Everybody hears a lot of the same stuff when their parents split up:

- We still love you.
- Things just didn't work out.
- We were way too young.
- I'm just not happy.
- We grew apart.
- We just don't love each other anymore.

As you can see, divorce is sad. It's sad for everybody. It's sad for your mom. Sad for your dad. Sad for their parents. It's sad for you.

I guarantee you: Nobody plans for their marriage to end when they are getting married. No one sets out planning to divorce when they are trying on that wedding gown or getting fitted with that tux.

Because your parents' marriage has ended, it is normal to feel a bunch of crazy, mixed-up emotions. It is as though an axe just keeps falling—again and again—cutting you in half, splitting you right down the middle. You feel torn with every new situation the older you get.

Caught in the middle between two people—both of whom you still love—forced to choose sides. You're not sure where your loyalty belongs. Your dad remarries and has a new family. It's prom night: whose house do you go to for pictures? You're getting married: who gives you away?

You feel *split*!

You think divorce sucks? God agrees with you.

"'I hate divorce!' says the LORD." (Malachi 2:16)

It breaks His heart! He didn't say He hates divorced people. When God says He hates divorce, one of the reasons is because of *exactly what you are feeling right now*. I don't know many people who like divorce either, especially those who are going through it. It is hard, gut-wrenching, and always leaves scars.

God designed marriage to be a relationship of commitment that mirrors His love and relationship with His children. That's a tall order! Unselfish love. Love without conditions. A love that gives instead of takes. Not a love that looks for a way *out* when the conflicts come—because they will—but a love that looks for a way *through*.

God hates divorce because the scars on His children are deep and ugly. And more than two lives are affected.

Just a little "Jimme" advice as you think about marriage:

Every marriage is hard work. Go into it expecting to be *incompatible* because you will be! Marriage is tough. It is the *merging of two flawed, broken people:* two wills and two backgrounds. Marriage is one of the *biggest tests of maturity* in your life. It will bring out the *best* in you, and it will bring out the *worst* in you! Marriage requires *two selfish people*—which we all are—to *grow up!*

Thankfully, God is a God of compassion. He hates divorce, *but never the people affected by it.*

Divorce, as ugly as it is, is *not the end of life.* It hurts because it is the *end of a marriage.* It is *extremely painful* because it is the *death of a family. Your family.*

So, the big question is: **How do I deal with the pain of my family being split?**

When we're hurt, it's easy to start reacting and lashing out. Listing our rights. You know, the things we're entitled to because we've been wronged. Like these things you've told me:

- I have the right to be really ticked off.
- I have the right to do whatever I d*** well want to do.
- I'll feel a whole lot better if I:
    - sleep around because I really just want someone to hold me.
    - numb my pain with drugs or binge drinking.
    - sneak out because nobody has the right to tell me what to do if they can't even keep their own freaking life together.
- I have the right to screw up right now because they sure did.
- I have the right to hold grudges and make life hell for everyone.

But clinging to your rights will only destroy you. Poor choices, done out of spite or because you are just plain frickin' hurting, are just gonna take you down and leave you with some horrible consequences to live with. I really don't want that for you because I care.

Let's talk about the lies that might be going through your headspace because of the divorce. Lies that will destroy you if you believe them. Areas where we need to ask God to bring healing to your broken-to-pieces heart, and massage healing salve into your deeply hurting, wounded soul. May I ask permission to speak life into your broken world and have a heart-to-heart talk—just me and you—about some lies you might be telling yourself?

1. I Caused It

Maybe deep down, you know it's not your fault, but you still get trapped into thinking if you could just do something to make them fight less, if you could just be better, maybe they could be happy together again.

2. I Can Never Trust Anyone Again

You put walls up and don't let people in because you are afraid of getting hurt again. So, you push them away and make it impossible for people to really care about you. Or you set impossible expectations for people in your life in order to *prove* that no one can be trusted.

Can I just let you in on a little secret? *Everyone you know and love will at some time disappoint you because they are human. So are you. So, you will also disappoint others. Often unintentionally. The only perfect one is our Perfect Father—GOD. And I'm certainly not God. Neither are you.*

Don't set your expectations at an impossible standard. The best of us will disappoint each other, even though we mean well. So, cut people a little slack! Don't demand perfection. No one is capable of that. Not even you. Allow people to love you. Love them back.

3. I Am Responsible for Getting My Parents Back Together Again

No, you're not. Take yourself off the hook. That is not your responsibility. They are two adults. Do not put yourself under that unrealistic burden.

4. I Am Guaranteed to Get Divorced Myself Someday

While it may be true that the divorce rate increases for those who come from split homes, you do not have to repeat your parent's mistakes.

Before you start dating, make sure you are emotionally healthy. You attract people who are as emotionally healthy as you are. So, get really healthy!

I often say, sometimes the best education you can get is what *not* to do. You know that you will repeat the behavior you have seen modeled in front of you unless you intentionally choose to be different.

The divorce? It was someone else's choice for your life. But, sooner rather than later, you've got to deal with unfair. *Life is not fair.* The healing truth is this:

> Brokenness has a purpose when it drives us to God.

God can use the huge pain of "unfair" to grab our attention and rivet our focus to Him.

> The LORD is close to the brokenhearted and saves those who are crushed in spirit. (Psalm 34:18 NIV)

> [The Lord] heals the brokenhearted and binds up their wounds. (Psalm 147:3 NIV)

God is the Great Healer. He really can bring healing to your mind and bring hope where there was despair.

There is nothing you can tell Him that would shock Him or make Him hate you.

> Run *to* God in your pain, not *away* from Him.

There is absolutely nothing you can go through that is not, as God's Book puts it, "common to man." "No temptation has overtaken you but such as is common to man" (1 Corinthians 10:13 NASB95).

So, don't be embarrassed or ashamed. You are not alone. There is nothing you could possibly tell God that He does not already know or get.

The truth is, every single one of us comes from a dysfunctional family. We are all dysfunctional! God knows we are all broken and can't fix ourselves. That's why we *must* have a Savior—to save us from ourselves. It is so vital to memorize and plant God's Truth in our minds so we learn to think right, get true perspective, and lean into all the great plans He has for our lives. So, we don't destroy ourselves and everyone around us!

God chose to tell us in His Book of Truth about families who were anything but perfect role models. God pulls back the curtains in the front window and allows us to take a peek inside the front door to see what these families were really like.

God shares real stories about real people so that we can learn how bad choices or good choices really do affect our lives and the lives of those close to us. Turns out that nobody is exempt—that means you too. I believe life can be summed up in two simple sentences!

LIFE IN A NUTSHELL

1. Make choices.
2. Live with the consequences of those choices.

Totally on point!
Good choices = Good consequences
Bad choices = Bad consequences

How many of you have ever watched shows like *Keeping Up with the Kardashians* or *Pawn Stars*? Well, they've got nothing on God! God shares with us snapshots of families that are more messed up than any of those "celebrities"!

On my website, download the gripping story of one majorly screwed up, dysfunctional family from God's Book: JimmelynnGarlandRice .com/Books.

Inside of you is a deep-rooted need to be loved. To be seen. God placed it there. Take comfort in the fact that *He is the God who sees you.* No matter your situation, you are not alone. He is the God who sees. He is the God who sees *you.* You probably feel caught in the middle. Maybe you want to run. And sometimes you need to function as the only adult in your family because your parent is acting like the child!

There is a very real, silent epidemic destroying families. It is called Parental Alienation. When one parent viciously turns their child against the other parent. Over 22 million families are going through this.

I am so sad and so sorry if you feel caught in the middle and sometimes get used as a pawn. I hate that your childhood has been robbed and you feel ripped apart and caught in the middle. That is a horrible place to be. A huge weight to carry on your shoulders.

All I know is that you don't have to carry that heavy weight alone. Jesus understands and is acquainted with our deepest grief, our deepest loss, our deepest pain, our feeling of being abandoned. Feeling like we are carrying the weight of the world on our shoulders.

His own Father had to turn His back on His Son when Jesus literally carried the weight of the world on His shoulders, took every one of our sins and all our wrongdoing upon Himself, and died a horrible crucifixion death to create a way for us to have a relationship and forever life with Him.

I love the lyrics of the touching gospel song "He Will Carry You":

> If He carried the weight of the world upon His shoulders,
> I know, my sister, that He will carry you.[2]

He truly is the God who sees. **Your** God who sees **you.**

He will tenderly pick up your broken pieces and put you back together again . . . His way.

Take hope in that truth. *Too often we try to use God to change our circumstances while God is using our circumstances to change us.* Run to Him in your pain, not away from Him.

David, a mighty king and warrior, led his nation and army well. He was also a fabulous musician and poet who wrote the book of Psalms.

He was hunted down to be killed by the former jealous king, and he experienced major heartbreak and loss—some of which was his own selfish fault. David desired another man's gorgeous wife, so he ordered to have that warrior, one of his own loyal soldiers, killed in battle in order to have the breathtakingly beautiful woman for himself. When David was confronted with his horrific acts of

YOU ARE NOT UNWANTED;
YOU ARE CHOSEN.
YOU ARE NOT UNLOVED;
YOU WERE TO DIE FOR
YOU ARE NOT ALONE;
YOU ARE HIS.

being not only a murderer but also an adulterer, he was humbled before God and repented of his wicked behavior, in essence, saying "My suffering was good for me, for it taught me to pay attention to YOU!"

You know what kind of person God loves—what type of person He is drawn to? Well, I'll let Him tell you in His own words:

> The LORD is close to the brokenhearted;
>   he rescues those whose spirits are crushed.
> —Psalm 34:18

> If your heart is broken, you'll find God right there;
> If you're kicked in the gut, he'll help you catch your breath.
> —Psalm 34:18 MSG

You might say: *"I don't have anything but God."* Really? Wow. What a safe place to be!

> YOUR SECURITY IS FOUND IN GOD ALONE.
> Not your mama or your daddy. HIM!
> Not your boyfriend or your best friend! HIM!
> The security you desperately crave...
> The longing you have to be loved deeply...
> The desire to be known and accepted for who you are...
> IS FOUND ONLY IN HIM.

He is the God who sees. *When no one else sees.* When no one else seems to care. *He is the God who sees straight into your heart.* Honestly, *our hearts are made to crave Him.*

I want to take a moment to say something very carefully . . . very tenderly. From my heart that cares.

Many of you girls are quietly hurting because your father—your own daddy—has deeply crushed you. You have this huge emptiness because after all this time, you still crave his approval. You want him to notice you. Not just his other kids—the new family he has with *her*.

You secretly long for him to reach out to you, to call you, to want to be with you. You crave his love. Maybe you find yourself doing crazy things to, somehow, be like him. Maybe things that you actually *despise* him for.

Can I just—very tenderly—share something with you? It might just be that your daddy does not have the capacity to love you appropriately. He does not know how to be a decent, good, caring father to you. He does not have the capability, because he, himself, is broken. There are things desperately broken inside of him that he may or may not realize. We can only trust that he, too, be changed by this same God who is changing you.

Do not destroy yourself because you desperately crave your daddy's love and he does not know how to give it.

A man will never satisfy your deepest longings. Whether that man is your daddy, your boyfriend, your best friend, or your future husband. It's not his job.

There is a hole in your heart that can only be filled by one. God.

He is the Relentless Pursuer.

His love is chasing you down.

Maybe you feel invisible. Like nobody sees you. Nobody in your family cares. No one can possibly understand.

Let your aching heart do one thing. Drive you to God. To the God who sees.

Remember:

> Forgiveness doesn't excuse their behavior.
> Forgiveness prevents their behavior from destroying your heart.

Forgiveness releases the poison of hatred from consuming and destroying you.

There is only one Perfect Father. God.

Do you know what name God calls Himself? Abba. Abba means "Daddy." A tender Father *who pulls his little girl into his arms* and *wraps her in His love.*

So call out to *your Abba.* Tell Him your heart is broken.

He will see you. He will hear you. He will heal you. From the inside out. He is on your side. The one who died for you is in the presence of God at this very moment sticking up for you.

Call out to Jesus, your Abba Father. Invite Him into your life. He sees you.

> The one who knows you the most loves you the best.

With more love than you can imagine,

 Jimme

9

Self-Worth | Dignity

My Dear Valued Struggler,

Unloved. Unwanted. A mistake.

Ouch. Piercing words that cut deep and ravage their way through every fiber of your being. Soul-damaging words that strip away your worth and begin to shape everything you think about yourself. Just ask Hope, one of my Girls Nite In girls who is a college student and shared this with me:

> Four years ago, my mama told me that she never wanted me, that I was a mistake. She said she only wanted my sister and that she wanted to have an abortion, but my dad wouldn't allow it. Unfortunately, I believed her words that I was a mistake and not wanted. I shut everyone out. I was at the lowest point I have ever been. Then, you showed up. Jimme, you and GNI have changed my life and I can't thank you enough. You gave me strength, faith, but most of all you made me believe in myself! I still have my weak days where all I wanna do is stay in bed and just cry. I may never know what happened and that  sucks. But, I do have a daddy and step mama who would do anything for me. Jimme, you taught me it's okay to trust someone again. It's okay to love someone. And mostly, that God has a plan for me!

Unloved. Unwanted. A mistake. Over time, Hope was able to sift through the pain of those destructive words and embrace the truth that the Source of her security, her identity, her value, her worth is found in God alone.

What about you? Where do you look to find your value?

If you're like me, sometimes you can feel *oh so small* in this big world with a lot of people.

Maybe you feel *useless*. God says you are *useful*.

Maybe you feel *worthless*. God says you are worth *everything*.

It's super important to recognize that, *yes*, there will always be somebody smarter, quicker, prettier, faster, or more talented than you. So what! At some point, you just learn to say, "That's okay! I still have something valuable to offer. I still bring something to the table!"

It is extremely important to recognize where your value comes from. God, your Creator, your Maker, has made only one *you*. Never has been, never will be another you. It is the privilege of a lifetime to be *you*. No one else gets that privilege. Don't waste it.

So, what are you gonna do with this one extraordinary life you have been given? How can you become the best *you* ever created? Stop a moment and think about your life purpose. Why are you here? What do you bring to this world that no one else does? When you get brutally honest with yourself to evaluate that answer, consider how God describes *His purpose for your life.*

> Make a careful exploration of who you are and the work you have been given, and then sink yourself into that. Don't be impressed with yourself. Don't compare yourself with others. Each of you must take responsibility for doing the creative best you can with your own life. (Galatians 6:4–5 MSG)

Here are two purposeful guidelines that can help as you seek your life purpose:

1. Don't *overestimate* yourself.

It is wrong to *overestimate* yourself. This means to be a bragger, conceited, and full of pride. Ever hear someone say, "She's just so full of herself!"

"Don't think you are better than you really are. Be honest in your evaluation of yourselves" (Romans 12:3).

2. Don't *underestimate* yourself.

It is equally wrong and damaging to *underestimate* yourself. To beat yourself up, to never feel worthy or good enough. Then, it becomes too easy to *just give up* and *never try*.

Both extreme behaviors will short-circuit the plans God has for you.

A number of years ago, a movie was produced called *Chariots of Fire*, which portrayed the true story of Eric Liddell, the famous British runner and Olympic winner of the men's 400 metres at the 1924 Summer Olympics in Paris. Against all odds, facing ridicule for standing true to his principles to honor his God, Eric announced to the world in his media interview: "I believe God made me for a purpose, but he also made me fast. And when I run, I feel His pleasure."

- God made me.
- God made me fast.
- When I run, I feel God's pleasure.

Wow. If you boil it all down, that's really what life is all about.

God made me. God made me good. When I run, paint, write, sing, or _____ (fill in the blank), I feel God's pleasure. What a healthy perspective and inspiring goal for each of us.

I really believe in the power of articulating, writing down the values you are trying to incorporate in your life. I thought I would share with you what I feel is my life purpose, my life mission.

Jimmelynn Garland Rice
Life Mission + Purpose

God created me.
God created me with a purpose.
He has placed within me all I need to fulfill that purpose.
My purpose and life will not look like anyone else's.
It is a privilege to be me.
I will not try to be someone else.
I will be myself. Everybody else is already taken.
I will set intentional goals to grow personally and professionally and to develop the leadership skills, talents, and gifts God has placed in me.
I will spend my life loving and serving others in order to make a difference in the short time I am on this earth.
The smile of God's pleasure over my life is my ultimate goal.
My life has value and worth because I reflect my Maker.
The Approval of One is all that matters.
I'm going to help other people value themselves.
I will help others discover and live their God-given purpose and calling.
My life mission is to intentionally share with everyone I meet:
You are *welcome.*
You are *wanted.*
You are *valued.*
You are *loved.*®

Maybe you don't feel *welcome* or *wanted* in your own family. Your mom has told you that you are a worthless piece of #@%! You've ruined her life. She wishes you had never been born. And you certainly never feel *valued* by anyone—your family or your friends. You never really *feel* what it means to be *loved.*

Oh, how I wish I could wrap my arms around you and tell you *how much you are loved. How much you are wanted. How much you are valued. How much you are needed. How much this world needs you.*

The way you view yourself is so very much influenced by your family.

135

Your relationship with your parents is one of the strongest factors in shaping *how you see yourself* and *if you value yourself.*

As a child, growing up, your emotions are tender and fragile. When you experience prolonged, persistent feelings of shame for not measuring up, your self-worth can be damaged and destroyed. Maybe this is how you feel inside:

A lot of days, I wrestle with feelings that I'm not good enough, that I'm worthless, that I'm never going to make it because I can't do anything right. Maybe I don't deserve to be loved.

Can I just tell you those feelings are telling you a lie? Let me help you as—*together*—we begin to work through those emotions and start on the path toward healing and becoming healthy emotionally. You *can* rewrite the script of your life. You do not have to be a victim of your past. You *can* choose your future. You are worth everything. You deserve love. You *are* loved.

Action Step 1: Evaluate the playlist of your childhood in your mind.

This is not a *dis* of parents. I am one! But, truth is: our parents greatly influence how we value ourselves. None of us escape that influence.

It is true that the messages you receive as a child repeat over and over in the playlist in your mind throughout your life. You internalize those messages and begin to believe them. Our goal is to analyze that playlist fairly and truthfully so that we begin to see ourselves as God sees us. God can help us to rewrite that playlist.

Maybe you are very fortunate because you have parents who raised you with affirmation, with healthy doses of praise and value. Go home tonight. Thank God and thank them.

But many of you struggle because the pattern in the messages one of your parents communicates to you leaves you struggling with shame.

- I'm stupid.
- I can't do anything right.
- Nobody could be as awful as me.
- Nobody could *love* someone as awful as me.

My daddy was an extremely difficult, demanding man to live with. Verbally and emotionally abusive. We walked a very thin tightrope, never knowing what would set him off next. On a daily basis, he was nearly impossible to please. A kind of Dr. Jekyll | Mr. Hyde where he could be charming, funny, humorous, and witty on the outside, but behind closed doors, it was very different. He had an inability to show affection, no question, and among other things, Daddy had an obsessive-compulsive disorder, making him even more rigid and demanding. We grew up with rules for everything. And I don't just mean the kind of rules like make your bed, take out the trash. I am talking about insane, rigid, drive-you-crazy rules. The problem was the harder you tiptoed around him and tried to keep from setting him off, the more impossible it was.

Every time I broke one of his rules (which was continually!), I got verbally lambasted with an angry, *"Hot Almighty! Get out of the way! What are you, stupid? You 'bout a dumb one!"* as he jabbed his index finger forcefully *into the side of my temple snarling, "You gotta think, think, think!"* (as he shook his head from side to side with total disgust at me).

If I got told that once a day, I got told it ten times! No matter how hard I tried, I couldn't do anything right. Mind you, I wasn't a disobedient, stubborn little hellion! I was very much a people-pleaser, follow-the-rules little girl. But, apparently, I didn't meet his approval—even though, God knows how hard I tried.

It could be just a simple thing like a door. God forbid that you actually open the door to your house and just walk in. No, first of all, line up all the passengers from the car; then barely open the door so everyone has to squeeze through the smallest opening possible so you don't let the heat or air conditioning out.

And for heaven's sake, don't let the door slam behind you. Turn the knob gently, so it doesn't make *any* noise as you ever so carefully twist it into the latch.

And while you're at it, now that you're inside, don't walk through the same room twice. If you came in through the family room, exit through the living room so you don't wear out the carpet.

Electricity brought a whole new set of rules. Don't open the refrigerator door unless you know what you want inside. Of course, the little girl inside me wanted to scream out, "How in the heck am I supposed to know what's in the refrigerator if I haven't even seen what's inside?" But

I didn't dare. I knew better. That would have set Daddy off, and his hand would've come up as though to slap me as he snarled with disgust, "You 'bout a dumb one! You stupid! Get outta the way!"

Daddy got furious at us for wanting to use a blow dryer to dry our hair before school. To keep his anger from exploding at us, many times I drove to school in the morning with my head hanging out the window, trying to dry my hair in the wind before I got to class.

When we took a shower, we weren't allowed to just turn on the faucet and let the water run until it warmed up. We kept a bucket in the bathroom to catch the cold water until it warmed. Then, that water was saved and used to water the grass outside. We won't even talk about rules for the toilet: how many times per day you could flush and for what reasons! I say we lived "green" before green was cool!

I can laugh about some of these things now; but the truth is, it wasn't so funny when I was growing up living it. I was afraid to be around Daddy; my stomach was in constant knots and filled with anxiety for fear of setting him off and making him angry. And in my head, I couldn't understand why Daddy seemed to dislike me so much.

But, one thing for sure, I learned about myself:

I'm stupid! I'm about a dumb one! I just need to get out of the way and let somebody more competent do it!

So, guess what playlist I have carried into my adult life and have to fight every time I mess up or don't do something right the first time. You got it! *"What are you—stupid? You 'bout a dumb one! Get outta the way and let somebody else do it!"*

I have asked God to help me reprogram, reteach, and retrain my mind by reading and devouring His Word, which is Truth. Some days I succeed. Other days I fail miserably.

The impact of words is powerful.

Life and death are in the power of the tongue!

Did you know words really are weapons—weapons of destruction or missiles of empowerment? Words *are* powerful. You can't control what has been spoken to you. But you can control what comes out of *your* mouth. You may become a parent yourself one day. How will you raise your children? Will you repeat and model the behavior you grew up with? How were words used in your home? *Will you use your words to give life or deliver death?*

You need to begin to make that choice now. Do you lift up or tear down others with your words? Do you encourage or discourage? How about the tone of your voice? Does it matter? You bet your life it does!

> Few forces have more impact than the words we speak.

On a side note: the older you get, the more you will try to understand your parents and even learn to forgive their actions because *maybe* the behavior that was modeled by *their* parents growing up shaped them too. You will learn to give them a little slack. 'Cause they're just as messed up as you are. [In fairness to my daddy, he modeled what he grew up with. He was raised by an alcoholic mother who was harsh and unnurturing, and a father who was cold and distant, selfish, and incapable of expressing love or affection.]

When you finally learn that a person's behavior has much more to do with their own internal struggle than it ever did with you, you will start to feel a little more grace.

The real truth is that every one of us is from a dysfunctional family in some way or another because we're all broken.

You may or may not ever hear the words of acceptance or affirmation from your parent that you long to hear. You may have to find grace, over time, to just let that go. Does it hurt? Yes. Is that hard? Yes.

However, don't use that as an excuse. Don't play victim. Use your energy to make a *positive out of your past* by choosing *now* how you want to raise your family one day. What can you learn? What things will you do differently? How can you break the cycle?

Action Step 2: Admit and confront feelings of inferiority.

Many girls wrestle with horrible, crippling feelings of inferiority. Perhaps, as you look at everyone around you, you feel like you will never measure up. Know what? You won't. Hate to disappoint you.

If your goal is to be someone else, it will never happen.
Step up to the plate and just be you.

> You were born an original.
> Don't die a copy.

I understand the whole inferiority thing! I beat myself up frequently too. I can think of a million other people who are more gifted and could do what I do better! People who are better speakers. Better leaders. More skilled. CEOs who graduated with a degree in business rather than music performance like I did.

But, guess what? God chose one little girl to grow up, to mature, and to accept the challenge of starting and leading this global mission and movement—Girls Nite In International. If I had let my insecurities and fear get in the way, you would not be receiving this help, hope, healing, love, life strategy, and guidance for your life. I would have been too afraid of everything I might do wrong instead of *valuing what I do right.*

My point is: fear of our weakness and what others think can absolutely paralyze us to the point that we cower down, shut down, and do nothing. You can only find healing from your insecurities by learning what God says about you.

> Your self-worth is not based on who those around you say you are
> but on who the Creator of the universe says you are.

God says: you are uniquely and wonderfully made. He oughta know. He's the One who pieced you together so carefully in your mother's womb.

Don't waste your energy feeling inferior. *No one* can do what you were placed on this earth to do.

When you really get that God loves you unconditionally, *other people's opinions of you will begin to matter less and less because you are fully loved, fully accepted, and fully valued by God.*

Action Step 3: Find your passion and develop the skills you have been given.

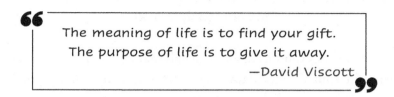

66

> The meaning of life is to find your gift.
> The purpose of life is to give it away.
> —David Viscott

99

Like Eric Liddell, discover how *God made you good*. Find your passion. Figure out the talents and skills God has so generously placed in you. Not so you become "full of yourself" and arrogant and boast about how great you are. But so you don't dis God by never becoming all He created you to be. How can you use your gifts and skill set to serve others and to serve Him? Love others. Love Him. True joy is found in serving and caring for others. The most bitter, miserable people are those who spend their lives investing in nothing but themselves—their looks, their career, their own self-absorbed self-interests. *"It's in Christ that we find out who we are and what we are living for. Long before we first heard of Christ and got our hopes up, he had his eye on us"* (Ephesians 1:11–12 MSG).

Action Step 4: Stop unhealthy comparing and competing.

Comparing and competing with others can get out of control and become destructive. If you are an athlete or a musician, healthy competition can spur you on to become better and "up your game." If you play basketball and see another girl who is a much better shooter than you, it can stimulate you to do drills and practice free throws until you improve. Maybe you're a singer and there is another girl who has an amazing voice. Instead of being jealous of her, work on your own skills. *Use that initial feeling of envy to spur you on to becoming better and more skilled.*

Action Step 5: Recognize that the goal for your life is progress, not perfection.

Life is about progress—not perfection.

Striving for perfectionism won't make you perfect. In fact, it will only make you feel inadequate. You are not worthless because you fail. You are simply *human.*

Yes, God does want us to grow up and mature, but He doesn't expect it overnight. Our Creator knows our weaknesses and He is patient and forgiving. When we fall, He wants us to come to Him for cleansing and then move forward. Each of us is a work in progress.

If your goal is perfection, it is impossible. You will continually *beat yourself up* and feel like a *failure.* You will become a *rigid perfectionist who never measures up nor allows anyone around you to measure up to your impossible standard.*

So, cut yourself and others a little slack.

You know the hardest person to forgive? Yourself!

Maybe you're thinking right now: *You are exactly right, Jimme. I hate myself. Why do I have to learn things the hard way? I'm just one big, screwed-up failure.*

Well, you're certainly not the first person to feel the pain, disgust, and shame of feeling like a colossal screwed-up failure. Download from my website (JimmelynnGarlandRice.com/Books) the true story of the hottest, sexiest couple on the planet, living in the most exotic location ever created . . . who made one horrible choice with devastating consequences causing them to feel the shame of being colossal screwed-up failures. In fact, they ran away and went into hiding. But God found them. Mercifully.

If God is calling you out, don't feel that you have to hide. Answer Him. Tell Him the truth. Own it. Take responsibility for your actions. I hid. I was afraid. I tried it my way. Epic fail! I admit it now. You are God. I am not. I want You to take over my life. I choose to trust You with the rest of my life.

Run to God for cleansing. When we come to God for cleansing, He forgives us and never throws it in our face again: "As far as the east is from the west, so far has [God] removed our transgressions from us" (Psalm 103:12 NIV).

Do not hold your past over your own head anymore. If God isn't, why are you? Do not continue to beat yourself up.

Can I give you some really practical advice from my heart?

- Keep short accounts with God. Tell Him when you're wrong. Ask for cleansing.
- Keep short accounts with each other. With the important relationships in your life, admit when you're wrong.
- Practice those six hard words: *I was wrong. I am sorry.*
- "Therefore, there is now *no condemnation* for those who are in Christ Jesus" (Romans 8:1 NIV, italics mine).

Walk in freedom with your head up. No more hiding.

I close with a story about my favorite mentor, Ruth Bell Graham, wife of Billy Graham.

One day Ruth was driving down the road through a heavy construction site. When she finally got to the end of the construction zone, Ruth tells of spotting a sign beside the road with these words: "End of construction. Thank you for your patience."

When she got home, Ruth immediately told her family that she had found the words she wanted written on her tombstone as her epitaph when she died.

Over Christmas break, I had the privilege to visit Ruth's gravesite at the Billy Graham Library in Charlotte, North Carolina. Sure enough, the words carved on the big slab of limestone lying on top of her grave were: "End of construction. Thank you for your patience."

My eyes filled up with tears as I stood there knowing the truth. We are all a work in progress. Under construction. Forgive yourself. Progress is the goal. Not perfection.

With that in mind, every day:

- Ask God for forgiveness.
- Forgive yourself.
- Forgive others.

My goal for my life and yours:

> Don't let yesterday use up too much of today.
> —Will Rogers

Every next level of your life will demand growth—a newer version of you. I can't wait to see who you will become.

With more love than you can imagine,

 Jimme

10

Dating Violence | Self-Protection

My Dear Terrified Survivor,

Not every person who *wants* to be in your life should have *permission* to be in your life.

One in three teens will experience physical, sexual, or emotional abuse from someone they're in a relationship with.

My goal is to help you protect yourself in dating relationships. We all long to feel safe, accepted, and loved.

That desire is good, normal, and healthy.

Knowing what a healthy relationship is and what an abusive relationship *looks* and *feels* like is hugely important. THIS LETTER MAY SAVE YOUR LIFE . . . LITERALLY! My goal is to challenge your thinking and bring awareness to *unhealthy*, *destructive*, and *abusive* dating relationships. To encourage you to think about how you want to be treated and what you *will* or will *not* accept. What behavior and treatment you *will* or will *not* allow. To help you see the 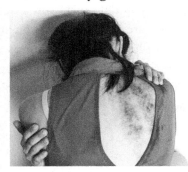 red flags and recognize if you are in a dangerous, abusive relationship and to give you the courage and the tools to get out!

What Is Dating Violence?

Dating violence is a *pattern* of abusive behaviors used to exert power and control over a dating partner. It's *not* an argument every once in a

145

while, a bad mood due to a bad day, or being told you're being oversensitive because it's that time of the month!

The one element that is common in most abusive relationships is that the violence escalates over time and becomes more and more dangerous for the victim.

What does dating violence look like?

- **Physical Abuse**: slapping, kicking, choking, spitting, punching, hitting, or pushing
- **Verbal | Emotional | Psychological Abuse**: threats, insults, monitoring or stalking, humiliation, intimidation, name-calling, mind games, or isolation from everyone around you
- **Sexual Abuse**: any forced sexual conduct, including touching intimate private parts, playing sex games, penetration, oral sex, showing porn, or any unwanted sexual activity
- **Economic Abuse**: taking your money, not letting you get a job, or causing you trouble at work
- **Digital Abuse**: using technology and/or social media to intimidate, harass, or threaten a current or former dating partner. This can include cyberbullying, sexting, excessive and threatening texts, and stalking on your social media accounts. If someone you date texts you a dozen times an hour to find out what you are doing or who you are with, that doesn't symbolize being "in love." It most often is a way to monitor and control your interactions with other people. It probably feels flattering at first, but in reality, it is manipulation and control of your actions.

The Four Red Flags of an Abusive Dating Relationship Are:

1. Lies
2. Control
3. Manipulation
4. Violence

Ask yourself: Does my boyfriend or girlfriend:

___ Look at me or act in ways that scare me?

___ Act jealous or possessive?

___ Put me down or criticize me?

___ Try to control where I go, what I wear, or what I do?

___ Text or IM me excessively?

___ Blame me for hurtful things they say or do?

___ Threaten to kill or hurt me or themselves if I leave them?

___ Try to stop me from seeing or talking to friends or family?

___ Try to force me to have sex before I am ready?

___ Tell me if I *really* love them, *I* would have sex with them?

___ Get me drunk or drugged to make me less resistant to having sex?

___ Physically hurt me in any way?

___ Tell me that I am worthless and no one would want me but them?

___ Throw objects or destroy possessions to intimidate me and make me afraid?

___ Demand to know my passwords?

___ Check my cell phone and social media without permission?

At the core of dating violence are two issues: power and control.

If you are feeling used or controlled by an abusive person, I want to talk real about some difficult decisions you may need to make. Steps you need to take to get your life back to a healthy place again.

It may be time to cut ties with that toxic, abusive person.

When you realize you are in an abusive relationship, it can be difficult to admit to yourself. Recognizing the truth, facing it, and admitting it to yourself takes time. It's a complicated process because you have so many conflicting emotions churning inside of you.

147

Fear: You may be afraid of what will happen if you decide to break off the relationship, especially if you have been threatened.

Believing abuse is normal: If you don't know what a healthy relationship looks like or grew up in a home where abuse was common, you may not recognize that this relationship is unhealthy and dangerous.

Embarrassment or shame: It's embarrassing to recognize you have chosen to be with someone who would abuse you. You feel shame and embarrassment that you must be a fool. No one wants to be a fool.

Low self-esteem or self-worth: It becomes easy to believe you are unworthy of love when your dating partner continually berates and belittles you. You begin to believe you are worthless and no one would want you but them.

Love: Because you genuinely care for and love the person who is abusing you, you keep hoping that they will change. That your love can cause them to change. Along with that, your abuser keeps promising to change, especially after an abusive encounter. You want to believe they will change. *You may only want the violence to stop, but because you think you love them, you don't want the relationship to end.*

May I have permission to enter your private, secret thoughts and share some advice that will help you?

1. You can never change another person.

You can't change another person. That's hard to accept, but it's true. The only person you can change is *you*.

Yes, you are with a very damaged, broken person who needs help and healing. But you are not responsible to fix them. In fact, you can't. You cannot change another person, no matter how hard you try.

You can only change you.

2. Ask for help.

Talk with someone you trust. There is no shame in admitting you feel trapped and you need help.

3. Don't allow fear to trap you and stop you from telling the truth and reporting the abuse.

I know you're scared. You fear for your own safety. Which is legit. You're scared to report the truth to an authority figure or the police because you fear losing confidentiality and what the law will require. You want your abuser to get help; but at the same time, you love this person, so you don't want them to get punished.

And to be straight-up real: you're terrified there will be revenge for you if you tell the truth and disclose the abuse.

The abuse is **not** your fault. Abuse is not "normal." Do **not** blame yourself! If you don't have the courage to report it, at least talk with someone you trust. Do **not** keep it all inside where it will destroy you and cause you to have thoughts of harming yourself or ending your life. *Please give yourself permission to get help.* **You deserve it.**

I need to share a most painful, gut-wrenching, heartbreaking story of one of my GNI girls, Heather Brown, whom I deeply love and will always love. Not only was Heather bright, beautiful, well-liked, fun, out-going, with a beautiful singing voice, she also came from a family who was close-knit, parents and four sisters who were very involved in one another's lives and was a vibrant part of her church and youth group. My point being: this can happen to you—even if you come from a good, respected family who loves you.

The saddest reality is that this story must be told from her mom, Shelly, because devastatingly, Heather is no longer with us. For this very reason, I am begging you to take the words of my letter to you seriously. If Heather's senseless death can help you avoid people who will destroy you and intentionally make changes in your life to protect yourself, it would at least make Heather's life have more purpose because it is helping you not to travel the same path.

Having the "wrong guy" in her life brought more wrong people into Heather's life. These people did not have her best interest at heart. They planned against her. They took turns raping her. They ultimately controlled every part of Heather's life. They told her what clothes to wear, how to wear her hair, if she was allowed to eat that day, and where she was allowed to go. If she did not do as they said, they told her they would come to our house and hurt her family and make her watch.

They also told her no one would miss her if she were gone. They told her to cut herself and bleed slowly until she died. They were horrible, awful people. Heather carried all this by herself for two years before she told me. These people trapped my girl until the only way out in her mind was death. The stress and fear stripped her of all courage and rational thought.

Heather finally told me what was happening and attempted suicide by taking an overdose of pain meds. After she was released from the hospital, we went to the police to make a report.

Heather ended her life on August 9, 2016. She was four days into her senior year. She went to work with me that day instead of going to school and wasn't herself. We had a pretty good time together. Little did I know Heather had planned out the day. Right before leaving the office, the police called and set up a recorded interview. It was their desire that Heather would have to tell only one time what these people did to her. That sent Heather into a dark place of terror, panic, and fear.

After getting home, her dad took our youngest daughter to softball practice, and I started dinner. After coming back inside from taking our dogs to the pond for a swim, Heather left the dogs outside to dry off. She took a notebook off the table. I asked her what she was going to do. She sighed and said, "Just going to clean my room, Mama." I saw no danger in that and continued to cook dinner. But after a little while, I realized I had not heard any cleaning noises coming from her bedroom, which was in the basement. No drawers closing, no music, no nothing, so I decided to go check on her. Her bedroom door was closed. I knocked and opened the door. Her room was still messy, and I didn't even see Heather in there.

I remember saying, "Heather, you're not getting very far in this room. Where are you?" As I pushed the door open to see if she was sitting on the floor at the foot of her bed, something caught the corner of my eye. As I turned to look again, I remember, it was like my soul left my body. I found her. She had hung herself from a rafter in her room. I couldn't form words . . . all I could do was scream.

That nightmare of pain and horror is something no mother should ever have to experience! The events following were so horrific that Shelly and two of her daughters—who saw Heather with their own eyes—have all struggled with panic attacks, flashbacks, difficulty entering into life again, and PTSD. It has taken years to rebuild their lives, knowing it will never be the same without Heather.

Shelly asked me to tell you that it's a lie to believe people will be better off without you. The pain they live with every day is ongoing and torturous to their minds. The pain didn't end when Heather took her life. It multiplied into the lives of so many who loved her. Shelly begs you to tell someone, even if you are being threatened. Don't let the tormentors cause you to feel trapped, with no way out. Shelly said the lies these people told Heather were vicious and wrong. Heather is terribly missed by so many . . . and Shelly will carry all of Heather's heartache to her grave, along with praying for justice for these perpetrators who caused Heather to end her life.

I, personally, will always do my part to honor Heather's life by telling her story and making sure she is not forgotten. Her life mattered so much, and we will make some good come out of this horrific, senseless tragedy if you will:

4. Set boundaries of protection around yourself.

Healthy boundaries keep you from being manipulated and controlled. Strong boundaries protect your mind, your body, and your heart. People treat you the way you allow them to treat you.

Decide how you want to be treated and what you *will* and *won't* allow. Set strong boundaries based on what your head, heart, and gut are telling you about what you want in a relationship.

Most importantly, choose someone who is running the same direction you are in life. Someone, like you, whose goal is to grow in your faith and please God with your life and choices. If the person you are with is leading you the opposite direction, run away from that relationship. Run away as fast as you can!

Like one of my friends says: "Your best equipment is your running shoes!" It might take a while to recognize that not everyone has your best interest at heart. You may need to distance yourself from so-called friends who manipulate, lie, and try to control or destroy you.

Not everyone deserves unedited access into your life.

As hard as it is, you do need to start putting boundaries of protection around yourself to protect your heart.

5. "When someone shows you who they are, believe them the first time."

Maya Angelou had it right! Quit lying to yourself. If your best friend or your boyfriend is jealous, critical, possessive, controlling, and manipulative, admit it to yourself. You do *not* have to put up with being abused, controlled, threatened, told you are worthless and useless, and treated like crap.

You are not worthless. Do not let someone stop you from seeing or talking with your friends or family. Do not let someone control where you go, what you wear, what you do. Do not let someone force you to have sex, blame you for hurtful things they do, threaten to kill you, or hurt you if you leave them.

That is not love. That is control.

You are not worthless. You do not deserve that. Do not be held hostage to that person. Tell someone. Ask for help. Get out. Don't be embarrassed.

> **Short-term shame is better than lifetime pain.**

When someone shows you who they are, believe them the first time.

6. Value yourself.

Love does NOT equal control.
In an abusive relationship, teens often mistake love for control.
Love does NOT equal possessiveness.

> **When you start seeing value in yourself, you won't tolerate toxic people in your life who do not value you.**

No person is worth sacrificing your dignity and values. Ever.

I often see girls tolerate certain behaviors within dating relationships or friendships, and I wish that I could pull each of them aside and say, *You are worth so much more than you are getting right now. If you could see the value I see in you, you would realize that you don't need to settle. You can set the bar so much higher with the people you let into your life.*

> **Cutting unhealthy people out of my life doesn't mean I hate them. It means I respect myself.**

If you are in a toxic dating relationship and you have legitimate fears for your safety because of the manipulation and control this person has over you, talk to someone you trust. You deserve help. You are not worthless and useless. You are *not* damaged goods.

How to Help a Friend Who Is in an Abusive Relationship

1. Be supportive and listen.
2. Don't judge.
3. Help your friend recognize that abuse is not "normal" and is *not* their fault.
4. Focus on your friend, not the abusive partner. Do *not* "dis" their abusive boyfriend or girlfriend.
5. Connect your friend to resources that can give them information and guidance.
6. Do not contact their abuser or publicly berate them.
7. Do not get discouraged. You may become deeply frustrated and feel helpless because your friend is not acting quickly and decisively when being abused.
8. Reassure your friend of his or her worth and that he or she is valued and loved.

loveisrespect.org: a great online resource for teens/young adults. A safe way to explore and face the truth of an abusive situation.

girlsnitein.org: A preventative mentoring and empowering program for young women providing tools to rescue them from self-destructive choices and empowering them to become strong, bold leaders.

Ten Things I Wish Someone Would Have Told Me

1. You are loved and valuable. Don't let anyone steal that from you.
2. When someone shows you who they are, believe them.
3. You can and will be fine without them. You will even thrive.
4. Don't settle for easy; the price is too high. Short-term shame is better than lifetime pain.

5. Your abuser will never change for you. The only person you can change is yourself.

6. Don't believe the lie that no one else would ever want you. Think about it. God wants you so you clearly have value. He sees your value. Can't you?

7. Don't let anyone isolate you from family and friends. Your partner should complete you, not isolate or control you.

8. Don't rush through life. Don't settle because you're afraid to be alone.

9. You hold the key to your life. You are in control. Don't give it away. It is very difficult to get back. So, just hang on to it.

10. Remember, you are precious, loved, and valued. Be the artist of your life. Create the canvas that you deserve—not someone else's design! You are the artist of your own life.

God has created and designed you for a purpose and a life *only you* can fulfill.

> Life is short.
> Spend it with
> people who make
> you laugh and
> feel loved.
> *Because you are!*

With more love than you can imagine,

Jimme

11

Self-Hate | Self-Harm

My Dear Self-Punishing Fighter,

These words from Shantell literally jumped off the page and arrested my attention:

> Cutting was a release because I wanted to cry so much, and I had stopped crying when I was 6 years old. The blood was like physical tears. At least there were drops. I think with cutting . . ., it's to be able to see the feeling of pain, or anger, or self-hatred. And it's really to punish yourself. We put the hatred back onto our bodies.[1]

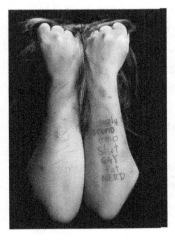

During our moments together, I want to pull back the curtain to expose this dark secret so it does not stay hidden any longer. Unless we start talking about it and make it acceptable for you to admit this is a struggle, it will remain in the dark: a secret—hidden—buried and clothed in shame.

I am deeply grateful to some of my girls who have generously allowed me to peer into the window of your private world in preparation for writing about this topic: self-hate|self-harm. You have taught me so much and I thank you. I have learned from you, from your honesty.

More than anything, I want you to know there is hope and there is a way out of and through your pain.

At the outset, I want you to know two things:

First, you are not alone. There are many of us who care about you and want to help. You do not have to struggle with this alone.

Second, your pain is real. I fully, fully recognize that. If you have started mutilating yourself in some way, it is because *you think the only way to feel better emotionally is to hurt yourself physically.* Cutting distracts you, momentarily, from what is bottled up inside. It provides a few moments of relief from the emotional pain that torments you inside. Cutting, actually reminds you that you're alive because inside you feel nothing but numb and dead.

Possibly you are one of those people who feels like you never do anything right. You're such a perfectionist that you can't live with yourself if you do anything less than perfectly. When you feel defeated because you didn't score enough points at the game or place first in the competition or score a perfect 100 percent on that exam, you may escape to your room, grab a pencil, and begin to rub burns all over your arms and your stomach because you're so disgusted with yourself.

Perhaps if you punish yourself enough, you'll get rid of the bad.

Or, God forbid, maybe you have fallen into the hands of someone who took horrible advantage of you, exploited you, or raped you. Understandably, your mind is tormented. You feel rage, anger, hurt, exposed, and betrayed. The pain is so overwhelming that you resort to scraping yourself with a sharp, broken shard of glass because the emotions are so intense. Or you hit and beat yourself again and again with a hard object—forcefully creating deep bruises—hoping to bring relief from the thoughts that torment you.

Although the subject of abuse is not what we are focusing on, I want to say loud and clear:

If you are being abused or have been violated in the past—you did nothing to deserve this abuse. Punishing yourself is not going to give you relief. Please, please talk to someone.

Someone you trust.

> Do not turn your pain inward. You are not the enemy!

When talking with some of you privately, I have asked what causes you to injure yourself, to harm yourself. Here are some of the things you have shared with me:

- I hurt myself because it is the one thing in my life I can control.
- I hurt myself to release anger.
- I hurt myself because it is better than thinking about all the bad memories I have.
- I hurt myself because I deserve to be punished.
- I hurt myself to get rid of guilt.
- I hurt myself because the outside pain hurts a lot less than the inside pain.
- I hurt myself when I feel like I have disappointed others I care about.
- I hurt myself because I hate my body.
- I hurt myself because it makes me feel things that I can't put into words.
- I hurt myself to feel alive again.
- I hurt myself because it keeps me from feeling numb and dead inside.

You may find yourself thinking, *I know someone who does that*, or *I do that, but so what? It's really not a big deal.* However, if you are torturing or damaging yourself with any type of self-harming behavior, it *is* a big deal.

The truth is, if you are cutting, burning, bruising, biting, yanking hair out, scratching, or purposefully harming yourself in any way, you are struggling with self-injury.

If you find yourself identifying with some of these behaviors, I really want to help you. I have some very intentional things to share. Let's explore why you self-harm, what triggers it, the truth about whether it's really "working" for you, healthy ways to handle stress and cope with life, and steps to begin breaking the addiction of self-harm.

Most importantly, I want to answer the vital question that haunts you: *Is there really hope that I can stop?*

We each have different ways to handle stress and cope with life. Injuring yourself is the way you have chosen to get relief from the pain in your life.

> The more pain you feel, the more pain you inflict on yourself.

One seventeen-year-old said,

> People who haven't cut can't understand how it can make you feel better . . . but it does. It's like bursting a huge bubble. You feel like you are going to explode and you don't know what to do with the emotional pain. When you cut, there is a kind of release or freedom in it. Then, it's like an emotional high. You release all this pain that's been building and building. Like any addiction, it's a coping mechanism. Skin is like a bulletin board. It broadcasts: "Can't you see how much pain I'm in?"

The bad news is that self-harm can only provide a temporary escape.

Yes, there is an initial rush of relief, but almost immediately you are overwhelmed with one very powerful emotion. Shame. Humiliating, suffocating shame. Shame that sneers and reminds you that you deserve punishment. Shame that compels you to hide and cover the scars with long sleeves. And so, the cycle of addiction begins. Self-injury begins to dominate your thoughts.

> You thought punishing and abusing yourself gave you a sense of control. Now "it" begins to control you.

The very thing you thought gave you power and control is now the very thing that has power and control over *you*.

Your mind has been taken captive. You have now become a prisoner in your own world. A prisoner held hostage by invisible chains. S–L–A–V–E. Your mind is a slave to this abusive behavior that controls you.

God's Book of Truth is filled with life-giving wisdom for our real lives. "For you are a slave to whatever controls you" (2 Peter 2:19).

> You are a slave to whatever controls you!

Abusing yourself can only provide a *temporary* escape—*temporary* relief.

After you've damaged yourself, you feel enslaved all over again . . . like a prisoner in the orange jumpsuit shackled in chains.

You feel shackled by two chains—one around each ankle—so to speak:

- The chain of pain
- The chain of shame

One girl verbalized it this way: *"Once you start, you can't stop. It starts with just a razor, then, it gets dangerous. I don't think my friends understand how it's like a drug. Cutting became an addiction. I craved it. I needed it. I couldn't go without it."*

This may sound like an extreme statement, but it is not. There is some truth that the endorphins released into your body when you self-injure can become quite addictive. That is why many times cutting is not something you can just "get over." It can become a compulsion. It really may be necessary that you seek the help of a medical doctor or a trained counselor to get the adequate help you really need to break this addictive cycle.

No matter how hard you try to stop, cutting is a behavior that is difficult to replace because it is so physically stimulating. You don't have the strength or the power within yourself; you will need the power and strength of God, which is available to you through Christ. "For I can do everything through Christ, who gives me strength" (Philippians 4:13).

There is HOPE! There is a way out. You do not have to remain a slave to this behavior that is controlling you. There is hope, and you can find lasting healing. The path to freedom begins with trusting Christ as your Savior.

I would not be honest with you if I did not tell you that meeting Jesus is the first step in the healing process. He is the Source of hope. Then, He will give you the power you need to overcome this self-sabotaging behavior that is now controlling you.

> You *can* recover because you have "the Healer" living and working inside you!

God can heal your mind and emotions, deliver you from the chains of this overwhelming addiction, and restore you mentally, emotionally, physically, and spiritually. He longs to make you whole.

He wants to bring joy into your life once again so your mind is no longer tormented by these obsessive thoughts.

Because I am all about being real, I want to help you develop a successful strategy: eight intentional steps to begin breaking free from this addiction that has a grip on you. I care about you and want to help you cope with life in a way that does not destroy you.

Strategy 1. Verbalize your pain.

You may feel scared to talk about your past. The very thought of saying things out loud may make you feel like throwing up. But, as long as you bottle everything up inside you, it will literally eat you alive. You will turn all that pain inward. The first thing you need to do is to admit your struggle. In order to deal with your emotions in a healthy way, you must first learn to talk about them. Talk to someone you trust. It will be hard at first. But it will get easier. Be patient with yourself. If it is excruciating for you to talk to someone, maybe you should write. Write down how you feel. Journal your thoughts. Express your feelings in a poem or a song. Sometimes, when there just simply are no words that can describe the depth of your pain, drawing or painting may be better.

Let yourself cry and feel the pain from past events that have traumatized your life. When you begin to acknowledge the pain and let yourself feel it, you are beginning the road to healing. Along that line, if you have been in the habit of harming yourself, make a choice to begin using your voice . . .

Strategy 2. Use your voice—rather than your body—to express yourself.

Use your voice, whether that is on paper or verbal. Use your voice—NOT your body—to express your pain. You do not gain anything healthy by punishing yourself. The only thing you gain is shame and even more despair.

An interesting suggestion to consider: When you are fighting the compulsion to injure yourself, take out your aggression on a safe, predetermined object instead of yourself.

One girl was fortunate enough to have her parents' support and assistance in overcoming her addiction. With their permission, she began to scrape slash marks on an old desk in her room instead of making slash marks on her body. Every time she felt the urge to cut, she sliced a gash into the desktop instead of herself. Just visually seeing those marks helped her begin to break the addictive cycle. When she saw how mutilated and beat-up the desk looked, she realized that was what she had been doing to her own body.

Strategy 3. Eliminate certain objects from your room that will cause you to struggle.

There are specific things that you cannot afford to have sitting around your room. They may not bother other people, but you know they are a temptation to you.

You have to avoid things that you would use to hurt yourself. If you were a smoker trying to quit, you certainly wouldn't want to have a carton of cigs anywhere near you. If you are aiming to become healthier and adopt good eating habits, you don't want a kitchen full of ice cream, chocolate chip cookies, or snacks that are high in calories. Similarly, if you are in the habit of cutting, burning, or hurting yourself in other ways, then you definitely don't want the objects you regularly use to hurt yourself anywhere close.

Get them out of your room. The things you use to hurt yourself—scissors, matches, razor blades, or whatever. Get 'em outta your sight!

Strategy 4. Avoid being alone when you know you are vulnerable.

If you are struggling, you will need to choose to surround yourself with support.

Your normal pattern is to isolate yourself and pull away from everyone. You don't want people too close 'cause you're terrified they might find out your secret. You're gonna have to choose to be vulnerable to someone. Confide in someone you do trust. Someone who is mature. Someone who can help you call out to God for help when you are hurting.

Strategy 5. Choose friends carefully.

Friends are hugely important. You become like the people you choose to spend time with. Choose friends intentionally and carefully.

Maintaining your freedom from self-injury will depend a lot on the friends you choose to be with. We become like the people we spend time with. Literally.

Tell me who you hang out with and I can tell you a lot about your choices.

Strategy 6. Create an emergency kit.

Another practical suggestion that I learned from you! Many people who are fighting the impulse to self-injure find it extremely helpful to create an emergency kit.

Create an emergency kit? I know that may sound odd.

An emergency kit is an actual box that contains items that will help you when you feel the urge to self-injure. A few of the items you might consider placing in your kit:

- A list of people you can call. People who know your struggle and care about helping you. People in your life who want you to become healthy and deal with stress in a positive way.
- A journal to write your thoughts and feelings in.
- A sketch pad for drawing or painting to express your thoughts.
- Calming, soothing music.
- A photograph of someone you love and who loves you deeply. Someone who cares for you and has your back.
- A stress ball. When you are feeling overcome with negative emotions, just the very physical act of squeezing and releasing a stress ball will help to relieve your tension and those emotions that are boiling inside you.

- Fidgets.
- Place an ice cube on the area you want to cut because it brings the same stinging sensation as when you harm yourself. Then, drip some red dye on that spot which will run downwards and symbolize blood to your mind.

Strategy 7. Find a replacement activity.

It is extremely important to find a replacement activity—something you can physically do when you feel the urge to self-injure.

Any time you are trying to break a harmful habit, it is not enough just to try to **remove** it from your life. You gotta **replace** it with something healthy. Remove and replace! That goes for just about any area of your life that you need to change.

A habit you're trying to change, a friendship that is bad news, a place you hang out that brings you nothing but trouble—remove the bad and replace it with good. A wholesome choice. In the case of self-injury, find a replacement activity that makes you think less about hurting yourself and do that activity until the urge to self-injure goes away. Play a musical instrument, jog, dance, exercise, walk your dog. Something physical.

Strategy 8. Identify the triggers.

It's important to analyze what feelings or situations trigger you to cut or self-harm. Let me list some possible triggers that may increase your impulse to hurt yourself:

- anger or rage over a situation that is horribly unjust and unfair
- pressure to be perfect and the disappointment when you're not
- a traumatic event totally beyond your control that has forever altered your life
- a painful loss of someone you love and cared for deeply

You want to begin to work on healthy ways to deal with your strong emotions. There is a better way to work through the deep hurts that have crushed you and devastated you for so long.

It is not true that the only way you can get emotional relief is to hurt yourself physically.

> You have to change the way you think
> if you are going to change the way you act.

As one thinks in her heart—so is she!
—Proverbs 23:7, paraphrased

What you think about really matters. What you obsess over. Because what you think, you become. That is why our minds have to be transformed with Truth. The most important thing you can do is to flood your mind with God's Book of Truth. Memorize some of these Principles of Truth we discussed. Say them out loud to yourself over and over. Those words have the power to transform your thinking and change your life. Remember: What you think about, you become. In the same way, if all you obsess about and think about is harming yourself, you will become just that: one who self-harms.

God's Book says we need to take captive every thought: "We take captive every thought to make it obedient to Christ" (2 Corinthians 10:5 NIV).

What does it mean to "take captive"? It means to take hostage, arrest, make a prisoner, control, seize. Take control and seize your thoughts. Every time you find yourself believing a lie, tell yourself the Truth from God's Word instead.

If you base your decisions on your feelings, you will choose wrong every time. Feelings lie. When you think: *Nobody can possibly love me. I'm just worthless and disgusting*, replace that with Truth from God's Word that says that you are valuable and matter to Him.

Nothing can separate me from God's love—not even myself. God has tenderly said:

> "I will never fail you.
> I will never abandon you."

So we can say with confidence,

"The Lord is my helper,
so I will have no fear.
What can mere people do to me?"
—Hebrews 13:5–6

Be patient with yourself. It will take time to renew your mind with God's truth to replace all the lies you have believed.

Perfection is not the goal. Progress is.

We are not capable of perfection. Regardless of how many times you screw up (because you will!), confess your wrongdoing to God. Then, get back up, dust yourself off, and start moving forward again!

"But one thing I do: Forgetting what is behind and straining toward what is ahead, I press on toward the goal" (Philippians 3:13–14 NIV).

When you decide that you're not gonna give in to the urge to self-harm, I guarantee you the battle will be very intense. You will have to face a lot of dark places in yourself and deal with things inside that are difficult.

But, as you run to God, He will give you the power to overcome. He will begin to change you from the inside out, to change your heart and your desires. He, alone, is fully able to help you because He created you. He made you.

One girl who has fully recovered wrote:

I did not do it alone; God was there to walk beside me. Freedom from self-harm started with my belief system. I began to understand who I was in Christ and continuing to self-harm did not line up with my new identity. I finally understood that I was worth more than that. *I couldn't stand there and say how precious I was to God and in the next breath say that I was a cutter and deserved to be hurt!*[2]

There is nothing God cannot deliver us from. Nothing! I believe that with every ounce of my being.

We think some of the problems we're dealing with are brand new and nobody's ever dealt with them before. That we're the only ones struggling. Not! "The temptations in your life are no different from what others experience. And God is faithful. He will not allow the temptation to be more than you can stand. When you are tempted, he will show you a way out so that you can endure" (1 Corinthians 10:13).

I love God's Book of Truth! He could have told us stories of perfect people who never screwed up. Who lived perfect lives.

But there are none!

Over and again, God shares real stories about real people.

Broken, messed-up people like me and you whom He has rescued. People He has restored. None of us are beyond hope.

I gotta tell you, I learned something recently that absolutely excites me to no end. Matter of fact, God is always teaching me something new about Himself!

I am so excited I can hardly contain myself. I could not wait to get to this point in my letter so I could share it with you!

Did you know that "cutting" is specifically mentioned in God's Book of Truth? I did not. *I honestly had no idea that God taught us about self-harm and cutting in His Word that was written over two thousand years ago! And we thought cutting was something new!* You gotta hear this. This, my friend, is our hope.

Here is the stunning, true story of a man tortured and possessed with evil spirits—basically a man who was considered a madman and mentally insane because of his unrestrained bizarre behavior. Until one day, he had an encounter with Jesus.

> When [Jesus] got out of the boat, immediately a man from the tombs with an unclean spirit met Him. He lived among the tombs; and no one was able to bind him anymore, not even with a chain, because he had often been bound with shackles and chains, and the chains had been torn apart by him and the shackles broken in pieces; and no one was strong enough to subdue him. **Constantly, night and day, he was screaming** among the tombs and in the mountains, **and _cutting himself with stones_**. *Seeing Jesus from a distance, he ran up and bowed down before Him. . . .*
>
> And the people came to see what it was that had happened. **_And then they came to Jesus and saw the man who_**

had been demon-possessed sitting down, clothed and <u>in his</u> <u>right mind.</u> (Mark 5:2–6, 14–15 NASB, emphasis added)

This man the Lord healed was actually cutting himself with sharp stones—the first cutter.

Christ can bring physical healing to our mind and the thoughts that obsess and torment us. But it begins with spiritual healing.

Don't be afraid of Him. Jesus Christ wants to rescue you. He wants to deliver you. Run to Him.

Look at His arms—outstretched on the cross—welcoming you. He's waiting for you and ready to save you.

Let me close with these powerful words from a former cutter who has been delivered and found healing. So can you.

> I was consumed with the power shedding my own blood gave me.
>
> My eyes were diverted from the cross!
>
> There had been something sickly therapeutic about seeing my own blood.
>
> I thought I could get better and bring healing to myself. . . . If I could just cut deep enough and often enough to get rid of the pain. . . .
>
> I didn't realize the story about Jesus dying on the cross was about me. His blood was shed for me.
>
> The Bible says, "Without the shedding of blood—there is no remission of sins." My blood has no power. His blood covers all my shame.
>
> There is only one blood that can heal.
>
> His body was broken—so mine could be healed![3]

It is not the cutter's blood that brings healing. It is the blood of Jesus Christ.

With more love than you can imagine,

Jimme

12

Eating Disorders | Unhealthy

My Dear Self-Critical Perfectionist,

You know what I would wish most for you? I would wish for you to be able to see yourself through kind eyes—not eyes of criticism and self-hatred, but eyes of tenderness, kindness, and love.

To be honest, one of the things that led me to start Girls Nite In International was spending so many hours after school mentoring girls who were making self-destructive choices or allowing someone else to do something to them that was destroying them. When I taught at the high school, I made the choice as a teacher to spend my breaks not in the faculty lounge but hanging out in the girls' restroom close to my classroom because I cared and wanted to know the truth of your world.

> You'll learn a lot in a girls' restroom if you have a heart to care.

Purging after lunch, girls viciously ripping into each other, with language that is not fit to repeat, all because of a dumb boy. Stories of cutting, addictions, toxic relationships, fear of being pregnant, or having an abusive stepdad surfaced again and again. Girls being humiliated, bullied, and made fun of because of their looks or their bodies.

Being a teen girl is tough. Your stomach stays in knots and is filled with anxiety because your world is not PG-13; you are trapped in R-rated and XXX-rated constantly.

Remember when you were a little girl and used to be so confident and carefree? Maybe playing baseball in the cul-de-sac or hide-and-seek with kids in the neighborhood? Or taking dance lessons? You were the little girl who would twirl around in her dress-up clothes or ballerina costume and make a funny face in the mirror. But now, your mirror has become *everyone else's eyes*! You constantly check the mirror of

their eyes to find out what you're worth! What *they* think about you! What their eyes convey to you tells you *everything*.

- If you measure up
- If you're beautiful or less than
- If you're graceful or a dork
- If you're accepted or rejected
- If you're smart or just plain stupid

You worry that you're not:

- smart enough
- thin enough
- rich enough
- strong enough
- pretty enough

1. You begin comparing yourself to other girls: her looks, her body, her brains.
2. You crave a certain guy's attention, but another girl is the one getting it.
3. You begin to look with disgust at your own body, at what you perceive as flaws.
4. You begin competing with other girls and never feel you measure up.
5. Or maybe, you are being relentlessly and unmercifully teased and humiliated about your body by a girl you admire or look up

to. That sting of rejection is one of the most powerful, destructive emotions we can feel.

> Feeling rejected by people from whom you crave approval can cause as much distress in the pain center of your brain as an actual physical injury.[1]
>
> As girls, we learn to do everything we can to avoid being the target of teasing and ridicule. Even if it means hurting ourselves.

An eating disorder can begin because you've been *teased relentlessly* about your body. Or perhaps what started out as just *harmlessly counting calories* now has taken a dangerous turn into a *harmful obsession with dieting and rigid control* of the type of food you allow yourself to eat, to the point that your thoughts are totally consumed with calories or purging.

Actress Portia de Rossi described her horrific journey through anorexia this way:

> I didn't decide to become anorexic. It snuck up on me disguised as a healthy diet, a professional attitude. . . .
> . . . Every time I restricted my calorie intake, I would binge immediately after. . . . I lived my life from day to day by weighing myself and measuring my success or failure solely on weight lost or weight gained. . . . I'd measured my accomplishments and my self-worth on that scale for my entire life.[2]

Maybe you totally identify. Those words sound painfully familiar. What once was a source of enjoyment and nourishment—that is, eating—has now become a source of torture.

> Eating has become your enemy.

What used to be a time of connecting and laughing—enjoying a meal with your family or friends—is now a ritual you will do anything to avoid.

Eating brings up horrible issues of control. And accusations.

- Why don't you eat more?
- Why do you have to be so picky?
- That's *all* you're eating?

My darlings! Please hear me. I wanna tell you something really important.

> There is nothing healthy about fearing food and using exercise as a whip.
> —Jess Zimmerman

That is a horrible way to live life. In fact, not much living is going on. So, if you find yourself at any extreme, whether:

- fearing food because you feel you will lose all control if you allow yourself to eat, or
- rigidly planning your day or week around exercise—not in a healthy way, but in an obsessive way, or
- abusing Adderall or laxatives to lose weight

then you may need to admit to yourself and then to somebody else: "I need help."

There is no shame in recognizing and admitting that. You do not need to feel all alone. You would be surprised at how many girls have struggled with exactly what you are struggling with. Please let us help you.

I want to be perfectly clear that overcoming an eating disorder may require professional help. We do have resources to get you help if you feel like you are drowning in this horrible, vicious cycle. Don't be afraid to ask for help. There is hope. There is healing. You don't have to feel trapped in this horrible cycle.

I remember my own daughter, Kristi, explaining to me after she recovered from her eating disorder:

> The issue is not food. It appears that way—especially to everyone around you who loves you and is scared sick for you. The issue is not food but rather control. The fear that if you ever start eating again, you'll never be able to stop. The obsessive thoughts in your mind that you can't get rid of. It is really a healing of the mind that has to take place.

That was a very powerful, arresting statement to me. It put everything in real perspective for me. If you are struggling in this area, I want to suggest some very practical truths that will help you begin to heal and move toward recovery.

Truth 1: Retrain Your Mind So Unhealthy Obsessions Don't Control You

A healing of the mind must take place. Every eating disorder starts in the mind, with how you view yourself and how you view food. Fighting the urge to binge and purge or starve yourself starts with identifying and changing your faulty thought patterns. You will have to retrain your mind to focus on the things you should obsess about, not those other thoughts you are obsessing about that are destroying you.

One of the toughest things about recovering from an eating disorder is that you must deal with food daily. You have to eat to live. When you're fighting an alcohol or drug addiction, eventually the drugs or alcohol will have to be removed from your life. But when you're battling an eating disorder, you can't eradicate food from your life.

Truth 2: Develop a Healthy Relationship with Food

You have to develop a relationship with food that is not based on fear. Your habits will have to be confronted and analyzed. Most people with eating disorders have very predictable patterns of thought and behavior. Certain triggers propel your behavior. The tension of living with those triggers can cause you to use food to try to control yourself and to control the situation or circumstances you are living with.

The real issue isn't food; it is loss of control.

Giving up control is a frightening concept. To begin establishing a healthy pattern of eating, you will have to take baby steps. Take a small risk. Go against that nervous voice in your head just a couple of times this week. Don't count. Don't measure. Don't consider the nutritional value. Just eat. And don't try to overcompensate by skimping on your next meal or exercising like a maniac.

You will see that the world does not end. You didn't automatically gain pounds just because you ate. You've got to take small steps.

If you want to have freedom from fearing food, you'll have to be a little looser, a little less rigid in your thinking. If you want to be the kind of person who can go to a party and not freak out about what will be served, you'll have to go to parties and learn to nibble, learn to socialize instead of isolating yourself.

You'll begin to change little by little. Every single day, just take small, baby steps. But, take them!

Truth 3: Reject the Lie That Your Value Is Based on Your Appearance

The way the culture around us defines attractiveness is so narrow that only a few select people could ever qualify. It is an absolutely unrealistic, unobtainable standard.

It is really dangerous to think that what you look like is who you are.

Until you are willing to go to war with the media and the voices of the culture around you, you will stay defeated and keep beating yourself up. Until you are willing to name a lie when you hear it or see it, it will be difficult to have a healthy attitude about your body. You will have to fight the message that says your value is based on your appearance.

I don't want you believing lies about yourself. Don't waste your whole life believing lies from the enemy of your soul—lies that are intent on destroying you. The enemy of your soul has one purpose: to kill, steal, and destroy you. He is thrilled when you self-destruct. On the other hand, Jesus Christ Himself came to give us life, but not only that, life abundantly. What a huge difference.

Do you ever wonder if anybody even cares about you, about whether you exist or not? Well, let me tell you. You do matter. Great care and detail were taken in creating you. Your Creator and Maker has a lot to say about how much He values you.

The Book of Truth, God's Word, tells us:

> You made all the delicate, inner parts of my body
>> and knit me together in my mother's womb.
> Thank you for making me so wonderfully complex!
>> Your workmanship is marvelous—how well I know it.
> You watched me as I was being formed in utter seclusion,
>> as I was woven together in the dark of the womb.
> You saw me before I was born.
>> Every day of my life was recorded in your book.
> Every moment was laid out
>> before a single day had passed.
> How precious are your thoughts about me, O God.
>> They cannot be numbered!
> I can't even count them;
>> they outnumber the grains of sand!
>
> —Psalm 139:13–18

So, if you are wondering if anybody really loves you, if anybody really cares, if anybody even knows you exist, look no further. Every time you see a little baby or pass a beautiful, pregnant lady and see her perfectly rounded tummy, let it remind you that God loves you.

You are valuable because you have been carefully crafted inch by inch. You, too, are exquisitely and wonderfully made.

Truth 4: God Had a Relationship with You Before You Were Born, and He Has a Purpose for Your Life

There is *nothing* you can do that will separate you from God's love or make Him love you any more or less than He already does.

He wants you to meet Him in a personal way. Not in a ritual way. It's not good enough to know *about* Him. You need to *know* Him as your Savior. God's Word says it simply: "He who has the Son has life; he who does *not* have the Son of God does *not* have life" (1 John 5:12 NKJV, emphasis mine).

You have to recognize that you need to invite Him into your life.

To call on Him and ask Him to be your Savior. "For 'everyone who calls on the name of the Lord *will* be saved'" (Romans 10:13 ESV, emphasis mine). If you have never done that, oh how I long for you to meet Him.

Until you recognize that you have a God-shaped hole inside your heart that can only be filled by one person—Him—you will keep craving to be accepted and loved by everyone else.

You will spend your life chasing every possible substitute, only to realize you are empty, empty, empty inside.

God's Book of Truth lovingly reminds us:

> Charm is deceitful and beauty is vain,
> But a woman who fears the LORD, she shall be praised.
> —Proverbs 31:30 NASB95

Another way of saying this is: charm is deceptive, and beauty is fleeting . . . fleeting . . . fleeting . . . but a woman who honors the Lord will be greatly praised.

Beauty is fleeting. You will grow old and you will age. All the things you spend every ounce of your energy on will begin to fade away. If that is all you have invested your time in, you will, guaranteed, feel empty inside and feel invisible and question if your life even mattered.

Let me tell you a little secret. If you seek your value through your friends' opinions of you, you will be disappointed. No person will ever meet all your needs or value you in the way that you so deeply crave! No person—ever. They're not supposed to. It's not their job. There is a God-shaped hole created inside every single one of us that can only be filled with one thing: Jesus.

It is your job to discover God's purpose for your life and to get busy being who He created you to be. God created only one you.

You are an original. Never has been—never will be—another like you. You do not need to compare yourself to anyone else.

> It's not who you are that holds you back.
> It's who you think you're not!

Just. Be. You. Nobody does it better.

Your assignment is to learn to accept yourself so you can get busy discovering your Creator's purpose for your life.

Truth 5: Learn to Accept Your Body Even if It Takes a Lifetime

I want to be perfectly honest and straight up. My goal is to be real and honest, and I don't ever want to paint a false picture. Accepting yourself and recognizing that your security is found in God is not a one-time event; it's a life-long process. You don't just wake up one morning and discover everything is perfect, discover that you no longer hear the critical voice in your own head, and never feel the urge to use your body for attention or wonder if you're pretty enough. You don't just wake up one morning and absolutely adore the person looking back at you in the mirror. Your assignment is to learn to accept your body, even if it takes a lifetime.

What is different is your response. The important thing is that you learn how to respond to those doubts and fears when they return.

Truth 6: Learn to See Yourself Through God's Eyes

We want the easy way out. We would love for God to just change our thinking overnight. But He will not do the work for us. You are going to have to do the hard work of changing your habits, changing your thinking by stopping self-sabotaging thought patterns. And you can only do that with the help of God.

He will remind you: Be yourself. Everyone else is already taken.

You may not love everything about your body. I honestly don't know that I have ever met one woman who does. But you can learn to accept your body and not spend a lifetime being paralyzed by what you don't like. The road to accepting your body begins with valuing it, not for its appearance but for the amazing, incredible functions it performs for you every day without you even being aware.

Value your body for its competence.

Gotta question for you: How many times have you breathed in the past three minutes? How many times have you swallowed? Blinked? How many times have you moved your arm or your leg? How many beats did your heart beat?

Have you stopped to say thank you to your Maker?

As I said at the outset of this letter, my hope is that you can begin to see yourself through kind eyes for the amazing, incredible work of God that you are. Pursue wholeheartedly and with passion the amazing plan God has for you. 'Cause you are the only *you* He will ever make. Don't miss out on His big assignment for you. I am waiting and watching expectantly.

Each day you must choose to see yourself through God's eyes—not through the eyes of everyone else around you while searching for their approval. You must train yourself and discipline your mind how to respond.

Seeing yourself through God's eyes instead of the mirror of other people's eyes will change your perspective and everyday decisions:

- Rather than thinking about food and exercise as a whip—a way to reach a certain size—you will view what you put in your body as a way to be strong and healthy so you can accomplish what God has designed you to do.
- Rather than continually checking yourself in the mirror to make sure your hair and clothes are just right, you will check yourself all day long to make sure your heart is right. The posture of your heart is everything! "As you think in your heart, so are you," says God's Book (Proverbs 23:7, paraphrased). So, how is your heart?
- Rather than worrying about whether the eyes of everyone else tell you you're beautiful, you'll be more concerned about the eyes of One. You'll be seeking the smile of God's pleasure.

If you want to feel rich, just count all
the gifts you have that money can't buy.

When you finally understand that your security and value are found in Christ, you will no longer be driven by the need for everyone else's approval. You have seen into the eyes of your Creator and found a place to belong that you never imagined!

Let me share a very candid, honest confession:

> For a long time I prayed that God would change the way I
> looked so I could learn to love myself. I asked God to help
> me diet, to find the right clothes, make me anyone but
> me. I had it all wrong. It was my heart, not my body, that
> needed to change.

Right this moment, you may find yourself deeply identifying with
those words. You might admit: That's me. I had it all wrong. It's my
heart—not my body—that needs to change.

He is the Relentless Pursuer. He is chasing you down. He knows
which buttons to push to get your attention. Don't be afraid of Him.
If God is tugging at your heart and creating a thirst—a hunger deep
within you to know Him—don't delay. Don't ignore His voice; you may
not get another chance to respond.

We enter into eternity only once. When we do, it will be to the
audience of One. The One who *knows you the most* and *loves you the best.*

With more love than you can imagine,

 Jimme

13

Loss | Grief

My Dear Heartbroken Friend,

Grief is like living two lives. One is where you pretend that everything is all right, and the other is where your heart silently screams in pain.

Grief is a million heartaches in the course of an ordinary day.

Grieving is like having broken ribs. On the outside you look fine, but with every breath, it hurts.

Grief takes so much energy. You feel it weighing down your whole body. The grief comes in such heavy waves you're not sure how you'll ever breathe again. You can't breathe without feeling all the feels: pain, sadness, exhaustion, numbness, anger, depression, lifelessness, hopelessness.

Grief is just so physical. Maybe you took a two-and-a-half-hour nap yesterday because your brain just stopped thinking. All you want to do is pull the covers over your head, sleep, and wish this horrible nightmare would just go away. Grief is so painfully physical that it sucks every ounce of strength just to open your eyes the next morning to your horrible new reality.

Grief is so heavy. You might do well for a little while and then bam! It hits you again out of nowhere. Every time the grief sideswipes or knocks you over, it's just evidence of your deep love. The deeper you love, the more painful the loss. Don't fight the emotions. Let your body, mind, and spirit grieve. Don't even try to put words to it.

The loss is so life-altering. You feel furious that the world keeps spinning around you when your grief is so devastating. That alone makes you angry, lonely, and feel like screaming or crying. Go ahead. **Scream. Cry. Grieve.**

Grief takes the floor out from under you without warning, just when you think you've found your footing again. One of my college students told me, *"After my mom died unexpectedly, I slept in my clothes.*

I didn't have the energy to dress or undress. Nothing mattered." Profound grief drains everything out of you.

It's disorienting. It's okay if you feel like you're walking on uneven ground. You are.

Our family was blindsided with the totally unexpected death of my thirty-four-year-old nephew, who just two weeks prior to his death was diagnosed with a silent, fatal disease if left untreated. He was husband to my precious niece Jennifer and daddy to their twin girls and his son. It has been gut-wrenching for her to become a widow at such a young age and try to keep going to support her family and care for her kids while battling severe health complications of her own. Life can be so unfair, yet they each are struggling to keep going.

Not long ago, I received the crushing, devastating news that a former piano student of mine decided to end his life. Apparently, he was caught up in some bad choices, hangin' with low-life, no-good losers, started using and dealing heavy drugs, got himself in major trouble with the law. Then, the feds were beginning to close in on him. David felt caught, and the only way out was to shoot himself. Sadly now his family and those closest to him are dealing with the heartbreaking reality of his decision, the horrific nightmare of the double life he was living of which they knew nothing, and the deep sadness that he felt he had no hope but to kill himself!

Sometimes, people refer to grief only in the context of the death of someone they love. *As you well know, loss is not limited to death and dying. Many of you, in the short lives you have lived, have experienced loss on many levels.*

The loss and the grief you feel may be because of your parents' *divorce*. The two people who brought you into the world cannot get along and live under the same roof and have deeply hurt each other and you. Everything that was familiar about family is completely, forever changed. New place to live, new custody arrangement in which you must go back and forth between two worlds, new stepbrothers and stepsisters. Maybe you are grieving because your life has been turned upside down. You had to move to a completely foreign city, leaving behind the house you grew up in, the friends you have played with since childhood, and the school and sports teams where you felt like you belonged.

Or maybe the deep grief and profound sadness you feel is because of *abuse*. You crave to know what it feels like to be deeply and appropriately loved. Someone who claims to love you is treating you in sick, disgusting, inappropriate, and vulgar ways. You feel violated and worthless.

Maybe you feel the pain of *abandonment*. You have been let down again by someone you loved and deeply trusted. You feel lonelier than ever and are not sure you will open yourself up ever again to trust.

Perhaps, at this moment, your heart is aching and feels like it is going to split in two because a family member you love deeply is facing a *terminal illness* and is not expected to live. You put on a good face on the outside 'cause you really don't want a lot of people asking you questions about something that is private and ripping you apart on the inside. You go to sleep at night sobbing into your pillow, feeling scared, worried about the one you love, afraid of what the future looks like.

Some of you have experienced the horror of a *parent dying* of an overdose.

Maybe right now you feel a deep sense of loss because someone you cared about was suddenly snatched from you—whether by a *horrible accident* that took their life, by a *disease or illness* that ravaged and consumed their body, or by an unthinkable choice someone you love made to *end their life*. You feel like you got sucker-punched in the gut and can't seem to catch your breath. The pain feels unbearable and like life will never feel normal again.

Can I say that there *is* some truth to that statement? Life may not ever feel like normal again. Not life in the way that you once knew it before. After a devastating loss, your entire life may change. As you grieve, your goal is *not* to get things back to normal. That's impossible.

But as you continue to process your deep pain and devastating loss, your focus becomes how to find a *different* normal from which to rebuild your life.

Out of a heart full of love and compassion, I will tell you this, my precious ones: there is hope for your future. There is every reason for you to have full confidence that life is worth living. To find a different normal even though your mind may be screaming at you otherwise.

If you will give me a chance—hang tight with me—I want to offer you hope to hang on to. I wish I could just wrap my arms around you and hold you in a tight hug—no words necessary.

Even though life may never look or feel the same, let's work together with intentionality to move toward that different normal. As we work through the process of these two goals, my prayer is that you will gain a stable and secure anchor to hang on to when you feel like you're drowning in a sea of grief. So, what are our goals?

Goal 1: Learn How to Cope. How do I cope? What can I learn about the tough process of grief that will help me better cope with it?

Goal 2: Find Hope. How do I find hope to move forward? What steps can I take to find hope for my future?

The honest truth is that grief is inevitable. If you are alive and breathing, you are going to experience some type of loss that is just devastating. No way around it.

And since every single one of us must confront the loss of someone or something we love, the message in my letter is for all of us. You cannot live without experiencing loss in a thousand different ways.

It could be something as insignificant and simple as losing that parking spot at the mall because another driver cut you off and bolted into the space ahead of you. Or grieving that you didn't come in first place at that competition you worked your butt off for. Or maybe the loss of your loved pet who has been a part of your family forever.

The point is: how we handle the "little griefs" in life will, to some degree, show us how we will handle the larger griefs when they come.

There are healthy ways and unhealthy ways to grieve. No two people grieve the same way. There is no right or wrong way. Grief is a long process.

Suffering is extremely painful and hurts like hell, but it does not have to completely destroy your life. Slowly, you can begin to experience healing and start the path to carve a new, albeit different, life.

If you have experienced a deep loss, you are going to experience some powerful emotions. Strong emotions that might make you feel like you're a bad person for having certain thoughts. Can I just assure you? You're not bad. You are *normal*.

Healing Step 1: Realize Grief Is Normal

Grief is a complicated set of emotions, all of which are normal. Grief is exhausting. It takes a lot of time and energy and can wear you out. No two people grieve the same way.

For instance, you might feel **guilt**. If the person you loved died suddenly, you might regret some of the things you said or didn't say. The scene will replay over and over in your mind. Maybe because you said some really hurtful, hateful things to the one you love and you wish like anything you could take those words back. But you can't. Or maybe it's what you *didn't say*. Maybe you never got a chance to say how much you really loved them and what a big impact they have had on your life. You keep beating yourself up for never sharing your true feelings with them.

Another emotion you may be experiencing is **anger**. Quite possibly you may feel intense anger at the hospital ER or doctor for what he didn't do 'cause things could have turned out so differently. There may be a million real reasons for which you feel anger and maybe even hatred.

Also, if you are really honest with yourself you have to admit you feel a little angry at God. I mean, after all, couldn't He have prevented it? If He is as powerful as He says He is, couldn't He do something?

Perhaps you also feel **extreme sadness**. Like on a dreary day. You know the sun is still shining and warming the earth, but the heavy, dark clouds are blocking you from seeing and feeling the warmth of the sun. You feel blanketed by a dark, heavy cloud of sadness. It is hard to make yourself get up and keep going. You're not sure you will ever feel right again.

I just want to assure you, these powerful, strong feelings of sadness, anger, or guilt may overwhelm you and even surprise you, but they are normal. You are not bad for feeling them. In fact, the worst thing you can do is to feel ashamed and try to deny your feelings or bury and suppress them. Admit them to yourself, share your feelings with God, and talk through them with a person you trust.

Healing Step 2: Feel the Pain

The intensity of your pain is normal, and you don't need to feel ashamed. Eventually, the intensity will begin to subside. The pain will probably never completely disappear, but over time, it will become more bearable.

The worst thing you can do is try to avoid dealing with the pain by burying it. Trying to avoid dealing with your emotions is only going to prolong your getting well and healing.

If you try to hide your feelings by pretending they don't exist, you are setting yourself up for other problems—emotional, physical, mental, and even your trust in God.

If you can encourage yourself to take some of these healthy steps toward healing, you will slowly begin a crucial path of healing and growth. You will begin to slowly feel alive again instead of feeling numb because your life was paralyzed by such a devastating loss.

I want to say something extremely important to you right now. If you hear nothing else I say, hear this:

> It is not disrespectful to the one you loved and lost to begin to rebuild your life again.

Fear makes us afraid that they will be forgotten by us or other people if we dare start to live life again. That is not true. You will carry them and their impact on your life forever inside of you.

It is not being disrespectful to work to heal and take steps to slowly move forward and rebuild your life without them physically here.

The real, harsh, painful truth is: we cannot, even with all the wishing and longing in our heart, bring them back to be with us. It is just not possible.

I have known too many people who have never given themselves permission to do this, and for the rest of their lives they remained paralyzed and frozen in time. A mother who lost her son cannot bring herself to touch anything in his bedroom and leaves it the same for thirty years and forbids anyone to touch it. Every day, she stands in the doorway to his bedroom and is paralyzed by her longing for it all to be so different. His room almost becomes a "shrine." As a mother, I totally understand that and my heart goes out to her. But realistically it is the worst thing she can do for herself and the rest of her family and those she loves because in all reality *her life ended when her son's life did.*

She, unknowingly, in her horrific grief, became part of the living, walking dead.

You may have heard of the psychological term *survivor's guilt.* It is when you feel guilty for living because the other person was not so lucky and didn't survive.

For instance, a lot of the survivors of the terrorist attacks on September 11, 2001, have had to deal with guilt because they survived that horrific day while others didn't. Another example is of soldiers who have served in Afghanistan, Iraq, or another war. Some of their buddies were killed in battle, yet they survived and came back home to their families. These soldiers have disturbing emotions to deal with because they survived while their buddy did not.

One of my son's best friends, Brian, has struggled deeply with this very thing. One of his close friends whom he convinced to sign up and join the marine corps with him was killed in Iraq. But Brian was fortunate and got to come home. He has had a tough time dealing with this. For a lot of soldiers, the only way they can get past this survivor's guilt is to talk out loud with a trusted counselor or friend and process their emotions and admit them. Otherwise, they come back home and never really "live again." Or they turn to self-destructive behaviors to cope. In essence, they must give themselves permission to actually be alive and live.

So, in the same way, you cannot put your life on hold because your sister was killed in a horrible accident or you were the driver who, innocently, hit another car and the outcome was the worst imaginable. A life was lost.

If a friend of yours feels no hope and makes the unthinkable choice to end her life, don't let yours end with hers.

If your parent is struggling with an illness for which there is no cure, you need to love on them and care for them while you have them and can do so. And both of you need to give yourselves permission for sometimes being short with each other, because you are both processing power-packed emotions, knowing your time with each other is limited. Because of that frustration, you sometimes unknowingly take it out on each other. Give yourselves permission to be human. But remember to apologize and start each day with a fresh slate of enjoying every moment you have.

Here is the harsh truth.

Last time I checked, I'm pretty sure we're all terminal!

I don't mean that to be, in any way, morbid—just a reality check. We're just not meant to live here forever. We are literally just passing through.

This place called earth is temporary. Eternity is forever. That's why your life here is literally preparation—the pregame warm-up—for the big event. For that really long life which is called "eternity."

You will face events in this life that cause you to wrestle. Cause you to question and doubt everything you have ever believed. Don't be afraid of wrestling. If each of us was honest, we would all say we have wrestled with the bigger questions:

1. *Why was I born? What am I supposed to do with my life?*
2. *What really matters? What is life all about?*
3. *Is this life all there is?*

That third question is one that you really wrestle with when you are faced with the loneliness of grief and loss. Is this life all there is? Life really is short. It's already over by the time you barely start living and begin to figure out the answers.

So that third question is the big one. 'Cause it is the most important one. *Is this life really all about me? Or is it* actually *all about God?*

How you answer the last two questions will shape your *entire life,* which is eternity-long. This short life is just a prelude. What matters in this life will affect how you live. How you grieve. If this life is all there is, that leaves you with little hope. When it's over, it's over. Pretty empty.

I happen to believe there is hope because this life is not all there is.

God's Book of Truth says this about our mourning: grieve, but don't grieve as those *who have no hope.* That gives us some answers regarding the shortness of this life.

1. **Grieve**. God has made you with the emotional capacity to experience all these powerful emotions that are necessary when you grieve because you have lost someone or something really important to you. Sometimes without warning, there wells up inside of you an uncontrollable urge to express the emotion that you are feeling.

   Sometimes
   the loss is too big,
   and the pain too deep
   to put into words.
   That's what tears are for.

2. **We've been created with tear glands for a reason.** So, for goodness' sake, cry! Please be extra gentle with yourself. It's okay! Tears are healing! They provide a physical release when you can't find the words to express your grief and you literally feel as though you are going to explode from all the emotions bottled up inside of you. Sleep as much as you can. Your body needs it. Rest, eat, drink, take care of your body and soul. Listen to your body and soul. If you wake up with the "I don't wannas," then honor the "I don't wannas." Grief is exhausting. Be kind to yourself. A soft blanket. A hot bath with Epsom salts. A grilled cheese sandwich. Whatever brings you comfort. Hug yourself, allow others to hug you and grieve.

3. **But we don't have to grieve as those who have no hope.** If we have invited God into our lives and have a relationship with Him, then we can grieve—but not as those who have no hope. We do have hope! We do have a future! We grieve but with hope. There is life beyond this one, and we will be reunited with the ones we love who know Him.

On the other hand, if this life is all there is, that doesn't give you much hope or give much meaning to life. Just stupid empty at the end.

That's why it is really important to wrestle with the big questions that are already tormenting your mind:

- Is there a God?
- What does He want from me?
- How do I find out?

The reason you can grieve with hope is because the Maker of you and the very life you live is the One who gives hope! Your main purpose is to seek Him and to learn what it means to have a relationship with Him. God is allowing this wrestling that is going on inside you to get your attention.

I call Him the Relentless Pursuer. He is chasing you down. He loves you and wants to have a relationship with you to give you true hope, life, and emotional healing. His love came in the shape of an object of torment and suffering for Him: a cross. Has someone ever said to you, *"I'd take a bullet for you"*? A phrase that means that person loves you and doesn't want anybody messin' with you or hurtin' you. If so, they'd take 'em down. "I'd take a bullet for you." Well, Jesus took a "bullet" for you. He has borne your grief and carried your sorrows in order to open up a way for you to have a relationship with Him.

The Creator wants a relationship with the "created." Unbelievable! What love!

What kind of love takes "my nails"—my bullet? I'll tell you. Listen to these words from Isaiah 53 describing Jesus Christ who took your nails—your bullet—for you:

He was despised and rejected—
    a man of sorrows, acquainted with deepest grief.
We turned our backs on him and looked the other way.
    He was despised, and we did not care. . . .
But He was pierced for our rebellion,
    crushed for our sins.
He was beaten so we could be whole.
    He was whipped so we could be healed.
All of us, like sheep, have strayed away.
    We have left God's paths to follow our own.
Yet the LORD laid on him
    the sins of us all.

—Isaiah 53:3, 5–6, 10

Me. You. Our hope is found in Christ Jesus. Our healing is found in Him. He lovingly tells us: "I will never leave you or forsake you. I know what you're going through. Trust Me with your life. I am your Refuge."

Blessed are those that trust in the Lord whose hope is in Him

Don't waste your life living for the wrong reasons only to find out at the end of your life that it was all a bust. That you have spent your whole lifetime on the wrong thing. This is the most important decision to settle now. Who is going to be your god? You . . . or God?

Healing Step 3: Accept Support and Comfort from Those Who Truly Care

Everything inside you will want to avoid people and isolate yourself. You won't feel like being with people or allowing them to see you hurting. Especially when you don't feel in control of your emotions. But isolating yourself is one of the worst things you can do.

I understand if at first you need some space and time alone. That's okay and necessary. But just don't let it turn into days, weeks, and months. That's when isolation becomes unhealthy for you.

Powerful, unwanted feelings may cause you to try to find acceptance and relief through hookin' up, having sex, or using drugs, porn, or some other coping mechanism that is going to leave you feeling worse about yourself than before.

So, it is enormously important that you don't withdraw from people who truly love you and care about you. Identify a few friends or adults you really trust who won't just offer cliché answers and quick solutions to your broken heart but will be patient and let you talk out loud when you feel like it. Even if what you have to say is ugly and you really don't mean it and it doesn't make sense. Because bottling up all those complicated emotions inside of you will eat you alive.

Grieving is hard work. If you bottle everything up, you will only prolong the process of your healing. Because the problem is: you won't escape it. Sooner or later, you will have to do the work of grieving. The stages of grief are different for everyone. Some people can work through things in a period of painful months while others take several years.

When someone has been incredibly important to us and a huge part of our lives for a long time, and they are taken from us, we suffer daily as we struggle to come to grips with the realization that they will not be returning in this life.

Healing Step 4: Choose to Be Open to New and Different Relationships and Experiences

During this heavy, difficult time, all you will want to do is run away from life. But you will have to choose not to become paralyzed in dark thoughts. Be willing to open yourself up to new experiences that will help to bring healing. That may involve meeting new people. Trying new things. Getting out in nature, which is so healing. Join a dance class. Start a new exercise or fitness routine. Just sheer exercise and physical activity can help you release anger and sadness.

Otherwise, your legitimate anger can remain inside you and turn that dark corner into bitterness. Bitterness and resentment that you can't let go of. Bitterness that ends up destroying you.

If you feel you have crossed the line after a legit time of trying to cope with the crushing loss, and you have settled into a deep depression and heavy sadness that never seems to end, or you have fallen into a bitterness that is destroying you and every relationship you have, don't be afraid to say, *"I need help. I am in a very dark place. Way beyond my control. I'm in a scary, very unhealthy place."*

Don't be afraid to reach out for help. Don't suffer alone. You might need the help of a medical professional to help you over the hump so that a needed healing of your mind can begin. I've had to do that. It's perfectly okay. You do it, darling. I want you to get well.

Healing Step 5: Accept that It's Okay to Be a "New You"

Please notice that I didn't say the last step is that you will become "your old self" again. Because that is absolutely *not* true. When we go through any significant experience of grief or loss, we come out of it a different person. And that's okay. It can actually be a good thing.

One of the most life-changing and riveting experiences for me was losing my daddy after he suffered for five very painful years from a severe stroke. Watching my strong, able-bodied daddy turn into someone who was paralyzed, confined to a wheelchair, and no longer able to care for himself was beyond heart-wrenching. I have never seen a man who had more willpower and did his dang-best to try to recover and "will" his paralyzed body to move again through excruciating physical therapy. Nobody ever worked harder than Jim Garland did. But it wasn't supposed to be. I miss him like crazy.

However, as a result of this horrible loss, I am a better person. More driven to build endurance, resilience, tenacity, and perseverance in my life. A better perspective on what really matters in life, and even more tenderness toward people who are "broken" in the eyes of the world. I am forever changed. Never, ever will I take my body for granted like I used to. Never, ever will I say I "can't" do something. I have watched sheer willpower at work against all odds. I have always had a tenderness toward people who are not considered "normal" or "fit in" in the world's eyes. But now I think they are some of the most beautiful people I know.

So, you have a choice.

> You can either become bitter or better.
> The only difference is the letter *I*.

Depending on the way you respond to the loss and grief in your life, you will become either a stronger person than you were before or weaker. You will become either healthier in your spirit and outlook on life or sicker and more bitter.

You will learn that brokenness can mend you, wounds can heal you, and the scars you bear can become a sign of healing.

The gaping wound that threatened to undo you when you faced the loss of someone you loved will become a scar that covers the raw wound. You will always have the scar with you. You will always see the scar. But the scar becomes part of your story. It reminds you of a deep turning point in your life.

You are an overcomer! And together we will become stronger.

We need each other. Scars included.

Scars can be a good thing.

Check out the hands of Jesus. They represent the deepest love. He took our "bullet." He took our "nails."

We show our scars. Scars are nothing to hide. They mean healing has taken place.

By His wounds we have been healed!

With more love than you can imagine,

 Jimme

14

Social Media | Influence

My Dear Susceptible Scroller,

> We're so connected, we're disconnected. Connected to screens, that is, and disconnected from each other.

Your cell phone may feel like the single item you can't leave home without, and when it gets lost, you go into full-out panic mode and feel like part of you is missing. Same! Me too! I can't tell you how many times I've had to turn around in my car and go back home to get my cell because I accidentally left it and knew I wouldn't have the info I needed to make it through my workday without it! So crazy how much we depend on that little pocket-sized thing!

> Most people under thirty have spent more time interacting with screens than they have interacting with people in real life.

Signs of Social Media Addiction:

☐ Changes in mood, particularly when not looking at social media.

☐ Compulsion to check social media.

☐ Spending long periods on social pages.

☐ Spending less time doing offline activities.

☐ Withdrawal symptoms.

☐ Conflict as a result of social media use.

Are you addicted to social media? Rather than being a useful tool that is handy to have, your phone becomes an obsession constantly stealing your attention. Many of us have allowed this to happen without really questioning it. The more time spent on social *media*—the more we miss out on an actual social *life* . . . in real time.

I realize you are bombarded with information overload. No other generation in history has been bombarded with constant information overload like you have.

It's impossible to imagine your life without social media. Before social media, there wasn't the constant barrage of information being thrown at you or the burden of all the horrific events happening all over the globe causing you anxiety.

Social media can normalize bad behavior.

- School shootings
- Wars
- Pandemic
- Racial tension
- Culture issues
- Crime
- Violence

It's *not* that horrible, vicious wars, shootings, racial tension, crime, and violence have not always existed. But, we didn't carry that information around in the palm of our hand 24/7.

I hate it because I feel like your carefree childhood was ripped away from you. Your childhood and teen years have been sabotaged by *extreme emotions* that no other generation has had to deal with 24/7 every single day. Rather than experiencing the joys of a carefree childhood, you feel as though you are carrying the weight of the world on your shoulders. No wonder anxiety has skyrocketed!

And if being overloaded with information from all over the world isn't enough, there is that constant access your friends *and haters* have to you through that little device carried in your hand.

All this information overload starts to mess with your mind, and you begin to have mood swings, feel anxious, depressed, overstimulated, overwhelmed, and angry! It's all *too much.*

Do you ever feel exhausted, like you're going crazy or you're gonna lose it? Ever feel trapped and wish you could run away from it all? Like you can't breathe? Well, I want to offer you an intentional strategy to keep constant phone use from consuming you, to discuss the importance of unplugging, and to discuss mindful ways to put your phone down and expand your life beyond it. I also want to give you purposeful steps to analyze your social media time, healthy phone-free activities to enjoy and make your life meaningful, and a way to reprioritize your actions and choices to gain some control again.

First, let's discuss some of the positive benefits of social media.

Fourteen Positive Benefits of Social Media

Of course, we know there *are* some great, positive benefits and life-changing options social media and technology have given you that no other generation ever had. For that, you should be truly grateful.

Say this list of gratitudes out loud. "I have the privilege to . . .

1. stay safe by being able to communicate with my family and friends."
2. have access to my friends to keep in touch."
3. meet new people."
4. connect with others who have the same interests I do."
5. feel more comfortable to ask for help, support, advice, prayers, love, and care."
6. connect with people I love who don't live close to me."
   - Military brothers, sisters, dads, moms, other family members
   - Parent or siblings who live away
   - Grandparents who live in another city
7. express my emotions."
8. feel less lonely."
9. find and get support from a community of people with similar experiences."
10. share good news about a hard-earned accomplishment or award."
11. share pics of fun events and special memories in my life such as birthdays, celebrations, softball tourneys, prom, award ceremonies, and college scholarship signings."

12. have instant access to important information."

13. learn new skills."

14. be entertained when I need to laugh."

Because of social media, online friendships are considered the norm.

A lot of these friendships are launched quickly, sometimes on impulse. It also only takes a millisecond to end a Snapchat friendship. True friendship is about more than likes and dislikes. It is more than shares or emojis.

We can be quick to IM or Snapchat new friends, but for a friendship to maintain value over time, true friends will show loyalty, love, compassion, sympathy, and honesty. Both of you will need to work to keep your relationship drama-free. That's why it's so important who you choose to be on *your team*. It takes a lot of effort to create and maintain lasting friendships. Friendships require time, good communication, and being there when it matters most.

Choose to invest your time in friendships that have a future, with people who share the same values and goals you have and will make you a better person mentally, emotionally, relationally, and spiritually.

Online-only friends usually lack true depth and are low in commitment.

Surround yourself with a team, a tribe, who will challenge and inspire you to become the best version of you, friends who will encourage your personal growth. Surround yourself with a tribe that is running the same positive direction in life that you are.

Now, let's turn the corner and discuss some of the *negative* effects of social media, which can influence your physical, emotional, and mental health.

The negative effects of social media on your brain have the power to change you.

Have you ever woken up in a pretty good, upbeat mood, then get on either Insta or TikTok, and immediately your mood and emotions change? Why? Because you start setting unrealistic expectations as you compare yourself to others and start belittling and hating yourself, beating yourself up because you don't compare to the images you just saw.

Social media can lead to negative feelings like depression, loneliness, isolation, lack of sleep, and vicious experiences like cyberbullying.

Ten Negative Effects of Social Media

1. Depression and Anxiety

Do you spend multiple hours a day browsing socials? Maybe you're not aware that spending too much time could be negatively affecting your mood and your health.

- Do you experience major anxiety when you have to speak face-to-face with other people?
- Do you have terrible anxiety over making a phone call?

If you are a chronic scroller, you are more likely to struggle with poor mental health conditions.

It doesn't take much to realize that comparing yourself to other people can lead you down a dark road, causing depression because you don't think you measure up to accomplishments you see other friends making or the "fake" standard of beauty on Insta feeds.

So, how do you use socials without harming yourself? Studies show the average teen spends two hours a day on socials, which is a large chunk of someone's free time!

Mental health experts say the amount of time that you *should* spend on social media is around half an hour per day.

That's thirty minutes! Eeeek! For real?! I was kinda stunned by this! But as with any other area, a healthy lifestyle is all about moderation. To start taking your power back and gaining control, moderation is the key. For example, if you eat too much, you may develop an eating disorder. If you eat too little, you may struggle with anorexia. If you exercise to the extreme, that is an unhealthy addiction. If you lie around on the couch all day and binge-watch Netflix, that is not healthy either.

Any of these things—eating, exercising, watching Netflix, or being on socials—if done in moderation, is good. On the other hand, excessive phone use is dangerous to your mental well-being. Moderation is the key to everything. The sensible thing to do is not to overindulge!

2. Fear of Missing Out

FOMO is just what it sounds like: a form of anxiety that you feel when you are terrified of missing out on something important. It makes you constantly check your messages or focus on your Instagram feed all day.

This fear receives constant fuel from what you see on social media. You know, the angst you feel when you see someone having more fun than you. The jealousy you feel when there's a party and you weren't invited. All your friends are in the pics, but not you . . . and *that* causes FOMO.

3. Cyberbullying

> It's a lot easier to come at somebody through a screen than face-to-face.

Cyberbullies often don't have the guts to confront you to your face, so they anonymously hide behind a screen to gain your trust and then start viciously attacking you, terrorizing you in front of your friends, stalking, or blackmailing you. Their goal is to destroy you and humiliate you online.

Cyberbullies create fake profiles and start out acting friendly; then, later on, they threaten and intimidate their online targets. Teens are often left with deep mental scars after these endless online bullying attacks. Some feel forced to commit suicide because they feel trapped, with no way out. Online abuse is vicious and terrorizing.

Please take care of you. Do not feel bullied or blackmailed into taking your life because of shame and embarrassment over something you have done or been forced to do because of this bully. Do not let them silence you if they threaten to hurt your family or someone you love. You are not alone. You need help. You deserve help. Tell someone you trust. Do not listen to their lies. You are loved and wanted. You matter. Your life matters. There is hope.

4. Unrealistic Expectations

Most people on social media only post their good side. Remember that social media is fake life, not real life. Particularly, celebrities who have perfect makeup and perfect bodies and live exotic lives.

People use Snapchat and Instagram to share pics of their exciting adventures and significant relationships. But the more you minimize your time on these socials, the less you'll become jealous or feel discouraged, defeated, and dissatisfied with your life.

5. Negative Body Image

Speaking of Instagram celebs ... if you look at popular Insta accounts and reels, you will see gorgeous celebs slayin' it wearing their trendy, posh, on point, crazy expensive threads on their perfectly hot bods.

Seeing people who are supposedly perfect can quickly make you feel self-conscious about how you look.

The reality is everyone is human, and no one wakes up every day looking like a supermodel. Lots of celebs chasing fame on social media have taken unhealthy paths to appear more attractive and beautiful.

It's so much better to surround yourself with people who love you for who you are and don't buy into the fake Instagram lifestyles.

6. Addiction

Social media can be more addictive than drugs or alcohol.

If you're not sure whether you're addicted to social media, try to remember the last time you spent your whole day without checking your social accounts. Just sayin'.

Social media creates an enticing lure to intentionally hook you into checking it all the time. Don't believe it? Take one hot minute to analyze your life. Are you low-key freakin' out if you leave your phone at home? Are you attached to your cell 24/7? Can you eat dinner and not scroll through your reels and feeds?

Social media keeps you away from important activities that matter.

Advertisers and marketers want to keep you addicted and scrolling so that they can flood your feed with lots of ads to make more and more money. The goal of social media networks is to keep your eyes on them for as long as possible. So, take my challenge to take a break from your cell. Even for just an hour. Let's take back control and say:

Nope.

Not today.

7. Disturbance in Sleep Patterns

An extremely damaging, negative effect of social media is lack of sleep. The major health impact most of you experience is sleep deprivation because you sleep with your phone beside you and are available 24/7, which keeps you from the sleep and rest your body and brain need. Did you know your brain does more work when you are asleep than when you are awake?! The human brain is probably the most complicated thing in the universe.

8. Barriers in Clear Communication

No doubt about it, socials are great when used in limited amounts and for good reasons. However, some serious dangers as far as close relationships are:

- It is too easy to hide behind your screen, rather than have the guts to have any meaningful conversation with those you love.
- Talking on social media is communicating indirectly—not face-to-face.
- Relationships can be damaged because messages are misinterpreted and misunderstood because there is no tone of voice in the message. Many arguments and hurt feelings result.

9. Time Suck

How many times have you caught yourself mindlessly scrolling through Insta posts and jumping up to check what time it is, only to realize that *two hours* have passed and you're PO'd at yourself for wasting that much time with nothing to show for it?

No doubt about it, too much time on social media is a major time suck that leads to decreased productivity and not accomplishing things you really needed to get done.

Wasting time makes you feel depressed, anxious, and frustrated because you haven't gotten projects done and haven't been working toward your personal goals.

Analyze the amount of time you spend on social media and change your habits. Spend more of your time on personal growth and developing strong character.

10. Predators and Pedophiles

One of the biggest dangers ... You may think you have found a legit friend or boyfriend who really cares about you. Unknowingly, however, it could be a predator posing and posting as a fifteen-year-old boy who is asking to meet up with you. In actuality, it could be an older man, maybe married, who has evil, wicked, horrific intentions and is trying to lure you. You'll deny it and try to cover up for him because you long to be wanted and loved so badly!

Indianapolis—where we live—is a major hub for human trafficking, particularly during the Super Bowl, Indy 500, and other major events. These scumbag pedophiles will comment on your post, telling you how beautiful and hot you are and how much they want you. They will lure you and bait you into meeting them somewhere private and insist you don't tell anyone where you are going. They might tell you they own a modeling agency and will introduce you to powerful people who will help you become a model making lots of money.

What girl doesn't want to be told she is beautiful and hot? Once you are lured and caught in their trap, you will be taken away never to be seen by your family again. You have just become the property of a pimp who will sell your body for sex and keep you locked up and trapped.

They will blackmail you and not allow you to have any contact with your family or friends who care about you. You have just become a modern-day sex slave.

PLEASE DON'T FALL INTO THIS TRAP. I know you want to be loved, but don't be naive. Wait for the right kind of person who has the same values you do and will not use and abuse you.

If you are caught in one of these fake relationships, please tell someone you trust who loves you. I can't bear the thought of you becoming a statistic. I love you too much!

After reading this list of the negative effects of social media, what are you going to do differently? What changes are you going to make? What new goals are you going to set for yourself?

Action Steps

My challenge to you is this:

- 💜 Live in real time more than screen time.
- 💜 Place boundaries on how much time you will allow yourself to be on social media each day.
- 💜 Real connection means *looking up* into faces when your tendency is to *stare down* at screens.
- 💜 Keep your phone out of your bed at night so you are not accessible.
- 💜 Get rest. Your brain and body need it.

> Laugh when you can.
> Apologize when you should.
> And let go of what you can't change.

Set one of these new goals for yourself. Take action and accomplish it! I believe in you!

Use the majority of your socials to make a significant impact focused *on others*.

> Don't live your life to make *an impression*.
> Live your life to make an *impact*.

Be you, bravely.
With more love than you can imagine,

 Jimme

15

Bullying | Boundaries

My Dear Hurting Sufferer,

Just so we're clear. There's girl drama, and then there's bullying.

I have counseled mean, vicious, self-proclaimed bullies, who trusted me enough to let me get close to them and go . . .

Inside the Mind of a Bully.

To say it was eye-opening and jarring is an understatement.

You might as well learn how to handle bullies now because, truth is, there will always be bullies in your life.

Not just in high school. There will be bullies at work. Bullies in the neighborhood. Bullies in your own home.

We're going to talk about not only dealing with bullies but also how to stop being a bully if you are one.

What do you do if you are being bullied? How do you protect yourself?

Statistics show that girls are more likely to be bullies than guys are. The main reasons for girl bullying are:

- Jealousy
- Attention
- Anger
- Fear
- Competition

A bully might take photos of another girl at school in a compromising position, perhaps in the bathroom. The bully holds her cell phone above the top of the stall door and snaps a pic of a popular girl in what

should be a private moment and sends that pic all over the school just for the heck of it with the caption, "Everybody touches you, but nobody wants you." Or a bully takes photos of a girl at an awkward moment in the locker room changing clothes and posts it on Instagram with the degrading insult "Even dogs don't like you. Now, I know why everybody talks about you behind your back."

Or sometimes, it may be a bad decision you made that started the bullying or you put yourself in a dangerous position to be bullied. Too many girls sext nude pics of themselves to their boyfriend. They break up. Then, he forwards that pic to all the guys on the football team belittling her. So, now she's the "ho" and the object of all kinds of crass comments and sexual jokes.

Question 1: What Is Bullying?

Bullying is any type of aggressive, insulting, or threatening behavior that is repeated over and over and aimed to hurt. Bullying is always intentional. Bullying always includes:

- Imbalance of power—*Bullies use their power to control or hurt people.*
- Intent to harm—*Bullying is done intentionally, not accidentally, to cause harm.*
- Repetition—*Bullies target the same person over and over.*

There are three types of bullying:

1. Verbal Bullying:
   - Name calling
   - Derogatory comments

- Insults
- Verbal threats
- Spreading lies, rumors, gossip
- Cruel jokes

2. Physical Bullying:
   - Poking
   - Hitting
   - Shoving
   - Pulling hair
   - Throwing items
   - Kicking
   - Grabbing
   - Pushing
   - Blocking someone's way
   - Intimidating someone physically
   - Defacing a person's belongings

More and more teen girls are engaging in vicious, physically violent behavior such as attacking another girl in gang-like packs, slapping, punching, biting, scratching, and kicking their victim. A lot of girl fights start because of gossip, relationship jealousies, looks, or status.

Apparently, there is a common "game" making its rounds in girls' restrooms of middle schools and high schools across the country. It's called "30 Seconds." For thirty seconds, bullies gang up and pick on a certain girl in the restroom. They take her down. Then they poke, hit, shove, kick, lift her head up and bang it up and down on the bathroom floor over and over to win and show dominance. They threaten her to keep quiet or else *"Snitches get stitches!"*

3. Cyberbullying:
   - Cruel texts and messages, or posting insults
   - Intimidation | harassment
   - Rumors | lies about the person
   - Compromising photos
   - Character assassination

A bully often excuses her behavior in a passive-aggressive way by blowin' it off—*"Yo gurl, ease up! I was just messin' wit ya!"*

The problem is that she wasn't joking, and it wasn't funny. A classic bully intimidates and harasses on purpose, avoiding owning up and taking personal responsibility for her actions.

The issue comes down to intent. Does the person want to intimidate or harm another person? If the answer is yes, then it's bullying.

One of the most painful things about bullying is that it just never stops. It's relentless. Just about anybody can take one or two times of somebody insulting and calling them names or being excluded or shunned from their group of friends. However, when it goes on and on, bullying starts to really mess with you mentally, emotionally, and physically. If you have been bullied, you know what it's like to have drastic anxiety and fear. You get stomachaches over the stress of having to go to school the next day or to the cafeteria at lunchtime. Maybe you even avoid going to the restroom all day because that's where your bully corners you.

So, how does a bully think? 'Cause if you don't figure that out, you'll never know how to deal with one and protect yourself.

Question 2: How Does a Bully Think?

Truth is: probably not like you.

Bullies operate by a completely different set of values and rules. Once you understand that, you can begin to understand their behavior. I'm not saying you will begin to condone or agree with their behavior.

But, once you get inside the mind of a bully and understand how they think, it will help you know how to deal with one. You can develop a specific action plan: what to say, what to do, whom to talk to, and how to get help.

The main goal of a true bully is:

- to intentionally inflict pain
- to intimidate you
- to gain power and control over you

To a bully, your pain is her victory. Your pain is her goal.

Aha moment: A bully is operating on a completely different set of values than you are. This was a huge eye-opener for me. How does a bully think? Not like me. Probably not like you. I cannot fathom hurting someone intentionally. Or getting joy from taking someone down!

But a true bully lacks empathy or compassion for other people. A bully is not reasonable.

How does a bully think? Their sole focus is to destroy other people; they don't particularly have to have a reason why. A bully gets great joy out of inflicting pain on you.

Our family had the unfortunate experience of living right next door to the town bully for eighteen years. Only this is an adult woman I'm talking about. I'm not gonna lie. It was not easy. There were many days I wanted to pack my kids up and move away. This evil woman was just not happy unless she was making everybody else's life miserable. The unbelievable level of hatred, selfishness, bitterness, and downright wicked and mean things she did to our kids terrorized us. I spent many sleepless nights and days brutally petrified and terror-stricken with stomachaches and fear.

My kids were literally terrified to go outside to play, and I was afraid to let them. Even the police and authorities hated dealing with her. It was not enough that she was miserable; she couldn't stand for anybody else not to be. I tried every tactic and idea possible to try to be nice to that woman. You know, kill her with kindness. Well, I am here to say that just plain does not work with everyone. In fact, God's Book of Truth is so honest about real life. Here's what it says: "If it is possible, *as far as it depends on you*, live at peace with everyone" (Romans 12:18, italics added).

The honest truth acknowledged here is that it is *not* possible to live at peace with everyone. But the directive is *as far as it depends on you*. You cannot make the other person's choice. You cannot change a bully. The only person you can change is you. Remember, a bully is not even operating by the same set of values you are.

Your best bet is to recognize that a bully wants nothing but complete control and power at your expense. Your pain brings her delight.

Question 3: What Is the Payoff for a Bully?

What payoff does a bully get that makes them want to continue behaving and acting that way?

> Payoff for a bully is power.
> They want to feel important.

Bullying is usually done for other people to see. Bullies don't just want to prove their power over you. They want to make sure other people know they have *control* over you. So, bullies usually play to an audience. Having an audience just adds to their feeling of being in control.

Bullies want attention. They think it makes them look powerful when they pick on you. They think it makes them look tough or funny.

The truth is: bullies have a lot of anger or sadness inside of them. Bullies have a tough time handling their emotions, so they take their anger or frustration or fear out on kids they think will put up with their abuse. They take out their anger on a less powerful person. They may be dealing with deep-down insecurities or possibly acting out because of abuse at home.

> Knowing how a bully thinks does not excuse their behavior. It only helps explain their behavior and how they think so you can protect yourself as much as possible.

Question 4: How Do You Handle a Bully?

You cannot control "mean." Your best option is learning how to manage *yourself* in the face of mean.

I read some thought-provoking, super helpful advice in a book called *Mean Girls* by Hayley DiMarco:

> The number one goal of the Mean Girl is to inflict pain. To her and her [friends], your pain is evidence of her victory. So in the game of mean, your pain is her point. . . . So your goal should be to make sure you don't give her any points. In other words, never let her see your pain. [That would] show her that she got to you and injured you, and *cha-ching!* Her point!

208

. . . Every time you get mad, cry, yell, shout, run away, retaliate, or do anything else in response to your pain, you've just let her get a glimpse of your insides and all the pain she's caused [(her goal)]. . . .

You see, mean is a living, breathing thing that grows and grows the more it's fed. It lives off the attention of girls just like you, loving your pain, your anger, and your retaliation. All those reactions just give mean a reason to live. Without them, what good is the attack? They need to see blood; they need to see pain; they want to know you are in agony. It gives mean wings. So if you want to put a stranglehold on mean, then you have to cut off its life force—your negative reaction.[1]

At home, alone in your room, or in a safe place with your family or close friends, you can break down and let it all out, but do all you can to stay calm in the presence of the Mean Girl or others who will report back to her. Any sign of pain or weakness, unfortunately, is a green light for more mean.

So, let me give you seven strategies. How do you handle a bully?

Strategy 1: Ignore

The first strategy: Ignore the bully. Pretend you didn't hear her. Don't even look at her. Just ignore her and walk away. Whatever! It definitely is not being a coward. Bullies thrive on the reaction they get, and if you just walk away and pretend to ignore them, you're telling the bully that you just don't care.

Don't acknowledge her or start shouting insults and fighting back. That will just ignite the situation, and then the bully has her payoff. She won.

What does that mean on Instagram or other social media? Don't join her game and start posting ugly, cruel insults back at her. Don't feed the drama.

Strategy 2: Don't Cry, Get Angry, or Show that You Are Upset

Remember the bully's goal: to get a reaction from you. Don't give her the satisfaction of making you upset.

Even if you're feeling really hurt or upset, which you probably are, do not let it show. You can talk about it, cry about it, scream about it, journal about it—later when you're at home in the privacy of your room or with your best friends. Bullies target girls who are anxious or get upset very easily or girls who don't have a lot of confidence and won't stand up for themselves.

Build an invisible wall around your body—in your mind. Imagine the bully's insults just bouncing off the invisible wall around you.

> **"** If someone treats you bad, just remember that there is something wrong with them, not you. Normal people don't go around destroying other people.
> —Unknown **"**

Strategy 3: Do Not Keep It Inside; Talk About It

Talk with someone you trust: a coach, a teacher, a mentor, or a safe adult. It's not being a snitch or rattin' somebody out. It's allowing people who love and care about you to give you help when you really need it. Sometimes, people in positions of authority can find ways to resolve dangerous bullying situations without the bully ever knowing how they found out.

Strategy 4: Do Not Plan Revenge Against the Bully or Take Matters into Your Own Hands

Do not tackle a bully on your own or try to take matters into your own hands. Don't attempt to fight back by screaming insults or physically retaliating. In whatever way you choose to deal with a bully, don't use physical force (like kicking, hitting, or pushing). Not only are you reacting in the heat of anger, but you can also never be sure what the bully will do in response. You are more likely to be hurt and get into trouble if you use violence against a bully.

You'll be the one who ends up getting expelled, not them.

However, if you are being bullied and threatened with physical danger or harm, you need to report that immediately to an appropriate authority. Too many teens and adults have died or committed suicide because of stalking, threats, or attacks that went unreported, and the silence gave the bully license to become more violent.

Please, please hear this and understand: You do not deserve to be bullied. No one does.

Strategy 5: Surround Yourself with People Who Care About You

The worst thing you can do is isolate yourself. Sometimes you feel embarrassed or ashamed. When you're being bullied, the despair you feel can take you to a dark place emotionally and mentally. You feel terribly alone, like no one can understand, and deeply depressed with no possible hope.

I want to promise you and reassure you, there is hope. There is help. Don't believe the lie in your own head.

Don't become a bully to yourself. Don't replay and repeat the lies of the bully: *You suck. You're a piece of crap. Nobody likes you. You're worthless.*

Do not repeat those lies to your own self and feel you are trapped with no way out. There is hope for you. Talk to somebody. You do not have to face this alone. You've got a room—a tribe full of people who care about you.

Strategy 6: Take Charge of Your Life

Don't be alone.

Surround yourself with friends. Don't walk down the halls at school alone. Don't be an easy target to get picked on. Bullies are less likely to pick on girls in a group.

Act confident.

Stand tall, hold your head up, and *act* confident. If you're slumping your shoulders, hanging your head down, you're just announcing that you are a bully magnet.

Fake it!

It may be the biggest acting role of your life. Tell yourself you're gonna take home an Oscar for being the Best Actor. Don't let your body show defeat. Fake it 'til you can make it. Until you begin to feel more confident. Don't obsess about the bully and let her control your life.

Don't let another person steal your joy.

Do things that bring you joy and make you feel good about yourself. Whether that is sports, art, horseback riding, music, singing, dancing, writing, designing, drawing, creating, coaching, caring for an older neighbor, or helping a little child, do something that makes you feel good about yourself, that reminds you: *you* are making a difference in this world.

> You're going to have critics all your life. The only way to avoid criticism is by saying nothing, doing nothing, and being nothing.

Strategy 7: Reminder: Revenge Is in God's Hands, Not Yours

> Never take your own revenge, beloved, but leave room for the wrath of God, for it is written, "VENGEANCE IS MINE, I WILL REPAY," says the Lord. (Romans 12:19 NASB 1995)

Don't try to take the matter into your own hands and get revenge on your bully. However, I didn't say don't confront your bully. I said, don't take revenge. Huge difference.

If you choose to confront your bully at some point, it is extremely important that you do it in a safe environment with other people present—not while the bullying episode is happening but later, when you are mentally and emotionally prepared to confront them.

I promise you it really is true. What goes around, comes around. What a person does eventually comes back to them. The key word is: *eventually.* Not on our timetable and not as fast as we would like. Sometimes it may take years. But it will catch up.

Advice for a Bully

Do I have anything to say to you if you are a bully? You betcha I do. Take a good look at that face in the mirror. You've got some serious issues to address in your life.

1. Get over yourself. It really is not all about you. Grow up.
2. Two words: Stop it!

Controlling others by putting them down is a miserable way to live. There may be a short-term payoff because you temporarily feel you have control. But you're going down. You will eventually lose every relationship that matters to you because of your destructive behavior.

Maybe name-calling, putdowns, or physical force are the norm in your family. You're just modeling behavior that you have seen at home. That's all you know. You've been pushed around, shoved, or bullied yourself by a parent, an older brother or sister, a neighborhood bully.

Maybe you're a bully because that's the only way you know how to protect yourself. Can I tell you from my heart full of love for you, there is a better way to live.

3. Ask for help. There is no shame in that.

We sign up for lessons to be coached in a lot of areas of our life: sports, gymnastics, horseback riding, singing, drawing, playing an instrument. There's nothing wrong with being coached in life skills.

I have mentors in my life who coach me in certain areas. I have so much to learn. So many ways I want to grow and improve. If you ever stop learning, you may as well stop living. Learn from someone positive you admire and start imitating them.

You could ask someone to coach you and to help you learn how to control your anger, how to resolve conflict, how to make friends, and how to take responsibility for your own behavior. You don't have to stay the way you are. Don't be afraid of being a "new you."

I'm not gonna lie. It's going to be the hardest work you've ever done in your life. But it is so worth it. Ask people you admire to help you change. You cannot do it by yourself. God accepts us just as we are, but He has very real plans to change us.[2] Ask Him into your life so He can change you from the inside out.

4. Learn positive, appropriate ways to get attention and respect.

Bullying and violence are never acceptable.

Advice for All of Us

Choose to make your life a no-bullying zone. No bullying allowed! I often say, "Leave your drama at the door!"

But I have a bigger challenge for you. Let's go deeper and take it to a new level.

I heard this statement and I love it!

> Bullies love an audience. Let's steal their show.

Let's become known as a family that doesn't tolerate bullying. A huge family that has each other's backs.

No one fights alone in this family.

You are part of our family, my dear reader! A global movement with a huge mission. Like a gang. But a gang for good. ☺ You know one of the most powerful aspects about a gang—the reason people want to be a part of one? A gang is a place where you feel accepted, like you belong and people will have your back!

So, let's have each other's backs. A Safe Refuge where we all belong. Where we feel loved, wanted, and accepted. A gang for good.

You can totally do this!

Use your power and your influence for good.
And steal the show!

With more love than you can imagine,

 Jimme

16

Courage | Perseverance

My Dear Daring Achiever,

Did you know statistics show that the most courageous thing you do every day is get into a car and drive down the street? Seriously.

How many of you have your driver's license? Remember the first time you climbed behind the wheel? You probably drove with a tight-gripped "9 and 3." You drove hella slowly, but you continued to get behind the wheel each day, even in your fear, because you knew the benefit of driving definitely outweighed the risk.

Now that you've been driving a while and are more confident, your grip on the steering wheel probably looks a lot different—maybe one hand or maybe even just a knee. I'm not sure if that's "courage" or crazy! ☺

How do you define *courage*?

> Courage is not the absence of fear, but the ability to act in spite of it.
> —Franklin Roosevelt

> Courage is the ability to do what frightens you. The willingness to confront fear, pain, danger, uncertainty, or intimidation.

To the brave and brokenhearted who have taught us to rise after a fall, your courage is contagious. #lifegoal #letsbuildcontagiouscourage

When you think of courage, are there certain people that come to your mind? When I think of fictional characters and courage, I immediately think of Katniss Everdeen. Love that girl!

Have any of you seen *The Hunger Games* movies? Or read the books? That girl is my daughter's hero. Like, Kristi wants to *be* her.

The truth is that courage does not always look like Katniss Everdeen. It doesn't have to be some huge act of bravery that saves a group of people.

Personally, I have always been inspired by *real people* who are heroes. I am inspired by *true stories* of women and men who face *adversity* and overcome incredible odds to *accomplish the impossible*, who make a *difference* in the world because of their *bravery and courage*. They inspire me to *never quit, never give up*, and to be *tenacious, resilient*, and a *warrior*.

I have a Post-it note on my desk with these words I wrote to remind myself every day of my life goal.

> **66**
>
> **My goal** at the end of my life is to be a **courageous leader** and **strong woman of bold faith** who **dared to believe** and **trust God for the impossible!**
>
> — ♥ Jimmelynn Garland Rice
> An Ordinary Woman Empowered
> by an Extraordinary God
>
> **99**

Courage is *not* built in the big moments of adversity. Courage is built in the small, everyday decisions you make to show up, hustle, work hard out of the spotlight when no one is looking, refusing to take the easy road and quit, acting in everyday small decisions with integrity and discipline. Bravery and resilience are built by building your courage muscle.

216

The *strength* of your courage is *revealed* when you are faced with horrific adversity and challenging obstacles that test every fiber of your being.

Remember, building your **courage muscle** starts today. Now.

> Courage doesn't always roar. Sometimes, courage is the little voice at the end of the day that says I'll try again tomorrow.
> —Mary Anne Radmacher

Courage for you might mean:

- Interviewing for that job you *really* want
- Finding your voice to *speak up* and *speak out*
- Trying out for the ball team or school play even though *you're afraid* of failing
- Deciding to befriend that girl who always sits alone at lunch even though you *might get made fun of* or *bullied* for being with her
- Not *giving in* to peer pressure—sexting, shooting heroin, sleeping around

Maybe you need to find the courage to:

- Make *better choices.*
- Find new friends or *break away* from toxic friends.
- Try something *new*, something you've *always wanted* but have *been afraid to try.*

On a much more serious note, perhaps you or someone you love deeply has been diagnosed with cancer or another serious illness that requires a *fierce kind of courage* and *bravery* that makes other things seem *lame* and *inconsequential* in comparison. No matter what you're facing: Courage is a choice. You must choose to have courage, despite your fears.

Having courage does not come naturally. Let's develop strategies to build courage and perseverance.

Strategy 1: The courage to be yourself is the biggest barrier you must first overcome.

> 66
> To be yourself in a world that is constantly trying to make you something else is the greatest accomplishment.
> —Ralph Waldo Emerson
> 99

Your time is limited, so don't waste it trying to live someone else's life.

Strategy 2: Silence the negative chatter in your mind.

You are your own worst critic. You are fighting "all the feels." You are your biggest opponent. The way you view yourself is often shaped and influenced by your family. Maybe it's time to re-evaluate that playlist from your childhood looping over and over in your mind.

It's true that the messages you receive as a child play over and over in your mind throughout your life. You internalize those messages and begin to believe them. Our goal is to analyze and release the power those words have on our view of ourselves so that we begin to see value in ourselves as God sees us.

Maybe you are very fortunate because you have a parent who raised you with healthy doses of affirmation and praise. When you go home, thank God and thank them.

However, many of you struggle because the message you heard growing up leaves you hurt, wearing shame, and feeling worthless:

- I'm stupid.
- I can't do anything right.
- Nobody could be as awful as me.
- Nobody could *love* someone as awful as me.

As I shared with you in chapter 9, my daddy was an extremely difficult man to live with. Verbally and emotionally abusive. There was only *one* way to do things—his way.

Courage | Perseverance

We grew up with rules for everything. And if we didn't follow them we got lambasted with being called stupid and dumb. He would forcefully jab his index finger into the side of my head and say, "You gotta think, think, think!"

I was afraid to be around Daddy a lot of the time; my stomach stayed in constant knots and filled with anxiety for fear of setting him off and making him angry! But, one thing for sure I learned about myself: *I'm stupid! I'm about a dumb one! I just need to get out of the way and let somebody more competent do it!*

So, guess what playlist I have carried into my adult life and have to fight every time I screw up or don't live up to other people's expectations?! You got it!

I have intentionally asked God to rewire, reteach, and retrain my mind through His Word, which is Truth. Some days I succeed at rewriting the playlist. Other days, I fail. Miserably.

> Your past does not define your future.

If you *give others the power* to determine your self-worth, you'll never feel worthy enough. Choose to find value and worth in yourself. Develop a belief in yourself; don't take on others' beliefs about you. Don't become a victim of your circumstances. You'll become a passenger in your own life instead of the driver!

Strategy 3: Just do it! Build your courage muscle.

> Courage is like a muscle. It gets strengthened the more you use it.

The more you exercise your courage muscle, the more confident you'll become.

> Choose to act in spite of your fear.

219

You can't conquer your fear or build courage by *sitting around thinking* about it. You have to *act*.

Pushing yourself through experiences where you are forced to face your fear is what really builds courage and confidence. There are no

shortcuts. Until you step out and move forward, leaning into your fear, you won't make any real progress.

It's easy to think that you have to conquer your fear before you act. Like, if you get anxiety around adults, you might think, I'll just wait 'til I'm older and hopefully my anxiety will go away and then I'll be okay. The truth is, you gotta take that step of courage and act first, and then, it gets easier. Not the other way around. The more times you force yourself to be around adults, look them in the eye, and have conversations, the easier it will get. Eventually, you won't even have to psych yourself up for it. It'll just be natural.

Sometimes, you have to take baby steps starting out. I've definitely had to take baby steps my whole life to build courage and become the woman I am today. I did not come into this position in life fully formed. I did not grow up feeling confident. I have *so* many insecurities and fears.

I choose to be intentional about working on self-improvement, personal growth, and leadership development *every single day* to become the *best version of me God has intended.*

While battling late-stage Lyme disease these past years, I have had to work my butt off to regain body and brain function that I *completely lost.* But also, I have had to *be patient* while my brain and body are *rebuilding, repairing, and healing* because it is a *slow* process. And *terrifying.* And *humiliating.* And exhausting. It has taken *courage, bravery, perseverance, resilience*, and everything I have *not to give up.* There have been many days I have not had much strength to endure and keep fighting to survive. Many days I wanted to give up and pull the covers over my head and say *I quit.* Many days I do not want to be in the public eye while fighting the complications of a vicious disease with no cure; I would prefer to be healing far away from public life and people's judgment and hurtful assumptions.

This daily battle has made other worries and concerns become unimportant and inconsequential in comparison. This disease has *tested my courage muscle to the max*, and I could not possibly survive or persevere without God's presence and strength. God has brought me so far. I am *the most grateful girl on the planet*.

Strong women aren't simply born. They are *made strong* by the storms they walk through.

Strategy 4: Don't be afraid of failure.

Failure will *not* kill you. Nor will *being wrong*.

Peter T. McIntyre said, "Confidence comes not from always being right, but from not fearing to be wrong."

You *will* fail. *Everyone* does. You have to go through the falling down in order to learn to walk. It helps to know that you survived it. There is *nothing* that you are presently doing that you did not have to *learn*. When

> **Don't be afraid to fail. Be afraid not to try.**
> —Michael Jordan

you realize that you're able to learn new things and handle new situations, you will stop fearing the future so much. If you approach life with the philosophy that failure is bad, you'll be too hard on yourself when things don't go as planned. You'll never learn from your mistakes. You'll never grow as a person. *You'll become so afraid of failure that you won't even try in the first place.*

> **Stop acting as if life is a rehearsal. Live this day as if it were your last. The past is over and gone. The future is not guaranteed.**
> —Wayne Dyer

To put courage and perseverance in perspective, let me share a couple of fascinating stories of two very well-known people who persevered.

Did you know that Walt Disney, creator of Walt Disney World, was fired from the *Kansas City Star* because his editor felt he "lacked imagination and had no good ideas"? REALLY?!

Hardly an hour goes by that you don't use something Thomas Edison invented or improved. Edison made a thousand unsuccessful attempts at improving the light bulb. When a reporter asked how it felt to fail a thousand times, Edison replied, "I have not failed. I've just found 1,000 ways that won't work."

Now, that's perseverance and resilience!

Are you scared to audition for a musical group or try out for a ball team? You will never know until you try. If you try, you at least have a chance of making it. *If you don't try, your chances of making it are zero!*

Are any of you upperclassmen scared to choose a major at college because you don't know if you'll like it? You're paralyzed in fear because you don't want to make the wrong decision.

Can I just share this advice? If you don't like your decision, *you can always change it!* Same for choosing a career. Just make a decision. **The only thing unchangeable is death!** Other than that, *if you don't like it, you can always change.*

Sometimes the very thing you are most terrified of ends up being one of the best decisions and memories of your life. Allow me to share with you my daughter Kristi's story:

During my junior year in college, I decided to study abroad in Australia. But I was the only one from my college who went to Australia. So I didn't know a single person. I remember feeling so alone and scared when I arrived at the university there. Back then, we didn't have cell phones! So I had to wait in line to use a public phone when I wanted to call home. For the first two weeks, every time I called home, all I could do was cry. As soon as I'd hear my mama's voice answer the phone, my throat closed up and I couldn't talk. All I could do was cry!

But that time in Australia ended up being one of the best experiences of my life. I wouldn't trade it for anything. In fact, I didn't want to leave at the end of the semester and almost signed up to stay another five months!

Attitude is everything. Build your courage muscle. The more confident you are, the greater your chances are of being successful.

Strategy 5: Prepare mentally.

Mental practice is just as effective as physical practice. Our brain doesn't know the difference! Ask any professional athlete or professional musician. Mentally going through the actions is astoundingly effective! As a professional pianist, I learned that I could "practice" playing the piece of music in my mind or by physically tapping the correct fingers on a desk. This type of mental practice was incredibly effective at learning and even memorizing a piece of music—without even touching a piano keyboard! The brain processes this as "muscle memory." And it works!

The more ways you prepare for situations that require courage, the more confident you will become.

For example, if you have to give a speech in class and you're terrified of public speaking, practice your speech in your room. Practice in front of your family or friends. Practice in front of your dog. ☺

Maybe you want to interview for a job in a challenging field. Prepare yourself. Do your research. Find a mentor. Meet with others who've done similar things. These actions will help build your courage and give you confidence.

Perhaps you need to prepare your exit strategy for the next time your friends ask you to shoot heroin and get wasted with them. Maybe you develop a code word with your mom so that she can pick you up from a party that has turned into illegal, risky behavior and you realize you need to get outta there! Or maybe you don't want to go to the party at all, and you need to plan how to say no when invited.

The more you prepare, the more you will be able to act confidently with courage.

Strategy 6: Stop worrying about what other people think.

Eleanor Roosevelt, former First Lady and wife of President Roosevelt, wisely said, *"You wouldn't worry so much about what others think of you if you realized how seldom they do."*

Most of the friends you have in high school, you probably won't even talk to ten years from now. Let's face it. Girls love drama. The "mean girls" are always going to find something or someone to talk about. Let them. Haters gonna hate.

At the end of the day, the only opinion that matters is that of your Maker and Creator—God. The only approval that matters is the Approval of One.

Strategy 7: Never give up.

Know your worth.

Stay humble, stay hungry, and hustle! Never give up. The most certain way to succeed is always to try, just one more time.

Never give up.

Every person faces setbacks and endures difficult obstacles and adversity.

> Winners are not people who never fail;
> they are people who never quit!

You can't beat a person who never gives up.

The key to perseverance? Stay hungry, remain humble, and never give up!

Well, I've shared proven strategies to build your courage and resilience. Now let's talk about what *really* matters.

Your True Worth

If you read this letter and you don't recognize where your real worth comes from, I have failed you big-time. We can take steps to build our courage, we can face our fears, we can prepare, and we can try to care less about what others think. But the source of our inner courage and confidence *must* come from Jesus Christ and our trust in Him.

The truth is, on our own, we are not much good. On our very best days, we are still probably going to mess up somehow, say something stupid, get a huge zit on our forehead, fail our pre-cal test, or let that stupid guy take advantage of us again because we are afraid of losing him.

We *are* going to fail and mess up. Often. Doesn't matter how many times we say stuff in the mirror like, "I am kind, I am important, I am beautiful," right?

If we try to find our courage only in ourselves, we are going to be hugely disappointed.

> Your only true security, confidence, and worth come from having a personal relationship with your maker, Jesus Christ, the One who created you, knows you, and loves you more than anyone. The God who values and adores you. Your self-worth is based not on who those around you say you are, but on who the Creator of the universe says you are.

Let me close with this story that will help put this truth in perspective.

My daddy grew up on a forty-acre farm in Hartsville, South Carolina. When his parents died, Daddy inherited the family farm. Well, Daddy had great plans for this little farm, and he started working on it as soon as he retired.

The farm property was divided down the middle by a creek. On the back half of the property, the farm fields encircled a perfect, beautiful, little oasis of tall pine trees and refreshing shade. It was my daddy's dream to create a little "park" in that area. He named it *Carolina Bay*. He built a fire pit and picnic tables and made plans for a gazebo. His dream was to make this a place where our family and all the grandkids could go hang out, have a bonfire, picnic, and be together.

Well, Daddy sadly suffered a series of very serious strokes, which left him completely paralyzed—except for his left arm. It was devastating and heartbreaking. He worked fiercely to try to rehab and gain any movement of his body. However, five years later, as his body continued to deteriorate, my daddy lost his battle and passed away.

He never got to finish his dream of completing *Carolina Bay*. But before he died, Daddy had a friend of his bring a dump truck–load of large, gleaming, shimmering quartz rocks that he was going to use to line the walking paths in *Carolina Bay*.

After Daddy died, I took my family to the farm to take one last look. There in the middle of the field in front of *Carolina Bay* was the huge stack of quartz rocks. Of course, I was fighting back tears like crazy thinking of Daddy and looking at the few winding paths and bridges we had worked together to create. Even though Daddy didn't get to complete his dream, he raised a little girl who loved nature, woods, paths, and rocks as much as he did. I can still see a blank canvas of land and woods and create a vision of what could be done.

That day, standing there with tears streaming down my face and seeing that enormous pile of rocks, I knew what I had to do. The plan became crystal clear in my mind. I just had some major convincin' and 'splainin' to do to get my boys on board with Mama's plan to get that huge pile of rocks back home to Indy with me. Just sayin' the hubs and my two sons were *not* feelin' it! Insert eye rolls and looks of pure disbelief (and, I'm sure, more than a few choice words under their breath). They did *not* share my enthusiasm.

"What? Take these rocks *home* with us? You've gotta be kidding me! We can just *buy* you some rocks when we get home."

"But you don't understand," I said. "These aren't just *any* rocks. These are my daddy's rocks."

So, yep! You know it! There we were, all pouring sweat in 100-degree sweltering southern heat and humidity, loading up these huge, heavy rocks in five-gallon buckets and piling them onto a flat-bed trailer. We pulled that trailer full of rocks behind my Jeep all the way from South Carolina back to Indy.

That summer, after we got home, I created a beautifully landscaped backyard retreat—complete with a curvy, winding walking path lined with those rocks—in honor and memory of my daddy.

Now, those rocks might not mean anything to anybody else, but to this one little girl who loved her daddy, those rocks mean everything. They are valuable and priceless and worth more than anything money can buy. They have value and worth because of *who* and *what* they represent to me—someone I love very much. You have value and you have worth for the same reason. You are valued and worth everything because you are loved by God.

Do you ever feel alone? Like no one really cares or understands you or knows what you're going through? Your friends try to be supportive, but they don't really understand. You know what? God knows. God sees. God hears. And God cares. He sees your tears. He hears your cries. And He knows your name.

> "The LORD who created you . . . the one who formed you says,
> 'Do not be afraid. . . . I have called you by name; you are mine.
> . . . I, the LORD, made you, and I will not forget you'" (Isaiah 43:1; 44:21).

So, when you feel scared, like you can't do this life anymore? Well, you're right. You can't. You were made to need God. This great big Creator of the huge universe wants to be your Savior, your Provider, your Guide, your Security, and your Protector. He cares about you and about the details of your life.

And He wants a relationship with you.

He loves you much more than I love my daddy's rocks. And that's a lot!

With more love than you can imagine,

 Jimme

17

Confidence | Goals

My Dear Brave Leader,

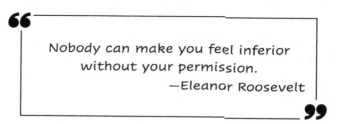

> Nobody can make you feel inferior
> without your permission.
> —Eleanor Roosevelt

You know that *intoxicating, invigorating* feeling you get when you do something *brave?* That *exhilarating rush* of raw adrenaline when you finally *find your courage* and *try something new that's not easy?* That's. . .

Confidence

Confidence gives you the power *to be your brave self— even when it's scary.*

I remember as a tiny little four-year-old girl begging my mama—persistently—to let me sing a solo at our church of five hundred members. I wanted to sing that worship song so badly I could taste it.

I remember having to meet and audition to see if I was "good enough" and to see if I would have the courage to actually follow through. My mama says she was sitting in her seat, holding her breath, scared to death for me. But I got up in front of our church congregation and sang my heart out. Afterwards, I felt so confident and grateful that I was allowed to do that and that I had pleased my God by singing my little heart out praising Him!

A couple years later, I was asked to sing a solo at one of our prominent South Carolina TV stations for a weekly program our church did. I sang that Christmas solo with all my worshipping heart, then right at the very end, my voice completely gave out, and I couldn't sing the last line of the song. Even though I was poised enough to stand there in front of the camera until the end of the song, that experience felt 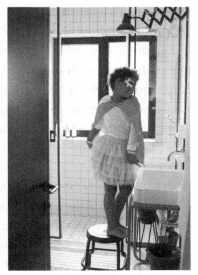 totally different. I felt thankful for being asked and for having the courage to do it but felt *humiliated* that my voice quit at the very end of that song while on live TV. I experienced a helpless feeling that there was nothing I could do to change what had happened, and I couldn't ask for a do-over! In my young mind, I failed.

However, now, as an adult, I look back and realize that was totally untrue. As an adult, revisiting those moments and writing this to you, I see that I never gave myself credit for all the rest of the song I sang well nor for the *huge accomplishment* that was for a young child. And, I am just now realizing that it took *bravery*, *courage*, and *confidence* to even do it!

Had I allowed that experience to completely give me stage fright to the point I would never take a risk again, I would have never had the incredible opportunities that being a professional musician, worship and band leader, production director, and accomplished pianist have given me throughout my life! I feel so truly honored and grateful for the unbelievable opportunities I have had and for the incredible musicians I have had the joy to direct and work with, along with the privilege of ministering and bringing joy and healing to so many people through the power of music!

I would love to share with you what I've personally learned about confidence, and then coach you so that you have a clear game plan to succeed, with great tools to become brave, become confident, and take action. Throughout this book, I've guided and helped you work through unhealthy thinking patterns, learn better coping skills, stop comparing and competing with others, and have the courage to be yourself. Now, I want to give you a clear game plan to become more brave and courageous, take action, learn not to be afraid of failure, and take risks that will grow your confidence.

Action Steps

Action 1: To become confident, you must take risks!

In taking a risk, sometimes you're successful and other times your voice gives out on you, and you experience what you consider failure.

Let me share something with you that will rock your world—and hopefully change your perspective.

> There is actual science that shows *failure,* of all things, *helps us become successful.*

Failure really does have an upside! It's not so much the actual failing but the *recovery, getting up, brushing yourself off,* and *trying again* that can be hugely valuable. It's all part of the critical process of building confidence.

Scared is what you're feeling.
Brave is what you're doing.
—Emma Donoghue

Tackle life.

One day at a time.

Action 2: Tackle life. One day at a time.

Someone very close to me sent me this encouraging card with this loving challenge and reminder when I was fiercely fighting for my life battling late-stage Lyme disease. Looking at this little pig-tailed pre-school girl dressed in her football uniform, with the black circles under her eyes—this determined little girl's fighting spirit and confidence gave me courage and confidence to keep fighting.

I LOOOOVE HER! Her face, grit, determination, steely eyes, adorable pigtails, dressed in her football uniform, standing in her tackling position, complete with the blacked-out eyes and unwavering confidence are inspiring! This card still sits on a shelf in my office to inspire me.

Why? Because I know the dreams God has placed in my heart are global-sized, God-sized dreams that can only be accomplished through dedication, determination, grit, perseverance, and confidence given by Him to accomplish the purpose for which I was born.

You have BIG, God-sized dreams placed inside of you too. And I am in your corner cheering you on with excitement and delight, believing in you and expectantly waiting to see the powerful difference you are going to make in this world that needs YOU! But before you can embrace those dreams, you have to first develop one trait: confidence. Some are born with it; others must consciously work to develop it.

If you know my little granddarlin', Trey, you know he burst into this world with confidence. A *lotta swagger* and *no fear*. Trey was born ready to conquer. No matter the question, Trey has a ready answer for anything and everything. He has a strong opinion, even if he knows *absolutely nothing* about the subject. When he tries a new sport or new endeavor, he says, "JiJi, I'm *bery* good at that!" No matter what the situation, same answer. "JiJi, I'm *bery* good at that!" Raw confidence.

I'm thinkin' to myself, that must be so nice. Perhaps you're more like me than Trey. Your own insecurities paralyze you. You don't feel good enough or feel that you measure up. Maybe you didn't grow up with the privilege of being affirmed and validated by your parents or anyone who matters to you. So, what are you gonna do? Don't allow challenges and obstacles to paralyze you!

Action 3: Take action to conquer self-doubt.

Just one small positive thought in the morning can change your whole day.

Do you ever beat yourself up? Wow, I sure have. And still do. All of us struggle at some point in our lives with self-doubt.

I sure wish I had someone to mentor me when I was a teen growing up, but I didn't. So, what did I do? Instead of spending my life feeling inferior and wallowing in self-pity, I made a challenging decision to follow the calling on my life and become passionate about giving YOU what I did not have! I want to inspire you to conquer and overcome your self-doubt.

So, how do we overcome self-doubt?

- Take action. Use the fear of *not* doing something and regretting it as motivation to overcome self-doubt.
- Think about how you'll feel if you don't do it, and use that feeling to help spur you into action. Do the thing you're afraid of doing.
- Start small. Make your bed every morning for a week. You'll build discipline, which will help you gain confidence.
- One small act every day for seven days can increase your ability to overcome self-doubt, just because you made a commitment to do something small for seven days and *you did it.* ☺

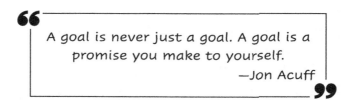

A goal is never just a goal. A goal is a promise you make to yourself.

—Jon Acuff

You'll get more confident because you did what you promised yourself you would do. Then, you'll gain confidence to tackle a bigger goal. If this feels like too much, think back to when you were a little kid. You learned to walk. You learned to ride your bike. You finished elementary school. That means you're capable of learning how to do the next great thing.

Action 4: If you fail, get up and try again.

And again! Like falling off your bike and intentionally climbing back on to try again. When you take a small action, it builds confidence, which is the opposite of self-doubt, and gives you the courage and power to go after a bigger goal.

Setting goals and building good habits are extremely important because they help you to build character and gain competence and courage.

Start small. Follow through. Become more confident. Go after your next goal. Because you kept your word to yourself on the last one, you will gain momentum and confidence to do the next big thing. You can do it! I believe in you!

Actually, let's try this! Pick *one* habit you want to incorporate into your life. Just one.

You can do anything for one day! Anything! Don't think too far ahead. That starts to feel overwhelming and impossible. We're just gonna do one thing—one day at a time. Pick just one habit. One goal. Go!

Okay. Let's say your goal is to make your bed. Do it today. That one thing.

Go for the win! You did it! You met your goal today!

That feels soooo good!

Now, in the morning, make your bed.

Go for the win to start your day feeling *ACCOMPLISHMENT*!

That will put you in a good mood and affect your perspective, attitude, and confidence the rest of the day!

'Cause you did it! Yes, you did! ☺

Be intentional. Your life does not get better by chance; it gets better by change.

Action 5: Do one thing every day that scares you.

DO IT AFRAID.

If none of the above have worked, and you're still terrified, *tell yourself you're going to DO IT AFRAID.*

Because you can't always wait for those nerves to go away. What if they don't? Admit you're nervous but decide to *act anyway*. Just shrug your shoulders and announce to yourself, "I'm just going to DO IT AFRAID!" That is one powerful phrase! Put that negative energy to good use! Use that energy to focus on the powerful decision you just made. *I AM* going to do it afraid. Take the risk and just do it!

> There's no way to think yourself into being confident while sitting in your comfort zone.

Action and risk are required, so let's just say it:

YOU GOTTA RISK MORE!

Visualize yourself doing what you're afraid of—successfully. Close your eyes and picture it mentally. Literally practice it mentally as though you were actually doing it in the moment. Like we talked about before, your brain is powerful. It doesn't know the difference between reality and visualizing. Imagine and feel the joy of doing it successfully! Give yourself a pep talk! Self-talk matters. Talk to your inner self and speak out loud those positive words. "I did it! I am so proud of myself for trying! Woohoo! Yes! You go, girl! You did it!"

God's Book reminds us of this hugely empowering truth:

> I can do all things through Christ who strengthens me.
> —Philippians 4:13 NKJV

I can do *some* things ... through Christ who gives me strength. *NOT!* I can do *all* things. *All means all.*

Not in your own power. But, through the One who gives you strength.

Action 6: Don't allow challenges and obstacles to paralyze you.

If you're not *failing* some, then you're *not learning*, you're *not growing* or becoming stronger, and you're likely not taking those important risks.

You're also not creating fun and adventure for yourself. You probably don't have to think too hard to remember moments when you've really learned from failure, like riding your first bike, falling down, scraping your knees, and then, getting back on it to try again!

Failure will happen. The key isn't to avoid it. The key is knowing what to do with it. *Let failure spur you on by challenging you to grow.*

Action 7: Listen to your brave side.

Your mind is either your greatest asset or your greatest liability.

Your mind will always believe everything you tell it.
Feed it FAITH.
Feed it TRUTH.
Feed it LOVE.

Believe in yourself. *Don't wear other people's limiting, negative beliefs about you or your life.*

You don't have to be defined by anyone else's version of what you should be.

- Learn to use *your voice*. Have *your own* opinions.
- *Invest in yourself.* Get a coach or a mentor to help you in an area you want to grow in and improve. Learn new things. Challenge yourself. I say all the time, *"If I ever stop learning, I might as well stop living."*
- Arm yourself with affirming Truth to make you stronger mentally.

If God has given you the ability to find a cure, solve a global need, break barriers that have never been broken—go for it! Don't let anything or anyone hold you back!

Dream BIG!

Major General Jessica Wright is one of the highest-ranking women in the US military. Even though she succeeds in a world of square-jawed generals and majors—mostly male—she manages to be utterly herself. And she kicks butt. She became the first woman to command an army combat brigade. Yet she still remembers when she was a brand-new lieutenant and one of her superiors told her up front that he was not in favor of women in the military. Not at all. "There were five hundred things going through my head," she said. "And I looked at him, summoned my courage, and said, 'You have an opportunity now to get over that. Sir.'" It worked. She won his respect and her career soared.[1]

Every day, women around the world are being brave, courageous, bold, strong, and daring leaders who are changing this world and making a monumental difference. You, my loves, have the capacity to be bold leaders who are courageously and compassionately changing our world—one life at a time.

Once you've experienced the courage to dream BIG, taken a challenging risk, slayed it, conquered it, you'll be totally stoked to grow your confidence muscle even more. Once you've had a taste of courage and success, you'll want more! And that's a good thing!

Be you—bravely.

With more love than you can imagine,

 Jimme

18

Life | Purpose

My Dear Adored Loves,

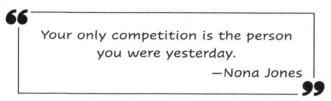

> Your only competition is the person you were yesterday.
> —Nona Jones

Here is my final challenge to you! The three Bs.

- **Be** yourself
- **Be**lieve in yourself
- **Be**tter yourself

Take my challenge, adopt these three goals, work on them over your lifetime, and you **will be**come that person you long to be! I will be so proud of you!

You've got one future.
Life is a vapor. Two seconds and you're gone.
You only get one shot at life. Are you taking your best shot?

Poet Linda Ellis has described our life as "the dash." On a tombstone are listed two dates. The first is the day you were born. The second is the day you died. Your entire life is *the dash*; the days lived in between. In the end, as Ellis said, "What matters is how we live and love and how we spend our dash." So, how are you going to spend *your* dash?

> The two most important days in your life are the day you were born and the day you find out why.
> —Attributed to Mark Twain

Want to know the quickest ways to *ruin* your life?

1. Spend your life craving the approval of others. Insist on pleasing everyone around you.

2. Do whatever it takes to get everyone's attention, even if it means doing what is not true to you.

3. Let an ugly, competitive spirit dominate you. It will drive away everyone you care about.

4. Refuse to trust other people or allow anyone to get close to you.

5. Park your mind in crippling thoughts that lead to depression and hating yourself.

Want to know the best ways to *improve* your life?

1. Take responsibility for your life. Own it.

2. Don't confuse *likes* with *love.* When you stay preoccupied with the opinions and approval of others, you will remain trapped in insecurity.

3. Don't live as a victim. Don't blame everyone else for your life. Fight and persevere through your obstacles and adversity. You will become stronger because of it and be able to help others who also struggle.

4. Set your goals high. Develop a strong work ethic. Nothing can beat the satisfaction and feeling of accomplishment when you prove to yourself that you can do what you set your mind to doing—and you slay it!

5. Be grateful. Expect nothing. Nobody owes you anything.

6. Your greatest test will be how you handle people who mishandled you.

7. Find your tribe. Your people. Keep being genuine. Your people will find you. *Beautiful souls recognize beautiful souls.*

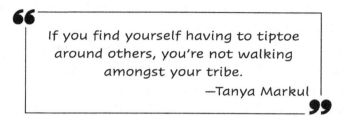

> If you find yourself having to tiptoe around others, you're not walking amongst your tribe.
>
> —Tanya Markul

Life is short. Spend it with people who make you *laugh* and *feel loved.*

Invest in yourself. Never stop learning. *You* are worth that investment. *You **will** achieve your life goals!*

> **Dream it.**
> **Believe it.**
> **Achieve it.**

> Before you can receive the truth that you are loved and approved of by God, you have to unfollow the lie that you need human approval.
>
> —Nona Jones

I thought it would be fun as I close this book to invite you over to my home to hang with me for the day. So, let's just imagine what that would look like. I'd greet you at the door with the warmest welcome, smile, and a big, tight *Jimme* hug, wrapping you in the warmth of a never-let-you-go embrace like long-lost friends. I'd grab your hand and invite you in as I tell you, "Just make yourself at home—'cause you are!"

As you glance around, you'd recognize right away that you have just stepped into a coastal, classy, casual, yet elegant beach-inspired home whose interior was designed by me, a Southern Belle, owner of *Jimme Design,* who just happens to live in Indianapolis. ☺ The "Y'all Spoken

Here" sign in the entrance would be a dead giveaway that you can take the girl out of Carolina, but you can't take the Carolina out of the girl. You'd be welcomed by our big, fluffy, English cream golden retriever, Bentley Tucker Blu. As you join me in our great room, you'd notice the tall palm trees on opposite sides of the room framing the enormous windows and soaring ceilings surrounding my cherished piano and favorite, cozy, charcoal-gray swivel chairs. I'd quickly tell you that our beautiful home belongs to my Daddy—Abba Father. We just have it on loan from Him for a while. I'd tell you how humbled and overwhelmingly grateful I am that God has allowed us to live in this healing home that feels like a retreat, because He knows we will openly, generously, and gratefully share it with others every chance we get, in every way we can. Yes, we pay the mortgage, but the real truth I am getting at is this fact: honestly, none of us ever gets to "own" land or a "home" really. We just purchase it and live there until God calls us to Glory—then, the next generation swoops in and does the same. Until their short life is done too.

Next, undoubtedly, I'd invite you into my delightful kitchen to have a seat with me around my big, round kitchen table, where I am known to say, "I *love* a round table because there's *always* room for just one more!" We'd sip on some sweet tea and then probably head back into the great room and snuggle next to each other in my swivel chairs that allow us to sit face-to-face as we share our hearts with each other. And there would be laughs. *Lots* of laughs. Hair. *Lots* of hair. White dog hair from Bentley Tucker Blu. I feel like Dr. Suess as I'm always saying and groaning, *"Hair. Hair. It's everywhere!"*

Then there'd be *lots* of talking, hugs interspersed with pats on your arm as I take delight in your company! *Lots* of deep, thoughtful questions I'd ask you. And then, I would *just listen*. Listen intently as though you were the only person in the world. Because to me, you are. You have my undivided attention. I am fascinated *with you* and *by you*. And the creative uniqueness with which God has made you and stamped you. We'd probably shed some tears as we talked about the real stuff of life and how it can flat kick your butt and knock your feet out from under you. Unexpected family issues, health struggles, emotional pain, deep hurt, abuse and betrayal, financial struggles, "friends" who really weren't, inner struggles, fears and doubts we are wrestling with.

We'd walk around my home, and you'd see all my favorite quotes hanging on my walls or sitting on a bookshelf and you'd ask the story of why each one has inspired me. Or how God has so kindly used my life to inspire others through one of my hard-earned life lessons, fierce health battles, or life quotes.

These favorite quotes, inspiring affirmations, along with positive promises from God, intentionally start my day off right by focusing my mind, challenging me, and shifting my thoughts into a positive mindset as I awaken to the **gift of life**—a *new day*!

> Today is a *gift* from God,
> that's why it's called the *present*.
> *Live* each day to the fullest
> And treat it as the *precious* gift it is.

I would share with you the importance of surrounding yourself with motivating words by allowing you a private peek inside my day.

When I climb out of bed in the morning, my eyes open to see these quotes:

1. Start each day with a grateful heart.
2. Every day is a fresh start.
3. Do small things with great love.

Then, I grab a cup of coffee and head to my favorite chair in my sunroom to cuddle up and meet with my Maker, Creator, and Savior. I *savor* God's Book of Truth—His love letters to me, which are endlessly fascinating and mind-boggling. *Radical love.* Countercultural love. Constantly teaching me about Him, speaking directly to my *soul.* Guiding me. Directing me. Challenging me. Calling me out on areas I need to *change.* I listen *quietly* to Him. Ask Him questions. Pray my worries and fears out loud to Him. Pray over relationships that have devastated and shattered my heart into a million pieces. Ask Him to bring healing and restoration. Pray for each of my family members and so many I love, their struggles and their *specific* needs. Search my heart to see where I have been wrong. Ask for His forgiveness. *Admit* where I'm hurting deeply and have deep wounds that need His healing. I ask Him to bring *healing to my soul.*

After that, I share with Him my plans and agenda for the day and ask the Spirit of God to give me *focus, clarity,* and *direction.* To guide me in every conversation. I pray and give Him full permission to change my agenda and exchange it for *His* agenda for me for that day. Change and disrupt *my* plan for *His* plan.

Each day I am greeted, along with my family, houseguests, and friends who come over to visit, with these inspiring quotes and artwork that I place with intentionality to remind me of my personal goals and life values. Since you are my guest, I thought I would share them with you because you may find one that inspires you just as much!

1. Be fearless in the pursuit of what sets your soul on fire.

2. If it doesn't CHALLENGE you, it won't CHANGE YOU.

3. It's never too late to start the day over.
Give yourself some slack. You're allowed a do-over!

4. Enjoy this day.
Be present.
Breathe deeply.
Show gratitude.
Live with intention.
Be fearless.

5. Choose joy.
This one is so important to me. After battling Lyme disease and the brutal treatments for so many years, it became difficult to "feel" the emotion of joy. That may sound crazy, but those of you who have experienced life-threatening disease or trauma understand what it does to the body. The body keeps the score, and there has to be healing of the mind, body, and spirit. I asked God to help me *feel* joy again, even

though I was *choosing* joy. One of the things I did was to purposefully *play* and do things I enjoyed as a child to rehab and retrain my body to experience that emotion again. Like skipping, riding bikes, diggin' in the dirt, planting and creating beauty out of nothing, designing winding paths with surprises around every bend, playing piano and singing, dancing alone, laughing and being insanely crazy with my friends, playing basketball, playing hopscotch with little kids, building sandcastles, and jumping waves at the beach on vacay—once my body had the stamina and energy to do so. Anything that made me smile and flooded my body with endorphins.

6. *Celebrate the little things, because one day you will look back and realize they were the big things.*

7. *Do one thing every day that makes you happy.*

Just one simple thing a day that makes you smile and brings you joy can be life-changing!

8. *Desire less.*
   Give more.

9. *Enthusiasm is contagious.*
   Endurance is rare.

10. *Don't take life too seriously. You'll never get out of it alive.* ☺
    —*Elbert Hubbard*

One life-perspective writing I have beautifully framed in my office, as well as in my home, is this writing by Mother Teresa that sums up an honest, healthy perspective on life's crushing disappointments, betrayal, and hurt. Immeasurable wisdom here.

Do It Anyway
People are often unreasonable and self-centered.
FORGIVE THEM ANYWAY.
If you are kind, people may accuse you of selfish motives.
BE KIND ANYWAY.

If you are successful, you will win some unfaithful friends
and some genuine enemies.
SUCCEED ANYWAY.
If you are honest, people may deceive you.
BE HONEST ANYWAY.
If you find happiness, some may be jealous.
BE HAPPY ANYWAY.
The good you do today will often be forgotten.
DO GOOD ANYWAY.
Give the best you have, and it may never be enough.
GIVE YOUR BEST ANYWAY.
Because in the end, it is between you and God.
It was never between you and them anyway.
—Mother Teresa

As our afternoon visit begins to come to a close, we would enjoy lively, spirited, stimulating conversation and lots of hugs. You would be inspired and challenged by the strategic quotes on the most important thing to me—my faith.

All of these and more are in my IV treatment room and on Post-it notes on columns, cabinet doors, and mirrors in purposeful locations. These powerful words sustain me, give me *hope*, and remind me that I am never alone. God will never abandon or forsake me, and He is the object of my trust.

1. *Fear not tomorrow;*
   God is already there.

2. *Under His wings you will find REFUGE. (Psalm 91:4)*

3. *I have heard your prayer, I have seen your tears: Surely, I will heal you. (2 Kings 20:5 NKJV)*

4. *She confidently trusts the Lord to take care of her. (Psalm 112:7, paraphrased)*

5. *You are*
   ENOUGH
   Because
   I AM.
   God.

6. *Trust in the* LORD *with all your heart,*
   do not depend on your own understanding.
   Seek his will in all you do,
   and he will show you which path to take.

—*Proverbs 3:5–6*

I have decided to close this book with a very intimate, personal story that is almost too sacred to share.

When I was so deathly sick, searching for answers, going to specialist after specialist, only to leave defeated because I was getting sicker and weaker and no doctor or test could give us answers as to why my body and my brain were shutting down and failing me, my husband took me to Myrtle Beach to visit with my mama and to see the ocean, which is always a healing place for me. As soon as we arrived at the beach cottage, my daughter, Kristi, called and said that Dr. Crozier was on the line and needed to do a merged call with me, Rodney, Mama, and Kristi because all my specialized test results had come back, and he needed to talk with us about my very serious diagnosis. After that forever life-altering phone conversation with my Lyme disease specialist, I knew I had to get to the beach because my whole head was spinning and dizzy as I tried to process the news I had just received and tried to make some sense of what was going on.

I will never forget that slow, unsteady walk in the sand, praying helplessly but fiercely while walking that familiar, usually happy beach, a beach that now felt anything *but* happy after hearing these words that turned my world upside down. Replaying that conversation over in my mind, trying to comprehend what this all meant, questioning why there was no specialist in Indianapolis who could treat me, I realized that I would have to leave my kids behind in Indy for seven months to begin the long process of intense treatment and that my life, as I knew it, had just come to a screeching halt. This horrific loop kept replaying in my mind along with the dreadful diagnosis. This doctor said he could help me, but I would have to get to his medical clinic *immediately* if I stood *any chance of survival* and begin these brutal treatments he referred to as "chemo on steroids" that made military warriors and grown men cry from the severity of the treatments.

With hot tears pouring down my cheeks, I begged God to confirm if I was to go to the medical clinic in Florida. If that was the *only path*, the only way I was going to be able to *survive and recover*. Prayer warriors around the globe were praying for God to spare my life and that He would direct my path by providing ONE. CLEAR. PATH.

Out of desperation and needing to hear from God, I did something I have never done in my entire life. I asked God if He would give me *one specific gift as a sign*. Not just any ol' gift or treasure from the sea. I prayed that He would grant me *one specific gift* that would give my confused, terrified heart confirmation that this *was* my ONE.CLEAR.PATH.

I knew I needed to trust in the Lord, with *all* my heart. Not to lean on *my own* understanding and reasoning. In *all my ways*, I would choose to acknowledge and *seek Him*, and He promised He *would* direct my path.

Because I was banking *all* my trust in Him and trusting Him with *all* my heart, I asked if He would please answer this little girl's prayer and help me find one *specific* thing, one *specific* gift that I would know was from Him to confirm my path: *a heart-shaped shell.*

I grew up in South Carolina, close to Myrtle Beach, and had walked that beach countless times collecting shells. But, I had never asked for a specific shell. And I don't remember ever having seen a heart-shaped shell. But, I asked the Creator, who can do *anything*, if He would please do this one specific thing to bring peace to my confused, fear-filled heart and confirm and direct my path. After all, He is the One who made that soothing, healing ocean. He created those shells and the salt water that brings healing and the grains of sand that massage our feet.

That heart shape would symbolize that I was *trusting* Him with my *whole heart*. That He *could* be trusted. And that I was to *go for treatment at this medical clinic in Florida.*

As I walked ever so slowly due to the excruciating pain of taking a step, there on the beach, in the sand, lay a **perfectly formed heart**. I was wrecked. Stunned. Ransacked and ruined. A hot mess of tears of gratitude that not only had my God heard me but that HE CARED. He *actually cared* for me and wanted to provide what my soul desperately needed—which was to hear from Him and be confirmed to trust that this was *the one path* for me. I knew that He would help me survive the brutal treatments that lay before me to start the path of healing from the ravages of this vicious disease.

When I bent down to pick it up and hold it close to my chest, one of the most fascinating things about that large, beautiful heart-shaped shell was that it fit perfectly in my hand. My fingers could wrap around it and grasp it tightly.

I literally held that heart during every single treatment as it fit perfectly to grasp one part with my thumb and wrap the palm of my hand around the other part. When I was in writhing pain during or after treatment, I held that heart to remind me of God's promise to never leave me or forsake me. To never abandon me. That He is the Healer. That He is my only Refuge, my Strength to endure, persevere, and fight fiercely in the battle for my life.

If my home were to catch on fire, and I could only grab a few things, this heart would be one cherished treasure that would go out the door with me. It is irreplaceable. What that heart signifies is worth more than anything money could buy.

I will tell you this. When God shows Himself to you in such a profound way when you are desperately seeking Him and He provides such an intimate, personal, custom-made-for-you answer, there are no human words to describe the depth of love you experience when you **encounter the Living God** and feel securely wrapped in a soothing blanket of His care and the warm embrace of His Love. My love for Him, my trust in Him will never be the same. I am forever changed.

My Abba. My Father. You have my full heart. You have my full attention and my full affection.

I have often wondered why God provided a heart-shaped shell that was actually a heart-shaped stone. I thought perhaps it was because that stone is a special type of stone made of certain mineral properties that bring healing. I have always wanted to have it analyzed to see if that is so.

However, just today—literally—as I am writing this, I realized for the very first time the significance of my heart-shaped shell being a stone.

- ♥ A stone is solid and unbreakable. If it had been a shell, that shell would have easily been broken. That shell would have been so fragile, especially since it has traveled back and forth with me to the medical clinic in Florida for these many years, has been in my suitcase, has been gripped tightly with my hand during intense, excruciatingly painful treatments—yet it still remains in a perfect heart shape.

- ♥ God is often referred to as our Rock. A firm, secure, immoveable foundation to cling to when the world around us is shaking in chaos and turmoil, fear clutching our throats.

- ♥ Often in God's Book, His people are told to set a memorial stone in place to mark where God showed up mightily. It was to be a reminder to them of God's faithfulness and that He would never leave them or forsake them.

- ♥ Most importantly, that memorial stone was a Stone of Remembrance. A story to be shared with their children and their children's children how Jehovah God had provided for them! A story that was to be passed down from one generation to the next and the next, to showcase the faithfulness of God, proof that He never breaks His promises to us and meets us in our darkest hour.

So, *this* is why God gave me not only the desperate plea and desire of my heart—this heart-shaped stone—but also this story to share with you, to pass down from one generation to the next so *you* would know: *your* God can be trusted.

God has graciously given me the gift of discernment to see deep into the eyes, heart, and soul of each person I meet and bring hope and healing not only through my words but also through the power of an appropriate, desperately needed hug. I have affectionately been dubbed "the Hug Whisperer" or "the Hug Healer." And my doorbell has rung more times than I can count by adults, teens, and children running over just to get a "Jimme hug" to know that everything would be all right. I thank God for empowering me with that beautiful gift. If I could speak no more words but could deliver that much-needed love—in this dark, hurting world—I would be honored to deliver God's love. Sometimes, we know God is there, but we just need "somebody with skin on." I am happy and honored to be just that.

After all these years, I realized my life purpose can be summed up in these four life-giving truths that God burned into my soul and that I chose to have trademarked as my life mission and why I was placed on earth. May I close with these life-giving words from my heart to yours to encourage you when you feel unseen, unheard, unaccepted, unloved, and wonder if you even deserve a place in this world:

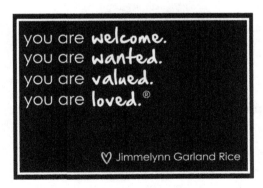

you are **welcome.**
you are **wanted.**
you are **valued.**
you are **loved.**®

♡ Jimmelynn Garland Rice

These life-giving words don't JUST come from *my heart* but from the *heart of your Maker.*

Whether spoken from a stage or one-on-one as I whispered in someone's ear and gently wrapped them in what has been affectionately been called "a Jimme hug," I have witnessed the power of these words over every precious person whose soul was moved deeply, with tears pouring down their cheeks, as I tenderly and lovingly spoke *to their wounded soul* and as a *blessing over them.*

I hope you feel that same warm hug and deep love as I close this book and send you a virtual hug through these pages painstakingly written to bring hope, healing, and life guidance to you.

> Your life is your story.
> Write well.
> Edit often.

I am in your corner cheering you on! Always.
Yours and His.

xxoo

With more love than you can imagine,

Jimme

Testimonials

Jimme is the most fiercely dedicated mentor, a wise counselor, and like the mother I never had. Toxic relationships have always been a part of my life, starting with my biological parents, who were drug abusers, mainly meth. My dad was a drug dealer, and my mom couldn't resist them. My dad and mom were both arrested for child pornography—and unfortunately, I was the victim. They both raped me starting when I was three months old, and my "dad" sold my body to his friends. They were arrested for the seven thousand videos and eighteen thousand photos they posted of sexual acts with me. My mom was forced by that man to take part in these acts. They are both in prison. I don't fault my mom as much because he drugged her, physically and sexually abused her, and forced her to participate. My grandmother has loved and raised me since I was six years old.

Jimme has made me feel like I am safe and not alone. I could be having the worst day ever, but as soon as Jimme walks through that door, with that worry-melting smile, and gives me one of her famous hugs, all my problems fade away. As soon as I first saw and met Jimme, I knew I had to talk to her and tell her my story. Not only is her laugh contagious, but so is her positivity.

I still find it stunning how engrossed people are when she speaks or counsels them one-on-one. Everyone immediately feels safe and loved, seen, and heard. I can totally be myself with her. I can tell the cringiest joke, and she will laugh uncontrollably.

Bad things happen, life sucks, but Jimme has helped me find healthier ways to cope.

She is helping me through the horrible trauma my body and brain have been through and to begin to heal. I still struggle; that's expected.

I battle with mental and emotional health, suicidal thoughts, self-harm, feeling worthless, and questioning my faith…like *where was God when I was being abused and why didn't He rescue me?* But Jimme is intentional about helping me through my horrific past, dark emotions, and demons that plague me. She has introduced me to a relationship with God, assured me that God has a plan for my life, and is guiding me to find my life purpose. I find purpose in helping others who are hurting and standing up to bullies or injustice of any kind, and I love working with service dogs and therapy horses. I plan to go into equine therapy when I graduate! —Riley, age 17 (name changed)

Jimme is the most genuine, compassionate, loving person that I have ever met. Once you are a part of GNI in any capacity, you become more than a broken soul or volunteer, you become a part of something big and special. She's modest despite the major impact she has contributed to young girls. She's just happy to know that she's changed lives. —Jessica, TEAM GNI mentor, Ben Davis High School Area 31 Career Center Teacher

The first time I ever heard you speak your touching trademark words of love, *"You are welcome. You are wanted. You are valued. You are loved,"* my heart immediately melted and I instantly felt *home*. Like I was wrapped in a warm, cozy blanket, fully accepted, and totally loved by you. After so many years of knowing you, admiring you, and calling you my close friend and pastor's wife (essentially half of my life now! ☺), you are and always have been a major role model and most influential mentor to me, someone I've looked up to, and someone I've wanted to be just like. You have the biggest heart of anyone I've ever known, and Christ's love RADIATES from you. It's impossible to know you and NOT want to be just like you. THANK YOU for loving me and everyone else so completely. Your impact on my life is immeasurable. —Kristen, 34-year-old wife, mama, and pharmacist

I just want you to know that I "idolized" you when I was a little girl sitting by you on that piano bench at your parents' house. I loved watching you put on makeup and riding with your family to church. I remember your wedding and crying afterward because I told my Mom I wouldn't see you any more and I was sad.

Thank you for being an inspiration to me many years ago as a child and thank you for being an inspiration to me many years later on a hot August night when you spoke about being sexually molested by your youth pastor. I never talked about what happened to me, but I feel safe and know I can trust you with opening a place in my heart that I have kept very closed. Love you always! —Your forever grateful piano student, mentee, and lifelong friend

♡ Gratitude ♡

Thank you, *Rodney*, my husband and teammate in life, leadership, and love. Your belief in me, your admiration and love you speak of me to everyone you meet, your unending support and cheering me on when I was beyond exhausted and weary has kept me from going under. For your concern and watchful care over me as my main caregiver so I could devote a year and a half to this project, I will forever thank you. You prepared gourmet dinners for me, helped with household duties that I had zero spare minutes to do, managed so much of our lives so that I could stay focused on this project amid the many demands on my time with all the leadership roles I wear. Thank you for continually telling me that *now* is my time to shine. That I have always been behind the scenes faithfully and happily helping to make all *your* calling and dreams come true, and that *now is your time to do that for me! ILY.*

Thank you, *Kristi Hardin*, my Director of Operations at Girls Nite In International. Your steadfast, dedicated work helped me create the capacity needed so none of the many balls I juggle across my various roles and responsibilities would drop while writing this. As my passionately loved and loving daughter, thanks for being one of my biggest cheerleaders! Your belief in me and the importance of this book have kept me going more times than you will ever know. You have encouraged and supported me in every possible way. Your hands-on work to help me compile the graphic artwork I wanted to include and being a sounding board when I needed fresh ears to listen to portions of the manuscript were an incalculable help and greatly appreciated. You have been with me every step of this journey, and I can never thank you enough. I am the most grateful mama on the planet to have you as my daughter. When I grow up, I want to be you. I love you and am so proud of the incredible woman and leader you have become. You are my heart. ILY.

Mama, thank you for believing in me and your affirmation and support of this book. I probably wouldn't have done it if you had not spoken your affirmation. Your confirmation was a deal maker for me that I should move forward because the message was so important and needed now more than ever. ILY.

Daddy, thank you for loving me the absolute best you could. Thank you for working exhaustingly hard, as a machinist, to provide for our family and our future . . . everything you could by saving frugally on a meager salary. I miss you. Only you would think it hilarious and a badge of honor when we told you people today would label you as having OCD—*obsessive-compulsive disorder*—and you thought we said **obnoxious**-compulsive disorder! To which, we said, *"Yeah, that is actually even more true!"* Then, you would wear that smirky grin, laugh, and find that something to be proud of! As you said of yourself, "I'm different." Yes, you were! I am so grateful you are whole, healed, and healthy now in Glory! ILY.

Angela, my sister, whom I love deeply; *Joey*, my brother-in-love; *Papa Jimmy*, my "bonus daddy," and *all* my family, thank you. ILY.

To *Charlotte Lucas*, thank you for your belief in me personally, my God-given talents and calling, and for being such a generous, humble, and selfless leader. I love how you describe our relationship: *"Jimme is the best friend you never knew you needed!"* It is with the deepest gratitude, love, and loyalty that I thank you for believing in my book, stating that it should be in *every* library. Thank you for generously investing a portion of the printing costs of this book knowing your *eternal investment* will point thousands to the True Hope and life strategy found in God's Book of Truth—and a life-pivoting relationship with Him. You have my deepest respect, admiration, and loyalty. *I will always have your back and love you more than you can imagine.*

Thank you to two of my dear friends who serve tirelessly with me in the mission of GNI but also are my caregivers in my battle against Lyme disease: *Cindy Modafferi*, my personal nurse who monitors my health and intense treatments, who shares the same passion I have for this mission—nurturing, caring, and loving others so well, laughing and finding joy together or working through heartbreak side-by-side—all of this while recognizing the high calling on my life and cheering me on always. For continually thanking me for being the best mentor by not only teaching but also modeling with my life. Thank you to *Sharon Hammer*, my personal and professional assistant, who shares the same passion for excellence I have, does many behind-the-scenes tasks anticipating my needs, and quietly takes things off my plate so I can focus on my "best yes." Watches out for my health struggles and manages the large daily number of supplements and medication I must take to keep my body functioning and my health from regressing, sends encouraging notes to remind me of the courage, bravery, determination, and resilience I have shown to write this book while fighting and persevering through many heartbreaks and the difficulties of this disease.

Thank you to my dear friends, both of whom serve on TEAM GNI: Cindy Barnard, who has encouraged me relentlessly to write this book and opened the door of opportunity by recommending me for a scholarship to attend a writer's conference—Speak Up Conference—where I was acquired for this book publishing contract. Thank you for kindly sharing with others the talents and giftedness God has placed in me, sharing how my boldness, vision, and faith have helped you grow, how God has used me in your life, for reppin' my speaking, writing, and musical ministries—and having the vision, along with others, to clearly see the future doors God was opening for me so that I would continue to *dare and believe*. To *Tammy Gordon*, who pursued tirelessly the best Lyme treatment options for me and used her gift of encouragement and humor to keep me fighting, recognized the visionary leader, creative entrepreneur, engaging worship leader, and worshipper in me, but most of all, my passion and love for my God and for every soul to know they are welcome, wanted, valued, and loved, especially those who feel unseen, unheard, and invisible. You continue to have big vision for how God will yet use me.

To my incredible *Girls Nite In International staff, Valeri Abbott, our deeply loved GNI donors and partners, my adored TEAM GNI leaders, mentors, and volunteers* who have advanced our mission in countless ways and work tirelessly to revolutionize the lives of young women in our backyard, across the nation, and around the globe. Teamwork makes the dream work. You prove that every day. *As I share with you often, this is not a one-woman band. I could not accomplish this global, God-sized vision without you. I truly believe the goal of a great leader is to inspire people with a vision so compelling that they become carriers of your vision—not just followers of your vision.*[1] It is my deepest privilege to lead and serve alongside the greatest team on the planet!

My tribe. My people. *You know who you are. The list is long. I am truly the most grateful girl on the planet. My dearest, closest friends whom I love deeply. I am truly blessed and so grateful for you.* My friends who circled the wagon and kept my hands lifted and rallied my spirit when I was so weary. You reminded me of the thousands of lives who have been changed, including yours—and how many more there will be once this book is released. ♥

To all of you I love and admired growing up. You saw value and leadership potential in me since I was a little girl who was scared to believe in herself. Your footprints are all over my life, and you have helped shape me into who I am today. I will always love you and never forget one single one of you.

Thank you to my army of war-room prayer warriors who have prayed for God to sustain me and my health and bring healing so I could finish this book project. Jean Capps and Alice Peacock, you led the charge—along with Shelly Brown, Chris Brady, Marcy Garrard, Tammy Patterson, *and a list so long it could circle the globe . . . and has. I am indebted to you and to God—the continual Healer and Restorer of my Soul.*

Thank you, *Suzanne Kuhn*, for immediately seeing the potential in me and wanting to acquire me to publish this book. Also, *John Herring*, CEO of Iron Stream Media, for offering the publishing agreement to sign me as an author and publishing my book. Thank you for recognizing I had a gift and spending countless hours on the phone providing guidance and answering a plethora of questions I had throughout this lengthy process.

Susan Cornell, my Senior Editor, I am so grateful to you for the guidance you have given, the tenacious work you have done in the editing process of this book, the the patience and genuine care you extended when I had health battles that caused unexpected delays in meeting a deadline. You offered grace and reminded me to offer my own self grace. Not only are you a spectacular senior editor, you have become a close, cherished friend! You are truly amazing! The best and an absolute joy to work with!

Michele Trumble, thank you for the tedious work you have done to make this book possible and for helping this first-time published author work my way through the multitude of tasks that must be done by an author, not just writing the book manuscript. I had no idea all that would be involved! You were a delight to work with!

Larry J. Leech II, a heartfelt thanks to you and all the wonderful team at Iron Stream Media who have their hands on this book project and are determined to ensure it is shared with the world—one beautiful soul at a time.

My book cover designer, *Ashley Day,* who took the design vision and color palette I created, collaborated so beautifully with me, and added her spectacular, creative talent to take this book cover to another level of unparalleled design, layout, and arresting beauty! A book cover for which I am extremely proud. I am forever grateful and indebted. You're stuck with me! We're gonna work on a lot of projects together! ☺ You are simply the best.

To my *many loved friends and supporters* who purchased this book before it was even released, I cannot thank you enough for your faith in me. You have no idea how much your gesture kept me going as we made our way to this day. You didn't have to do it, but you did. And I am so grateful to all of you.

Finally, to my *family* and my *friends* whom I have coffee or hang out with, that hasn't happened as much as it has in the past, *because of having to spend time with this manuscript that I would normally spend with you.* Especially my adored family—I can't wait to give you all the love and focus I desire and you deserve. As soon as I hit Send and this book goes on its way, *I'm all yours again!* Can't wait for my granddarlins' sleepover that is long overdue! 🖤

🖤 My Love. My Legacy. 🖤
Twelve of our family of eighteen

Notes

Dedication

1. Attributed to Tim LaHaye.

1. Anxiety | Fear

1. Mike Ronsisvalle, "Ronsisvalle: 90 Percent of What We Worry About Never Happens, so Why Do We Worry So Much?" *Florida Today*, October 26, 2021, https://www.floridatoday.com/story/life /wellness/2021/10/26/most-what-you-worry-never-happen-these -tips-help/6123169001/.

4. Sex | Self-Respect

1. Juanita Bynum, *No More Sheets: The Truth About Sex* (Maryland: Pneuma Life, 2000).

6. Depression | Suicide

1. Ann Voskamp, "What the Church and Christians Need to Know About Suicide and Mental Health," Huffpost, August 14, 2014, https://www.huffpost.com/entry/what-the-church-and-chris_b _5676318.

2. Ann Voskamp, "What the Church and Christians Need to Know About Suicide and Mental Health."

7. Jealousy | Envy

1. Corrie ten Boom, "Guideposts Classics: Corrie ten Boom on Forgiveness," *Guideposts*, https://guideposts.org/positive-living/ guideposts-classics-corrie-ten-boom-forgiveness/.

2. Susan Cheever, *A Woman's Life: The Story of an Ordinary American and Her Extraordinary Generation* (New York: William Morrow, 1994).

8. Divorce | Blending Families

1. Tim Baker, *Broken: Making Sense of Your Life After Your Parents' Divorce* (Colorado Springs: TH1NK, 2006).
2. "He Will Carry You," by Scott Wesley Brown, track 6 on *Sparrow: Double Play*, Sparrow Records, 1988.

11. Self-Hate | Self-Harm

1. Lauren Greenfield, *Thin* (San Francisco: Chronicle Books, 2006), 56.
2 Nancy Alcorn, *Cut: Mercy for Self-Harm* (Enumclaw, WA: WinePress Publishing, 2007).
3. Alcorn, *Cut*.

12. Eating Disorders | Unhealthy

1. Ethan Cross, Marc G. Berman, Walter Mischel, and Tor D. Wagner, "Social Rejection Shares Somatosensory Representations with Physical Pain," *PNAS* 108, no. 15, March 28, 2011, https://doi.org/10.1073/pnas.1102693108.
2. Portia de Rossi, *Unbearable Lightness: A Story of Loss and Gain* (New York: Atria, 2010), 277, 294–95.

15. Bullying | Boundaries

1. Hayley DiMarco, *Mean Girls: Facing Your Beauty Turned Beast* (Grand Rapids, MI: Revell, 2008), 26–27.
2. Attributed to Graham Cooke.

17. Confidence | Goals

1. Katty Kay and Claire Shipman, *The Confidence Code for Girls: Taking Risks, Messing Up, & Becoming Your Amazingly Imperfect, Totally Powerful Self* (New York: Harper, 2018), 92–93.

Gratitude

1. Attributed to Brian Houston.

About the Author

Jimmelynn Garland Rice—speaker, author, professional musician, recording artist, worship and pastoral leader—is a visionary leader who coaches organizations in culture development and team building.

A passionate lover of people, Jimme has a heart as big as the globe. Gifted with a discernment to see deep into the soul of everyone she meets, she immediately captivates you with her huge, welcoming hug and makes you feel safe, understood, accepted, and deeply loved. Jimme's passion is to be a world changer, bringing a message of HOPE, healing, life guidance, and God's love to everyone she meets.

Working through her own childhood trauma has given Jimme compassionate insight into emotional, mental, and spiritual health struggles while equipping her with a voice to articulate the pain and conflict churning inside broken, confused, hurting souls.

Her life mission is to intentionally share her life-giving words she coined to breathe hope, healing, and value into every single soul:

You are *welcome.*
You are *wanted.*
You are *valued.*
You are *loved.*®

Jimmelynn's life became permanently altered in 2015 when she was diagnosed with late-stage, chronic Lyme Disease and began a fierce battle fighting for her life.

A courageous, unrelenting fighter, Jimme became a brave warrior determined to inspire others to persevere and fight their own battles through keynote speaking engagements, life-coaching, and teaching resilient faith through her GOD'S NOT DONE® movement. A leader of mentors, Jimmelynn has committed her life to empowering, equipping, and deploying a global network of leaders to dramatically impact this generation!

For speaking engagements | team building + culture development | music events + worship concerts, email JimmelynnGarlandRice@gmail.com.

JimmelynnGarlandRice.com
jimme@girlsniteininternational.org
www.girlsnitein.org

Made in the USA
Columbia, SC
24 April 2024

34511759R00153